Beyond the Notes

Beyond the Notes

Teaching and Learning Music at Historically Black Colleges and Universities

Paula A. Grissom-Broughton

United Kingdom – North America – Japan
India – Malaysia – China

Emerald Publishing Limited
Emerald Publishing, Floor 5, Northspring, 21-23 Wellington Street, Leeds LS1 4DL

First edition 2026

Copyright © 2026 by Emerald Publishing Limited.
All rights of reproduction in any form reserved.

Cover photo: iStock/cidonia

Reprints and permissions service
Contact: www.copyright.com

No part of this book may be reproduced, stored in a retrieval system, transmitted in any form or by any means electronic, mechanical, photocopying, recording or otherwise without either the prior written permission of the publisher or a licence permitting restricted copying issued in the UK by The Copyright Licensing Agency and in the USA by The Copyright Clearance Center. Any opinions expressed in the chapters are those of the authors. Whilst Emerald makes every effort to ensure the quality and accuracy of its content, Emerald makes no representation implied or otherwise, as to the chapters' suitability and application and disclaims any warranties, express or implied, to their use.

British Library Cataloguing in Publication Data
A catalogue record for this book is available from the British Library

ISBN: 978-1-80592-590-3 (Print hardback)
ISBN: 978-1-80592-592-7 (Print paperback)
ISBN: 978-1-80592-589-7/978-1-80592-591-0 (Ebook)

Typeset by TNQ Tech
Cover design by TNQ Tech

CONTENTS

About the Author .... *vii*

Prelude .... *ix*

Introduction .... *xiii*

PART ONE: HISTORICAL AND SOCIOCULTURAL PERSPECTIVES ON MUSIC EDUCATION AT HBCUS

1. The Historical Foundations of HBCUs *3*

2. Ebony Towers: The Missions and Relevance of HBCUs *25*

3. Echoes of Heritage: The Musical Traditions of HBCUs *47*

4. Entwined Realities: Curriculum, Community, Challenges *67*

5. Music at HBCUs: Consciousness and Cultural Empowerment Pedagogy *85*

PART TWO: EXEMPLARS OF TEACHING AND LEARNING MUSIC AT HBCUS

6. Affirming Identity *107*

7. Valuing Cultural Assets *131*

8. Transformative Empowerment *153*

9. Implications, Recommendations for Policy and Practice................ 171

Postlude: Homecoming 193

Appendix A: List of Historically Black Colleges and Universities........... 195

Appendix B: Profiles of Eight Historically Black Colleges and
     University Exemplars... 199

Appendix C: Historically Black Colleges and Universities accredited
     by the NASM 201

ABOUT THE AUTHOR

Paula A. Grissom-Broughton is an assistant professor and former chair of the Department of Music at Spelman College, where she teaches courses exploring the intersections of women, race, and music. A dedicated scholar and researcher, her work centers on race, gender, and identity in music education, with a particular emphasis on Black feminist pedagogy.

A proud product of Historically Black Colleges and Universities (HBCUs) and a member of a multigenerational HBCU family, Dr. Grissom-Broughton is deeply invested in the study and preservation of HBCU music programs. Her research highlights how these institutions cultivate cultural pride, challenge dominant narratives in music education, and empower students as artists and leaders. Her book *Beyond the Notes* reflects her ongoing commitment to documenting and honoring the rich musical and educational traditions of HBCUs.

Prior to her role at Spelman, she taught piano, music theory, and history at Winston-Salem State University. She has also served as a music educator in Atlanta and Fulton County Schools, developing music programming for K–12 students. A former Atlanta Steinway Piano Competition winner, she remains an active collaborative pianist, guest clinician, and speaker. Across her teaching, performance, and scholarship, Dr Grissom-Broughton continues to open doors for future generations of culturally grounded music educators and scholars.

PRELUDE

U-A-P-B! Who are you rootin' for... U-A-P-B!!!!
U-A-P-B! Who are you rootin' for... U-A-P-B!!!!

Before I fully understood the significance of higher education, the rallying cry of the University of Arkansas at Pine Bluff (UAPB) was already a familiar sound. Originally called Arkansas Agricultural, Mechanical, and Normal State College (Arkansas AM&N), UAPB is the second oldest land-grant institution in Arkansas. The first, the University of Arkansas in Fayetteville (established in 1871), is situated in the scenic Ozark Mountains of northern Arkansas.

Although the University of Arkansas was ostensibly open to African Americans, entrenched social norms and stringent laws substantially hindered their access to higher education in the state. Moreover, the post-Civil War climate of vigilantism in the Ozarks added a layer of peril for African Americans seeking education. In 1875, under the directive of Governor Augustus H. Garland, Joseph Carter Corbin established UAPB specifically for African Americans, then referred to colloquially as Negroes. This mission would lay the groundwork for a profound legacy of education and empowerment.

As a girl in Pine Bluff, I became intertwined with UAPB culture unknowingly. My childhood home on Fluker Street was a stone's throw from UAPB's campus. The adjacent North Hickory Street, tranquil and undisturbed during the late 1970s, became an impromptu rehearsal ground for UAPB's marching band, The Marching Musical Machine of the Mid-South. As a child, I would excitedly run to the corner just to hear the band and watch their high-stepping routines set to the latest funk and R&B tunes. My friend Sylento would mimic the drum majors, while I mimicked the dance line, Golden Girls, who twirled and moved their hips to the beat. I would scan the rows of saxophones to spot out my sister, Alvena, proudly playing as part of the esteemed ensemble.

Alvena was just one of several siblings who attended UAPB, drawn by scholarships, proximity, and affordability. Seven of my eleven siblings were educated at UAPB. Another sister, Phyllis, received a choir scholarship to attend UAPB and was crowned Miss UAPB; she represented the college as an ambassador at various civic and community service events. My father, Allen Grissom, a son of sharecroppers and an Army veteran, also walked its hallowed halls. A beneficiary of the G.I. Bill, his educational journey was a testament to the transformative power of access and opportunity. Graduating in 1953 amid family and work commitments, he epitomized the resilience and dedication that faculty and administration instilled in its students. His subsequent pursuit of a master's degree and careers in teaching and counseling marked a lifetime devoted to education as a teacher, principal in segregated schools, and counselor.

Our home's proximity to the college meant we were intimately connected to its community. My mother, warmly known as Mother Grissom, demonstrated othermothering (Case, 1997; Collins, 2000) long before the term was introduced to pedagogical research. She frequently cared for the children of single mothers studying at UAPB, and our house was a regular overnight stop for my siblings' friends following their lengthy band rehearsals or study sessions.

Homecomings were especially unforgettable, transforming our home into the meet-up hub, a gathering place for these celebrations. Homecomings were like week-long family reunions, with alumni flocking back to their alma mater to rekindle friendships and revisit cherished memories with former classmates and professors. The spontaneous step shows by Greek fraternities and sororities would erupt anywhere and attracted crowds that cheered them on. The halftime shows, often the highlight of the football games, showcased exceptional musicianship and unforgettable entertainment. These homecoming festivities enlivened the entire city, engaging community leaders and local business owners who joined in on the celebration.

The fabric of my formidable community was intricately woven within the Historically Black College and University (HBCU) heritage. My neighbors on Fluker Street and North Hickory, such as Gladys Alley, who taught at Philander Smith College in Little Rock, were all proud graduates of AM&N. My foundational music education began with Mittie Robinson, another AM&N alumna, who introduced me to the world of music notation. My journey continued under the guidance of Lola Gordon, who provided my first formal piano lessons, and Juana Johnson, who led the community youth choir where I honed my skills as the piano accompanist. Aria Thorns, who operated one of the first culturally responsive preparatory schools in Pine Bluff, offered me my first music teaching role while I was still in high school. There, my musical abilities were further refined under Michael Bates, a long-time member of UAPB's music faculty. These individuals, among many others, enriched my upbringing with their profound knowledge and exemplary leadership, all rooted in their AM&N or UAPB education.

When it came time to choose my own path for higher education, I was drawn to UAPB, the University of Arkansas at Fayetteville, and Spelman

College. Despite offers of full scholarships closer to home, a visit to Spelman decided me. Viewing images of powerful African American women displayed around campus such as Ida B. Wells, Maya Angelou, Sojourner Truth, Leontyne Price, Jessye Norman, and Ella Fitzgerald awakened a profound connection to a heritage of empowerment and excellence. At Spelman, I saw that Blackness was celebrated, women empowered, and greatness expected. Spelman became the incubator that shaped my sense of a Black womanhood, developed me as a critical thinker, and inspired to leave a lasting impact on those I encounter—influences that would later define my professional and personal identity.

My principal teaching mentor, Joyce Finch Johnson, a distinguished alumna of Fisk University and one of the longest-serving faculty members at Spelman College, exemplified the quintessential HBCU music educator. She was instrumental in refining my musical abilities and broadening my horizons with a wealth of experiences and opportunities. Johnson was my first and most impactful example of how transformative teaching can extend far beyond mere musical notes. Johnson exemplified that impactful teaching transcended beyond mere instruction; it shaped character. Our post-lesson discussions emphasized pursuing excellence: "Paula, we must strive to be better than the best," Johnson would insist. She seized spontaneous moments in the hallways for personal encouragement. A quick glance into the practice rooms was not merely a check-in, it was a reminder that the standards were high and that exceptional musicianship and scholarly excellence was expected, despite *any* adversities.

My personal journey is more than a backdrop; it is the driving force behind this book. I am a living testament to the transformative experience that takes place in a nurturing environment, absent of gender and racial stereotype threats, taught with a culturally inclusive curriculum with positive professor-student interactions (Stewart et al., 2008). *Beyond the Notes* delves into the transformative role HBCUs play in cultivating skilled musicians, educators, and scholars, and examines both their pedagogical practices and their challenges. Through these explorations, I celebrate HBCUs' profound impact on education and aim to inspire a new generation to continue this legacy of excellence.

References

Case, K. I. (1997). African American othermothering in the urban elementary school. *The Urban Review, 29*(1), 25–39. https://doi.org/10.1023/A:1024645710209

Collins, P. H. (2000). *Black feminist thought: Knowledge, consciousness, and the politics of empowerment.* Routledge.

Stewart, G., Wright, D., Perry, T., & Rankin, C. (2008). Historically Black colleges and universities: Caretakers of precious treasure. *Journal of College Admission, Fall, 201,* 24–29.

INTRODUCTION

Along with the growing body of literature indicating that attending a Black colleges and universities offers students benefits not found at predominately White institutions (Gasman & Esters, 2024; Hale, 2023; Koch & Swinton, 2022; Palmer, Hilton, & Fountaine, 2012; Williams & Ashley, 2004), Audre Lorde (2007) remind us to consider how differences can bridge gaps rather than widen them. In music education programs in institutions of higher education, Historically Black Colleges and Universities (HBCUs) have played an integral role in the musical development of African Americans since the 19th century. The implications associated with differences (i.e., understanding people more holistically, embracing broader viewpoints) need to be assessed and utilized to understand the teaching of HBCU students in music programs. Such an approach provides the necessary insights to further understand the implications of incorporating expanded research methodologies outside of traditional disciplinary boundaries (e.g., areas of study limited by social and cultural constraints) in HBCUs.

The omission of HBCUs' from mainstream music education research diminishes both the visibility and the perceived legitimacy of their vital contributions to music education. Specifically, the experience of African Americans in HBCU music programs remains underexplored. With the ever-increasing racial diversity of the college environment, such challenging issues demonstrate a need to examine how HBCU students experience their music programs. To gain further perspectives on whether broadly accepted methodological teaching and learning tools, including African American cultural phenomena (e.g., oral traditions), need to be studied or will continue to remain absent from or underutilized in the major research literature.

Marybeth Gasman is a leading scholar of minority students in higher education with a focus on the contributions and benefits of an HBCU education. Gasman has conducted numerous studies of HBCUs to better document the role these institutions continue to play in shaping higher education and contributing to the success of their students (Gasman, 2009; Gasman &

Esters, 2024; Gasman et al., 2007). Yet, Gasman (2025) and other HBCU scholars (Allen et al., 2018; Hale, 2023; Palmer & Young, 2023) suggest that not enough is known of how HBCUs' unique environments translate into their graduates' academic and later professional success. One goal of *Beyond the Notes: Music at Historically Black Colleges and Universities* is to expand this knowledge base, especially as it relates to teaching and learning music at these institutions (See Appendix A for a list of all HBCUs).

A second goal of this book is to further demonstrate that nontraditional, less prevalent models of teaching can impact the broader society. Understanding the historical and socio-cultural influences of HBCUs as told by those who reflect the experiences in the musical world can help clarify why systematically oppressed groups have been left out of the musical canon and how the past still influences current professional practices. Coeyman (1996) notes that the voices of systematically oppressed people are often excluded from music education research. The author suggests that critical dialogue regarding the position of underrepresented students can address marginalized voices in music classrooms. This means examining the structures of formal music education, systems of thought and actions that have historically and systematically oppressed voices, and diverse ways of knowing in the field.

A third goal is to focus on how certain educational practices, particularly those found in music education, exclude certain voices while privileging others. These practices position certain kinds of knowledge as objective, devoid of dynamics of race, gender, class, and sexuality. In addition, the exclusion of particular issues from the curriculum continues to perpetuate the silencing and further marginalizing of collective voices. *Beyond the Notes* is thus structured into two parts and will provide in Part One, a historical and sociocultural critique of HBCUs and their music programs, and in Part Two, teaching and learning exemplars of eight HBCU music programs.

In Part I, which encompasses Chapters 1–5, I examine the pivotal role of HBCUs in nurturing African American musical talent, and I highlight their unique position in broader narratives of higher education. Chapter 1 provides a historical and sociocultural context for the founding of specific institutions dedicated to educating African Americans and highlights the conditions that necessitated their creation. Chapter 2 examines the missions of HBCUs in order to offer a deeper understanding of how these institutions intentionally create intellectual spaces in which students can critically analyze their unique positions in society. Chapter 3 explores the significant contributions of HBCUs in shaping diverse music genres and fostering cultural expression, positioning these institutions as vital forces in the development of American musical identity. In Chapter 4 I investigate the evolution of music curricula at HBCUs and address the challenges these programs face in adapting to contemporary educational demands, integrating technology, and staying responsive to the shifting dynamics of the music industry.

Rather than provide a historiography of the teaching and learning experiences at HBCUs, I further investigate this phenomenon through the pedagogical practice of what I call cultural and consciousness empowerment, a transformative pedagogical approach grounded at the intersection of three foundational theories: W. E. B. Du Bois' concept of double consciousness (1903/1994), Tara Yosso's model of community cultural wealth (2005), and Barbara Omolade's Black feminist pedagogy (1987). Chapter 5 explains how together these frameworks provide a holistic lens to understand empowerment, identity, and resistance within historically and systematically oppressed communities.

Part II (Chapters 6–9) is devoted to the fact that, while cultural and consciousness empowerment can be traced in nearly all HBCUs (and several will be mentioned in this work), the following eight colleges have been identified for their importance among HBCUs: Fisk University, Florida Agricultural and Mechanical University, Howard University, Jackson State University, Morehouse College, Spelman College, Tennessee State University, and Tuskegee University (See Appendix B for an overview of the eight HBCU exemplars highlighted in this book). They represent a unique musical quality in the American higher educational system. Part II's chapters highlight the cultural and consciousness empowerment's converging themes of affirming identity, valuing cultural wealth, and transformative empowerment. Finally, Chapter 9 offers an explanation as to how these eight institutions reflect a broader vision for music education and how they serve as templates for challenging negative ideologies in the field.

My hope is that *Beyond the Notes* will provide a comprehensive understanding of the experiences and perspectives of the individuals involved in music at HBCUs in the 21st century. I seek to acknowledge both the triumphs and challenges faced by these institutions and to highlight their resilience in overcoming obstacles to foster artistic and educational excellence. More importantly, I aim to shed light on pedagogical practices that contribute to their unique educational impact. Through these pages, we celebrate the profound impact of HBCUs on their communities and beyond and underscore their critical contribution to both musical culture and higher education in America.

References

Allen, W. R., McLewis, C., Jones, C., & Harris, D. (2018). From Bakke to Fisher: African American students in US higher education over forty years. *RSF: The Russell Sage Foundation Journal of the Social Sciences, 4*(6), 41–72.

Coeyman, B. (1996). Applications of feminist pedagogy to the college music major curriculum: An introduction to the issues. *College Music Symposium, 36*, 73–90.

Du Bois, W. E. B. (1903). *The souls of Black folk*. A. C. McClurg & Company. (Reprinted by Dover 1994)

Gasman, M. (2009). Historically Black colleges and universities in a time of economic crisis. *Academe, 95*(6), 26–28. http://www.jstor.org/stable/20694590

Gasman, M. (2025). *Why historically black colleges and universities matter: 25 years of historical research for justice.* Teachers College Press.

Gasman, M., Drezner, N. D., Jackson, J. F. L., & Terrell, M. C. (2007). Call for community-based education: The state of public safety issues at minority-serving institutions. In M. C. Terrell & J. F. L. Jackson, (Eds.), *Creating and maintaining safe college campuses* (1st ed., pp. 150–172). Routledge. https://doi.org/10.4324/9781003443742-11

Gasman, M., & Esters, L. T. (2024). *HBCU: The power of Historically Black colleges and universities.* Johns Hopkins University Press.

Hale, F. W. (Ed.). (2023). *How Black colleges empower Black students: Lessons for higher education.* Routledge.

Koch, J. V., & Swinton, O. H. (2022). *Vital and valuable: The relevance of HBCUs to American life and education.* Columbia University Press.

Lorde, A. (2007). *Sister outsider: Essays and speeches.* Crossing Press.

Omolade, B. (1987). A Black feminist pedagogy. *Women's Studies Quarterly, 15*(3/4), 32–39.

Palmer, R. T., Hilton, A. A., Fountaine, T. P., & Boykin, T. F. (2012). (Eds.), *Black graduate education at historically Black colleges and universities: Trends, experiences, and outcomes.* Emerald Publishing Liniuted.

Palmer, R. T., & Young, E. (2023). The uniqueness of an HBCU environment: How a supportive campus climate promotes student success. In T. L. Strayhorn & M. C. Terrell (Eds.), *The evolving challenges of Black college students* (pp. 138–160). Routledge.

Williams, J., & Ashley, D. (2004). *I'll find a way or make one: A tribute to historically Black colleges and universities.* HarperCollins.

Yosso, T. J. (2005). Whose culture has capital? A critical race theory discussion of community cultural wealth. *Race, Ethnicity and Education, 8*(1), 69–91. https://doi.org/10.1080/1361332052000341006

PART ONE

HISTORICAL AND SOCIOCULTURAL PERSPECTIVES ON MUSIC EDUCATION AT HBCUs

CHAPTER 1

THE HISTORICAL FOUNDATIONS OF HBCUs

ABSTRACT

Chapter 1 explores the historical and sociocultural foundations of Historically Black Colleges and Universities (HBCUs) and emphasize their role as counter-institutions to the exclusionary practices of early American higher education. Beginning with the colonial period, the chapter reveals how the nation's first colleges were built on wealth generated through slavery and upheld academic traditions that reinforced racial hierarchies. In contrast, HBCUs emerged as a response to systemic barriers that denied African Americans access to education, becoming critical spaces for intellectual growth, cultural affirmation, and social advancement.

The chapter also examines the founding of early HBCUs, the significance of the Morrill Acts of 1862 and 1890, and the impact of pivotal legislation such as the Civil Rights Act of 1964 and the Higher Education Act of 1965. It traces how policy shifts, abolitionist movements, and racial segregation laws shaped access to education and led to the development of parallel institutions for African Americans. Despite ongoing challenges—including underfunding, marginalization, and opposition to affirmative action—HBCUs have remained vital in educating generations of Black students and affirming their cultural and intellectual identities.

By situating HBCUs in a broader historical and policy context, this chapter underscores their enduring significance as sites of resistance, resilience, and educational justice. It lays the groundwork for understanding how these institutions continue to shape music education and affirm Black excellence in American academia.

Music at Historically Black Colleges and Universities (HBCUs) is a testament to the school's resilience, cultural richness, and legacy. One cannot engage in a meaningful discussion about the current state of music education at HBCUs, however, without exploring its historical and sociocultural context. To fully appreciate their unique role in music education today, we must investigate the past to uncover academic traditions and how they intertwine with the African American experience and shape a distinctive educational and musical landscape. Examining the founding principles of higher education is essential to comprehend how HBCUs have contributed to music education in the United States.

Research suggests that to fully appreciate the complexities of HBCUs, it is crucial to recognize their historical origins and development (Brown et al., 2001; Drewry & Doermann, 2001; Ricard & Brown, 2023). HBCUs have played a significant role in the landscape of Americas colleges and universities since the 19th century, but, despite their profound contributions to academic excellence, cultural enrichment, and the advancement of social justice, they are often erased from the historical narratives of higher education institutions. We must explore the historical and sociocultural reasons behind the establishment of specific institutions for African Americans.

Chains and Colleges (1619–1830)

Systematic oppression in higher education in the United States is a deeply entrenched national phenomenon rooted in the foundational educational and social systems established during the colonial period when the earliest colleges and universities were founded. When enslaved Africans were trafficked to the ports of North America in 1619, they quickly understood that education was the pathway to freedom in a new land (Hannah-Jones, 2021). Proponents of slavery also knew this. A mere 17 years after the first trafficking of enslaved Africans to Jamestown, Virginia, in 1619, the establishment of higher education in the United States began. In 1636 Harvard University in Cambridge, Massachusetts, was founded. Using the model of European academic institutions as their template, Harvard and its fellow colonial colleges were established to provide education to predominantly White middle- and upper-class men, preparing them for clerical and civil service positions. This alignment with European traditions not only shaped the curriculum and ethos of these institutions, but also reinforced existing social hierarchies and exclusionary practices.

The classic text *A History of American Higher Education* Thelin (2019) looks at how America's colleges and universities were founded, their triumphs and challenges, as well as how these institutions have evolved. Thelin (2019) explains that the students who attended colonial colleges were a "relatively privileged group of young men who were expected to be serious about their studies and their religion" and that the "family background of these students at colonial Harvard, Yale, and Princeton tended to be one of mercantile wealth" (p. 24). What Thelin did *not* mention was that the mercantile wealth acquired by these colonial families was directly tied to the trans-Atlantic slave trade.

In the groundbreaking book *Ebony and Ivy*, Wilder (2013) chronicles that "The first five colleges in the British American colonies…[were] instruments of Christian expansionism, weapons for the conquest of indigenous peoples, and major beneficiaries of the African slave trade and slavery" (p. 17). Wilder further asserts that these schools exhibited the

> institutional ownership of slaves; the use of enslaved laborers to build and serve institutions; students, faculty, administrators, and trustees who were enslavers and slave-traders; acceptance of donations from those involved in the transatlantic slavery economy and "triangle trade," such as merchants, insurers, shippers, investors, and plantation owners. (p. 67)

Ironically, or perhaps not, the economic prosperity that fueled the establishment of institutions such as Harvard, Dartmouth, and Princeton was built and maintained by the violent human trafficking of Africans and the disruption, dominance, and dispossession of Indigenous people from their lands (Stein, 2022). In addition to the financial backing from plantation owners and other trades involving slave labor, America's first institutions used labor to maintain daily operations and the functionality of the colleges and universities (e.g., groundskeepers, maids, and cooks). In fact, the use of slave labor in colonial colleges was a common practice (Edwards-Ingram, 2019; Wilder, 2013, 2019). Much work needed to be completed daily, and enslaved people were designated to carry out the most labor-intensive tasks. These persons were typically housed in designated slave quarters located on campus.

The entrenchment of systematic oppression was experienced by students and faculty at these institutions. Perhaps more astonishing than the visible signs of systemic oppression that took place on the outside, such as on-campus slave quarters, were the teachings inside the classrooms. The production and reproduction of knowledge rationalized scientific racism as proof of non-White inferiority. Scientific racism, as taught during the colonial era, was a pseudoscience that promoted the superiority of White people (Jackson et al., 2005). Harvard's anatomist John Collins Warren, founder of the Harvard Medical School, taught multiple courses that placed the physical development, cultural accomplishments, and intellectual potential of White men as God-ordained and supreme (Wilder, 2013). These ideas lasted for decades, well into the 20th century. Harvard President Abbott Lawrence Lowell (1909–1933) implemented the creation of a residential college system that excluded Black students and was a leader among Harvard faculty supporting eugenics (Presidential Committee on the Legacy of Slavery, 2022). Blacks were believed to be naturally placed at the bottom of humanity. Other colleges often used false sciences, theologies, and manipulated histories to justify the supremacy of Europeans above non-Europeans. Unfortunately, these views distorted science, theology, and history. Harvard and other Ivy League schools sustained a deeply ingrained narrative that reinforced systemic norms of oppression, and left a lasting impact on American academia.

Enslaved Africans came to North American as accomplished scientists, mathematicians, and virtuoso musicians, fluent in multiple languages of their indigenous regions. They did not initially speak English, however, and eugenic teachings and restrictive laws were established to keep them illiterate in the English language, often preventing them from even considering attendance at America's first colleges and universities (Williams, 2007). Both enslaved people and even many freed Blacks were subject to educational restrictions enforced by deliberate policies and slave codes. These restrictions extended to those who attempted to teach them to read and write. For instance, in Maryland, teachers could be fined for assembling Black students in school settings. South Carolina and Georgia followed suit by enacting laws that made educating Blacks on any level illegal.[1]

> According to Juan Williams and Dwayne Ashley in *I'll Find a Way or Make One* (2004),
> if slaves couldn't read [English], they wouldn't know a better world was out there. And if they couldn't write, they couldn't forge travel passes that would allow safe travel to freedom. Literacy—education—was a way to escape slavery... it was a way out. (pp. 20–21)

Ultimately, enslavers viewed literacy and education as a threat to the slave-based economy, believing it would lead to insurrection (Williams, 2007). As the desire for literacy among newly freed Blacks became an insistent demand, Black schools were established to offer basic literacy and math skills, but also training in social and trade skills. These early educational establishments for Blacks received crucial support from anti-slavery abolitionist groups who bravely faced arrest, persecution, and even death to fight racism in order to provide education for enslaved and freed Blacks. These abolitionist-educators who established schools for Blacks knew of the eventual need to create Black institutions of higher learning because

Southern Whites, as well as many Northern Whites, did not want Black people in their schools (Williams & Ashley, 2004).

During the Revolutionary War period (1775–1783) and its aftermath, a significant movement appeared aiming to end slavery and improve the status of free Blacks, particularly in the realm of education. A growing conflict emerged between Christian beliefs and the practices of slavery. Many Christians, influenced by the teachings of equality and compassion in their faith, began to see the inhumane treatment and enslavement of African individuals as fundamentally incompatible with their religious principles. According to Williams and Ashley (2004) "both Blacks and White educators pushed aside any fear they had for their own safety and followed their moral and biblical convictions" (p. 14).

A notable example of this collaboration was the attempted founding of the first college specifically for African Americans. In 1829, Samuel Cornish, an African American newspaper editor, and Simeon Jocelyn, a White minister at a Black congregationalist church in New Haven, conceived the idea of the Negro College. Jocelyn was a Yale alumnus, so they chose New Haven because of its established higher education environment. Despite securing financial backing for land and construction, the proposed college faced a formidable obstacle: entrenched interests from local White educators. Influential Yale alumni, faculty, and administrators, fearing competition for resources and prestige, fiercely opposed the new institution. Resolutions were passed to bar the college from the town that prioritized the financial well-being of existing institutions over the potential benefits of a new educational venture for Blacks.

The antislavery movement in the North, which advocated for educational opportunities for all people, began to place pressure on colonial colleges that had previously excluded Negroes. This advocacy paid off in 1828 when Dartmouth College admitted its first student of African descent, a milestone followed by Harvard University in 1847. its These moments set a precedent for other institutions to follow. Many colleges, especially those founded on Christian principles, came to realize the moral inconsistency in barring African Americans. The interplay of "moral philanthropy and racial animosity" in these institutions, as noted by Wilder (2013, p. 262), underscores the complexity and contradictions in early American social and educational ethos. Years of deeply ingrained social constructs posed challenges to Blacks' full integration. In many cases, oppressive social constructs prevailed over moral Christian standards.

The positions of Black women in higher education must be recognized. Before 1800, women of all backgrounds—White, Black, enslaved, or free—were systematically excluded from colleges by statute (Thelin, 2019). Instead of chartered colleges, many early institutions for women's formal education began as academies or teaching seminaries, offering curricula at a level equivalent to secondary schools. Oberlin College's (established in 1833) forward-thinking community was among the most progressive and inclusive of its time. Oberlin was coeducational from its inception and began admitting Black students in 1835 and its first group of Black women in 1837. In the same year, Mary Lyon founded Mount Holyoke in Massachusetts, where an unspoken rule had dictated that Black women not be admitted (Perkins, 1997). This policy was formally adopted in 1845 when the trustees voted against admitting Black women.

The pathway to formal education for Black women was significantly advanced by Myrtilla Miner, who established the Miner Normal School for Colored Girls in Washington D.C. in 1851. Miner was a pioneer in education for Black women who believed that if the influential men running the country could see that African American women were capable of intellectual and industrial achievements, they would support Black educational institutions (Williams & Ashley, 2004).

The drive to uplift African Americans through education was often tainted by pervasive racial biases and exclusionary practices. The admission of Black students into predominantly White institutions, although a progressive step, was not universally welcomed in these academic environments. As a result, many such students endured overt discrimination and sometimes violent treatment. For example, in 1832, a year after the founding of Wesleyan University, the institution accepted its first Black student, Charles B. Ray. He became a prominent abolitionist in the North. It would be encouraging to report that Ray's experience at Wesleyan set a positive precedent for other institutions, but the reality was far different (Work, 1919). His enrollment was met with such intense, and sometimes dangerous, protest from his peers that Ray left the university only seven weeks after his arrival. This episode is one of many that illustrate the profound challenges African Americans faced when attending traditionally White colleges.

Hurdles to Liberation (1830–1890)

Unlike the colonial colleges and universities, which trace their origins to 1636 with the founding of Harvard University, Historically Black Colleges and Universities (HBCUs) would not emerge until nearly 200 years later. The period between 1830 and 1865 was a time of significant societal transformation in U.S. higher education. Debates about how to treat African Americans, particularly in terms of education, intensified. Despite many obstacles, Northern Blacks and supportive Whites found ways of educating African Americans. In the North, several elementary schools were founded that focused on literacy and mathematics. In the South, however, no colleges were created for African Americans during this time. Access to any form of formal education was primarily at the discretion of the plantar aristocrats.

In the South, slave labor was the core of the economy, and in many southern areas where plantations thrived, slave masters were adamant about keeping their slave labor illiterate of the English language. They felt that educating their slaves would fuel their dissatisfaction and that they would be influenced by the growing abolition movement. While some urban Southerners believed that Blacks should receive a basic education and even risked their lives to teach them to read and write, most of the South resisted (Anderson, 1988). African Americans nevertheless found ways of learning to read and write. Despite the many risks of physical abuse through whippings, lashings, and other violent acts, even death, African Americans in both the North and South found ways to learn to read and write, demonstrating resilience and a deep desire for education.

In New England, increasing numbers of European Americans came to view slavery as morally reprehensible and incompatible with prevailing societal values. The abolitionist movement gained considerable traction, especially in New York and Massachusetts. A key milestone during this era was the establishment of the American Anti-Slavery Society in 1833, which coincided with Britain's abolition of slavery. This organization played a pivotal role in educational reform in the United States by promoting the inclusion of African Americans in higher education, thus catalyzing a crucial shift in the educational landscape. Northern abolitionists promoted education as a liberating force that could enhance the movement, which they believed could improve the quality of life for people regardless of race (Williams, 2007). With the support of abolitionists and ministers, the first HBCUs were founded: Cheyney University (1837) and Lincoln University (1854) in Pennsylvania, and Wilberforce University (1856) in Ohio. For the first time in the history of U.S. higher education, these institutions offered educational opportunities to free people of color. By 1860 4.4 million Black people lived in the United States, the majority of them in Southern states.[2] Only about 40 Blacks had graduated from colleges and universities, all of which were in the North (Drewry & Doermann, 2001). Given the United States's nearly 230-year history of higher education at that time, this translates to an average of only one African American graduate every five years from *all* colleges combined.

In an effort to provide opportunities to those previously excluded from higher education, Senator Justin Morrill of Vermont proposed that the government donate funding and public land to every state to provide colleges for the benefit of agricultural and mechanical arts. After many failed attempts to pass the bill, Abraham Lincoln, shortly after assuming the Presidency in 1861, was able to sign the Morrill Land-Grant Act into law in 1862.

This act enabled states to establish public colleges through the development or sale of federal land grants. Contrary to common belief, the act did not provide the actual land for campus sites. Instead, it allotted so-called land scrip certificates representing 30,000 acres for each senator and representative in Congress from the states, intended for sale.

Lee and Ahtone (2020), Stein (2022), and Nash (2019) assert the need to recognize that the designated public land was in territories inhabited by Indigenous peoples, the original stewards of these lands, forcibly taken to build these colleges. Approximately 10.7 million acres seized from nearly 250 tribes, bands, and communities through over 160 violence-backed land cessions (Lee & Ahtone, 2020). Despite these troubling origins, the establishment of this network of public state colleges and universities became a cornerstone of American public higher education, profoundly shaping the educational landscape of the United States. Important to note is the fact that these institutions primarily benefited White students, which reflected the racial inequalities and the exclusionary practices of the time. The free labor of Blacks was used to cultivate the very land that violently dispossessed of Indigenous people, yet neither group was allowed to attend these institutions.

Whereas the Morrill Act of 1862 in theory prohibited racial discrimination, it did not keep states, particularly in the South, from rejecting Negro students. For example, in 1870, following the Civil War, the University of Mississippi resumed operations. Despite constitutional prohibitions against racial discrimination, the chancellor and faculty continued to deny enrollment to Negro students. They believed the University of Mississippi was established exclusively for Whites and that they should not be required to admit Negro students (Lovett, 2015). As a result, Mississippi established Alcorn Agricultural and Mechanical College for Negros, the first HBCU to be designated as a land-grant institution under the Morrill Act of 1862.[3] Despite Alcorn College being entitled to its fair share of funding, the legislature reduced its appropriations, leading to over a quarter-century of neglect for the institution (Lovett, 2015). In fact,

> as Reconstruction came to a close and wealthy planters of the South regained control of local and state governments and the lands seized during the Civil War, federal funds intended to be used to educate all of the South's residents were funneled to white-only institutions. (Williams & Ashley, 2004, p. 97)

These actions left few funds for HBCU land-grant institutions. Unfortunately, the deliberate reduction of appropriations for HBCU land-grant colleges would persist, another manifestation of bias, well into the 21st century.

Although Cheyney University, Lincoln University, and Wilberforce University were all established before the Civil War and Alcorn University, Hampton Institute, and Claflin University immediately following the War, formal education was not customarily available for most of the Black population. Due to financial regulations and other systematic restrictions that kept Blacks economically crippled, few free people of color were able to afford these first HBCUs. The financial assistance of Northern abolitionists, generous benefactors, and other organizations made it possible for these free people of color to attend college at little or no cost.

One notable organization was the American Missionary Association, established in Albany, New York, on September 3, 1846. A Christian organization with close ties to the Congregationalist Church, the Association was committed to the belief that educating and assimilating Black individuals would effectively counter White supremacy and slavery, thereby positioning education as a critical weapon in the battle against systemic oppression (Williams & Ashley, 2004). Similarly, the Freedman's Bureau, established by Congress on March 3, 1865, under An Act to Establish a Bureau for the Relief of Freedmen and Refugees, was another abolitionist organization that prioritized the education of African Americans along with providing food, shelter, clothing, medical services, and land to displaced Southerners, including newly freed slaves. With substantial financial support from the Association and the Freedman's Bureau, a significant number of HBCUs originated during the years from 1865 to 1885. The greatest number of HBCUs were established in 1867, two years after the Emancipation Proclamation. Although now legally emancipated, these Blacks still faced severe restrictions in legal, educational, economic, political, and social environments.

Most of the first HBCUs were private, nonprofit institutions; that is, they were established and funded without state government support. For several years after the Emancipation Proclamation, Southern states refused to integrate, and many Northern schools still functioned under the unspoken cultural rules of segregation. Financial contributions from religious and abolitionists organizations such as the American Missionary Association began to dwindle. In 1872, the Freedman's Bureau officially ended due to corruption and the misappropriation of funds. As a result, many schools founded under the Freedman's Bureau and the Association were taken over by the states. These colleges and universities became normal and industrial institutes focusing more on teacher training and trades than on the classical education favored by Northern missionaries (Williams & Ashley, 2004). Despite these financial and organizational hurdles, the following HBCUs were founded by or with assistance from Association or Freedman's Bureau: Alabama State University (1867), Atlanta University, now Clark Atlanta University (1865), Avery Institute (1865, now closed), Barber-Scotia College (1867), Berea College (1855, no longer considered an HBCU), Dillard University (1869), Fayetteville State University (1867), Fisk University (1866), Hampton University (1868), Howard University (1867), Huston-Tillotson College (1875), Johnson C. Smith University (1867), Lemoyne-Owen

College (1862), Morehouse College (1867), Morgan State University (1867), Saint Augustine's University (1867), Talladega College (1865), and Tugaloo College (1869).

Separate and (Un)Equal (1890–1965)

By the end of the 19th century, many US colleges and universities continued to resist integrating African Americans. Despite the progressive intent behind the Morrill Act of 1862, which opened higher education to many people historically and systematically oppressed, the act did not guarantee universal access for *all* people. In the North, racial discrimination often prohibited Blacks from taking part of these new educational opportunities. The situation was more dire in the South, where state legislation enforced racial segregation and excluded Blacks, frequently still enslaved, altogether. These laws were part of broader efforts to maintain White supremacy, particularly in higher education (Chun & Feagin, 2021; Harper et al., 2009). Leedell Neyland (1990) note that

> [S]ince approximately 90 percent of the 4,000,000 blacks in America were in slavery, and since the approximately 250,000 'free Negroes' in southern states were highly circumscribed in their social interaction with whites, the early land-grant colleges became white bastions, barring blacks from admission by both custom and law. (p. 2)

The second Morrill Act of 1890 was seen as a way to address the loopholes of the first Morrill Act of 1862, specifically by stipulating that African Americans were to be included in the United States land-grant university higher education system without discrimination. The 1890 Morrill Act provided federal funds, not land, for both Black and White schools in the segregated educational system. To address racial segregation in higher education, the Morrill Land-Grant Acts forced states with segregated systems to establish separate colleges for Black students. The statute stipulated that

> No money shall be paid out under this act to any State or Territory for the support and maintenance of a college where a distinction of race or color is made in the admission of students, but the establishment and maintenance of such colleges separately for white and colored students shall be held to be in compliance with the provisions of this act if the funds received in such State or Territory be equitably divided. Morrill Act of 1890, P.L. 37–130.

The Morrill Act also prohibited the distribution of federal funding to states that made distinctions of race in admissions unless at least one land-grant college for African Americans was established (Allen & Jewell, 2002; Redd, 1998). In other words, for states to keep receiving federal funding, they had either to demonstrate that admission to a land-grant school was not restricted by race or to create a college to train Black students in agriculture, mechanical arts, and architecture. Most states chose the latter.[4]

The willingness of Southern states to offer educational opportunities to African Americans—solely under conditions of racial segregation—was a precursor to the Jim Crow ideology that the Supreme Court would later endorse through the infamous *Plessy v. Ferguson* (1896) decision. That "separate but equal" doctrine legitimized racial segregation through laws that purported to provide comparable public facilities and services for both African Americans and Whites. This meant that Blacks may have been given the right to a free and public education, but it did not mean that their education was to occur in the same institutions with Whites (Noltemeyer et al., 2012). De facto segregation had become the way of life in many parts of the country, and the *Plessy* decision provided its legal justification.

For more than half a century, numerous colleges and universities across America operated under the "separate but equal" principle. Segregationist laws were only overturned in 1954 by the Supreme Court in *Brown v. Board of Education*, which declared such "separate, but equal" practices in public K–12 schools unconstitutional. Although colleges and universities were not the specific focus of the *Brown* decision, fundamental similarities exist between the public K–12 schools referred to in the *Brown* decision and the public, land-grant schools for Blacks. All public educational institutions are funded primarily by state and federal dollars. Like many of the K–12 schools in 1954, the Black land-grant institutions were never funded on par with their White institution counterparts.

Historically Black Colleges and Universities were founded under the 1890 Morrill Land Grant have never received resources at the level of the 1852 land grant institutions, nor have their faculty and students benefited from the same opportunities (Harris, 2021; Martin & Hipp, 2018; Massy, 1996). Such disproportionate funding persists today[5]: Several Black land-grant universities continue to experience underfunding or even the complete withholding of government allocations (Cooper, 2023; Watkins, 2024; U.S. Department of Education & Agriculture, 2023). At the time of the *Brown v. Board of Education* landmark decision, segregation was as prevalent in higher education as it was in K–12 systems; the vast majority of African American students received their undergraduate education in HBCUs.[6] Some colleges and universities, entrenched in the ideology and practices of racial superiority, overlooked the ruling's broader implication for equity and were not readily amenable to integration. Despite expectations for a significant rise in Black enrollment at predominantly White institutions after the *Brown* decision, the majority of Black college students for several years afterward opted for HBCUs.

By the 1960s, America was at the height of racial unrest. The Civil Rights Movement was a nationwide effort to achieve equal rights for African Americans and an end to racial segregation and exclusion across the United States. It is seen now as the apex of the attempt to dismantle more than 400 years of sociocultural, political, and economic practices stemming from slavery, racism, and White supremacy. In June 1963, President John F. Kennedy asked Congress for a comprehensive civil rights bill, induced by massive resistance to desegregation and by the murder of civil rights activist Medgar Evers. After Kennedy was assassinated in November 1963, Lyndon Johnson vowed to carry out his proposals for civil rights reform. The next year, he United States Congress enacted one of the most monumental pieces of legislation in American history, the Civil Rights Act of 1964. The legislation outlawed discrimination based on race, color, religion, sex, and national origin. It also prohibited unequal application of voter registration requirements, racial segregation in schools and public places, and employment discrimination. Tile IV—Desegregation of Public Education of the Act states:

> "Public school" means any elementary or secondary educational institution, and "public college" means any institution of higher education or any technical or vocational school above the secondary school level, provided that such public school or public college is operated by a State, subdivision of a State, or governmental agency within a State, or operated wholly or predominantly from or through the use of governmental funds or property, or funds or property derived from a governmental source.

The Civil Rights Act represents the most significant civil rights law enacted since Reconstruction, marking a crucial advancement by removing racial barriers to educational access for African Americans. Despite this progress, African Americans still faced considerable challenges in gaining access to predominantly White institutions in the years following the Act. As Gbemi (2016) notes, these institutions saw minimal shifts in their cultural norms and overall character. For example, in the North, often seen as more progressive than the South, African Americans were frequently excluded from living in dormitories with White students. Moreover, they experienced social alienation, not only in shared spaces like cafeterias but also in classrooms, thus affecting their educational experiences and integration into campus life. Black students nevertheless persisted in attending colleges despite facing persistently hostile campus environments, where White students, faculty, and administrators actively questioned both their right to be there and their intellectual capabilities (Williamson, 2013).

One year following the Civil Rights Act of 1964, President Johnson signed two critical pieces of legislation that significantly influenced the accessibility of higher education for African Americans over the next six decades, the Executive Order 11246 and the Higher Education Act of 1965. The Executive Order, also known as the Equal Employment Opportunity order, mandated non-discriminatory hiring and employment practices among U.S. government contractors. It required these contractors to take "affirmative action" to ensure that employment practices were conducted without discrimination based on race, color, religion, sex, or national origin (Part II, Subpart B, Sec. 202(1)). Johnson's commencement address at Howard University on June 4, 1965, underscored his commitment to affirmative action and to creating educational opportunities for all Americans.

> "Freedom is not enough," he proclaimed. You do not take a person who, for years, has been hobbled by chains and liberate him, bring him up to the starting line of a race and then say, "You are free to compete with all the others," and still justly believe that you have been completely fair. . . . We seek not just legal equity but human ability, not just equality as a right and a theory but equality as a fact and equality as a result.

A few months after signing Executive Order 11246, President Johnson signed the Higher Education Act of 1965 that ensured that every individual had access to higher education. The law was intended "to strengthen the educational resources of our colleges and universities and to provide financial assistance for students in postsecondary and higher education." It increased federal money to universities, created scholarships, gave low-interest loans for students, and established a National Teachers Corps. These two federal initiatives have played a foundational role in democratizing higher education in the United States, breaking down barriers for African Americans, and creating broader educational opportunities for all citizens.

The 1954 *Brown* ruling and the Civil Rights Act of 1964 significantly expanded educational opportunities for Blacks previously denied access. In the years following these two rulings, a record number of Black students gained access to numerous institutions formerly closed to them. In some ways, however, this situation presented both benefits and drawbacks. Whereas African American students found new educational opportunities at White institutions, enrollment at HBCUs began to decline because they could not compete with the scholarship and financial aid offered by predominantly White schools (Williams & Ashley, 2004). Some HBCUs were compelled to merge with, or were absorbed by, local White institutions. Despite these challenges, HBCUs continued to forge influential spaces in higher education, providing nurturing environments for intellectual growth for African Americans.

Access Granted, Equity Denied (1968 to the present)

In the wake of Dr. Martin Luther King, Jr.'s assassination in 1968 and the extensive racial unrest from the Civil Rights Movement, numerous colleges and universities initiated policies to foster racial diversity and ensure wider accessibility (Thelin, 2019). The landmark *Adams v. Richardson* case in the 1970s challenged predominantly White institutions that had historically discriminated against African Americans, threatening the loss of federal funds unless they desegregated. This mandate compelled such institutions to open their doors wider to African Americans, viewed by many in academia as a minimal step toward fairness in admissions. The introduction of affirmative action was a significant response to this mandate, yielding remarkable improvements in access for African Americans and other minority groups.

HBCUs faced considerable obstacles during the 1970s and 1980s. Continued unequal funding from the state government crippled public, land-grant HBCUs, while private HBCUs grappled with shrinking endowments and philanthropy. This financial stranglehold limited scholarships, hindering HBCUs' ability to compete for talented Black students.

Whereas affirmative action played a crucial role in providing opportunities in higher education for Black students, it also brought significant challenges. Particularly at predominantly White institutions, many Black students encountered substantial inequities. While open admissions policies at non-competitive institutions have broadened access to higher education in various ways (Boykin, Hilton, & Palmer, 2017; Iloh & Toldson, 2013), the representation of Black students at selective colleges and universities is still concerning (Baker et al., 2018; Jones & Nichols, 2020).

Black students at predominantly or historically White institutions frequently experience racism and systematic oppression, which can significantly affect their academic and social experiences (Guiffrida & Douthit, 2010; Kelly et al., 2017; McGee & Martin, 2011). These policies soon faced legal challenges, however, with cases questioning the legality of affirmative action measures such as *Regents of the University of California v. Bakke* (*2013*)1978), *Grutter v. Bollinger* and *Gratz v. Bollinger* (both 2003), and *Fisher v. University of Texas at Austin* (2013). These cases highlighted the ongoing national debate over the balance between rectifying past injustices and ensuring equality in higher education.

In the 1990s, students and alumni at several major, historically White state universities, such as the University of Georgia, University of Texas, and the University of Michigan, became increasingly vocal in their opposition to affirmative action programs. While many viewed affirmative action as a necessary measure to correct long-standing racial inequalities, its application in higher education continued to face significant opposition (Byrd-Chichester, 2000; Long, 2004, 2007). One prevalent critique argued that affirmative action led to reverse discrimination against Whites (Messer-Davidow, 2021; Wilson, 1995). Consequently, Black student enrollment notable declined at many competitive, White institutions (Moses & Farley, 2011). This trend led many Black students to reconsider Historically Black Colleges and Universities (HBCUs), attracted by a desire to connect with their cultural heritage and traditions (Freeman, 2012). HBCUs had long included elements of Black culture in their curricula, but they lacked formal programs. In response to this growing interest, HBCUs began to expand their offerings by developing comprehensive African American Studies and other related programs.

The resurgence of interest in Black history and culture during the 1990s was partly fueled by popular culture, notably through the television series *The Cosby Show* and the hit sitcom *A Different World*, which prominently featured HBCUs. The television series *A Different World*, under the guidance of producer and Howard University alumna Debbie Allen, offered an authentic and engaging depiction of Black college life, inspiring a new generation of students to explore HBCUs. Former Dillard University President Walter Kimbrough highlighted this phenomenon in a *New York Times* interview, noting significant enrollment increases at HBCUs during the show's run and their slower growth following its conclusion:

> From the debut of "The Cosby Show" in 1984 until the end of "A Different World" in 1993, American higher education grew by 16.8 percent. During the same time period, historically black colleges and universities grew by 24.3 percent—44 percent better than all of higher education. But in the 11 years after "A Different World" ended, while all of higher education grew at a robust 20.7 percent, historically black colleges and universities grew only 9.2 percent. (Gasman & Kimbrough, 2010)

The positive portrayal of HBCUs in the entertainment industry continues to have a direct impact on generating interest in these institutions. Television series such as "Black-ish" and "This Is Us" maintain this trend by depicting HBCUs in a favorable light, presenting them as attractive options for prospective African American students.

The 2000s

The first decade of the new millennium presented significant challenges for most colleges and universities. Financial strains such as diminished endowments, reduced federal and state appropriations, and fewer donor contributions affected academic programming. Beginning in 2000, HBCUs experienced a slow decline in student enrollment. The 2008 recession had a disproportionately adverse impact on HBCUs (Gasman, 2009). These institutions often rely heavily on tuition for funding and, since many HBCU students come from low-income households, these families had fewer resources to mitigate the effects of the economic downturn. Additionally, HBCUs typically have smaller endowments compared with other institutions, rendering them more vulnerable to economic fluctuations. As a result, many low-income African Americans opted for community colleges or historically White state institutions, which offered relatively lower tuition costs (Gasman, 2009).

The events of the early 2020s served as a pivotal and revealing moment in American history, underscoring the country's enduring issues with racism, especially in the realm of law enforcement. A first responder shot in Breonna Taylor in home during a no-knock raid by the Louisville Metro Police Department, and the horrifying killing of George Floyd, who died after a Minneapolis police officer knelt on his neck for almost eight minutes—an act captured and widely disseminated by a bystander—underscored the urgent need for systemic change. These incidents catalyzed colleges and universities nationwide to critically address racial inequalities in their institutions. Many college leaders published statements condemning White nationalism, White supremacy, and police brutality toward Blacks (Meikle & Morris, 2022). Other colleges acted by removing Confederate monuments and other explicit symbols of racism and White supremacy (Cox, 2021). Moreover, some colleges called for new and often far-ranging efforts to admit more Black applicants and hire additional Black faculty—not under the umbrella of non-discrimination or affirmative action, but in the names of equity, inclusion, and antiracism (Rosenberg, 2021).

Critics viewed public denunciation of racism and the removal of symbols of racism as merely performative, which prompted widespread debate about whether these measures truly addressed the underlying issues and whether they would have a lasting impact (Blair, 2021; Crenshaw, 2011; Ekpe & Toutant, 2022). This debate was brought into sharp focus by a landmark Supreme Court affirmative action decision in the cases of *Students for Fair Admissions, Incorporated v. Presidents and Fellows of Harvard College* and *Students for Fair Admissions, Incorporated v. University of North Carolina* on June 29, 2023, which ruled that race-based affirmative action in higher education violates the Equal Protection Clause of the 14th Amendment. This decision underscored the persistent influence of exclusionary practices, deeply rooted since the era of slavery, in the fabric of American higher education. In addition, it highlighted the ongoing need for policymakers in both the public and institutions to address the structural barriers that perpetuate racial disparities in college access (Harper et al., 2009). This ruling effectively ended race-conscious admission programs across the country, stripping both public and private institutions of the ability to consider race as one of several factors in admissions decisions, a practice believed necessary to ensure diversity and equity in higher education.

For many families, HBCUs emerged as appealing choices due to concerns about racial hostility and students' feelings of isolation at predominantly White institutions, along with evolving perceptions of what constitutes the pinnacle of higher education. These factors, combined with a shifting landscape that values diverse educational environments, have once again positioned HBCUs as favorable alternatives. Much as in past decades marked by racial and civil unrest, HBCUs remain intellectual sanctuaries for students seeking an educational experience in which they feel safe, welcomed, and affirmed.

Notes

1. South Carolina enacted a bill for the better governance of Negroes, the South Carolina Act of 1740, known as the Negro Act of 1740. In general, the law prohibited enslaved Africans from growing and earning a living off their own crops, from moving and traveling freely, from assembling in groups, and from learning how to read.
2. U.S. Department of Commerce, Bureau of the Census, *The Social and Economic Status of the Black Populations in the United States: An Historical View, 1790–1978* (Washington, D.C.: U. S. Government Printing Office), Series P-23, No. 80, p. 11.
3. In the 1870s, Mississippi, Virginia, and South Carolina each assigned one African American college land grant status. These were, respectively, Alcorn University, Hampton Institute, and Claflin University.
4. A total of nineteen new land-grant HBCUs were established under the Act. The majority of HBCUs established during this time evolved out of state desires to avoid admitting Blacks to existing White institutions.
5. An analysis by the U.S. Department of Education revealed that 16 out of 17 states have consistently underfunded their historically Black land-grant colleges, with the cumulative shortfall exceeding $12 billion over several decades. Such chronic underfunding has significantly affected various academic programs, including music. While predominantly White land-grant institutions have often used their full government allocations to offer substantial scholarships and build state-of-the-art facilities to attract students, Black land-grant colleges have had to navigate these financial constraints while still managing to provide quality music instruction. This disparity raises important questions about the potential impact its music programs could achieve at these institutions if they received equitable funding.
6. Approximately 90% of Black college graduates earned their degrees from HBCUs prior to the *Brown ruling* (Harper, 2019; Kim, 2011).

References

Allen, W. R., & Jewell, J. O. (2002). A backward glance forward: Past, present and future perspectives on historically Black colleges and universities. *The Review of Higher Education, 25*(3), 241–261.

Anderson, J. D. (1988). *The education of Blacks in the south, 1860–1935*. University of North Carolina Press.

Baker, R., Klasik, D., & Reardon, S. F. (2018). Race and stratification in college enrollment over time. *AERA Open, 4*(1), 2332858417751896.

Blair, K. (2021). Empty gestures: Performative utterances and allyship. *Journal of Dramatic Theory and Criticism, 35*(2), 53–73.

Boykin, T. F., Hilton, A., & Palmer, R. (Eds.). (2017). *Professional education at historically Black colleges and universities: Past trends and future outcomes.* Routledge.

Brown, M. C., Donahoo, S., & Bertrand, R. D. (2001). The Black college and the quest for educational opportunity: The Black college: New perspectives and emerging possibilities. *Urban Education, 36*(5), 553–571.

Byrd, J. (2000). The federal courts and claims of racial discrimination in higher education. *The Journal of Negro Education, 69*(1/2), 12–26.

Chun, E. B., & Feagin, J. R. (2021). *Who killed higher education?: Maintaining White dominance in a desegregating era.* Routledge.

Cooper, J. N. (2023). Battle of the lands: The creation of land grant institutions and HBCUs: Fostering a still separate and still unequal higher education system. *Washington and Lee Journal of Civil Rights and Social Justice, 30*(2), 247–287.

Cox, K. L. (2021). *No common ground: Confederate monuments and the ongoing fight for racial justice.* UNC Press Books.

Crenshaw, K. W. (2011). Twenty years of critical race theory: Looking back to move forward. *Connecticut Law Review, 43.*

Drewry, H. N., & Doermann, H. (2001). *Stand and prosper: Private Black colleges and their students.* Princeton University Press.

Edwards-Ingram, Y. (2019). Scholars, lawyers, and their slaves: St. George and Nathaniel Beverly Tucker in the college town of Williamsburg. In L. M. Harris, J. T. Campbell, & A. Brophy (Eds.), *Slavery and the university: Histories and legacies* (pp. 211–231). University of Georgia Press.

Ekpe, L., & Toutant, S. (2022). Moving beyond performative allyship: A conceptual framework for anti-racist co-conspirators. In K. F. Johnson, N. M. Sparkman-Key, A. Meca, & S. Z. Tarver (Eds.), *Developing anti-racist practices in the helping professions: Inclusive theory, pedagogy, and application* (pp. 67–91). Springer.

Freeman, K. (2012). *African Americans and college choice: The influence of family and school.* State University of New York Press.

Gasman, M. (2009). Historically Black colleges and universities in a time of economic crisis. *Academe, 95*(6), 26–28. http://www.jstor.org/stable/20694590

Gasman, M., & Kimbrough, W. (2010, March 11). Part 4: Answers on historically Black colleges and universities. *The New York Times.* https://archive.nytimes.com/thechoice.blogs.nytimes.com/2010/03/11/hbcu4/

Gbemi, O. (2016). Examining primarily White institutions of higher education: Black student experience in the 1960s. *Binghamton University Undergraduate Journal, 2*(1), 1–18.

Guiffrida, D. A., & Douthit, K. Z. (2010). The Black student experience at predominantly White colleges: Implications for school and college counselors. *Journal of Counseling & Development, 88*(3), 311–318.

Hannah-Jones, N., & The New York Times Magazine (2021). *The 1619 project: A new origin story.* Random House.

Harper, B. E. (2019). African American access to higher education: The evolving role of historically Black colleges and universities. *American Academic, 3*, 109–128.

Harper, S. R., Patton, L. D., & Wooden, O. S. (2009). Access and equity for African American students in higher education: A critical race historical analysis of policy efforts. *Journal of Higher Education, 80*(4), 389–414.

Harris, A. (2021). *The state must provide: Why America's colleges have always been unequal--and how to set them right*. HarperCollins.

Iloh, C., & Toldson, I. A. (2013). Black students in 21st century higher education: A closer look at for-profit and community colleges (Editor's Commentary). *The Journal of Negro Education, 82*(3), 205–212. https://doi.org/10.7709/jnegroeducation.82.3.0205

Jackson, J. P., Weidman, N. M., & Rubin, G. (2005). The origins of scientific racism. *The Journal of Blacks in Higher Education, 50*(50), 66–79.

Jones, T., & Nichols, A. H. (2020, January 15). *Hard truths: Why only race-conscious policies can fix racism in higher education*. The Education Trust. https://edtrust.org/rti/hard-truths/

Kelly, B. T., Segoshi, M., Adams, L., & Raines, A. (2017). Experiences of Black alumnae from PWIs: Did they thrive?. *NASPA Journal About Women in Higher Education, 10*(2), 167–185.

Kim, M. M. (2011). Early career earnings of African American students: The impact of attendance at historically Black versus White colleges and universities. *The Journal of Negro Education, 80*(4), 505–520.

Lee, R., & Ahtone, T. (2020, May 8). Land-grab universities should acknowledge their debt to Indigenous people. *High Country News*. https://www.hcn.org/articles/indigenous-affairs-land-grab-universities-land-grant-universities-should-acknowledge-their-debt-to-indigenous-people/

Long, M. C. (2004). Race and college admissions: An alternative to affirmative action?. *The Review of Economics and Statistics, 86*(4), 1020–1033.

Long, M. C. (2007). Affirmative action and its alternatives in public universities: What do we know?. *Public Administration Review, 67*(2), 315–330.

Lovett, B. L. (2015). *America's historically Black colleges & universities: A narrative history from the nineteenth century into the twenty-first century*. Mercer University Press.

Martin, M. V., & Hipp, J. S. (2018). A time for substance: Confronting funding inequities at land grant institutions. *Tribal College, 29*(3), 50–57.

Massy, W. F. (Ed.) (1996), *Resource allocation in higher education*. University of Michigan Press.

McGee, E. O., & Martin, D. B. (2011). "You would not believe what I have to go through to prove my intellectual value!" Stereotype management among academically successful Black mathematics and engineering students. *American Educational Research Journal, 48*(6), 1347–1389.

Meikle, P. A., & Morris, L. R. (2022). University social responsibility: Challenging systemic racism in the aftermath of George Floyd's murder. *Administrative Sciences, 12*(1), 1–19. https://doi.org/10.3390/admsci12010036

Messer-Davidow, E. (2021). *The making of reverse discrimination: How Defunis and Bakke bleached racism from equal protection*. University Press of Kansas.

Moses, M. S., & Farley, A. N. (2011). Are ballot initiatives a good way to make education policy? The case of affirmative action. *Educational Studies, 47*(3), 260–279.

Nash, M. A. (2019). Entangled pasts: Land-grant colleges and American Indian dispossession. *History of Education Quarterly, 59*(4), 437–467.

Neyland, L. W. (1990). *Historically Black land-grant institutions and the development of agriculture and home economics, 1890–1990.* Florida A&M University Foundation.

Noltemeyer, A. L., Mujic, J., & McLoughlin, C. S. (2012). The history of inequality in education. In A. L. Noltemeyer & C. S. McLoughlin (Eds.), *Disproportionality in education and special education* (pp. 3–16). Charles C. Thomas Publisher.

Perkins, L. (1997). The African American female elite: The early history of African American women in the seven sister colleges, 1880–1960. *Harvard Educational Review, 67*(4), 718–757.

Presidential Committee on the Legacy of Slavery. (2022). *The legacy of slavery at Harvard: Report and recommendations of the Presidential committee.* Harvard University Press.

Redd, K. E. (1998). Historically Black colleges and universities: Making a comeback. *New Directions for Higher Education, 1998*(102), 33–43.

Ricard, R. B., & Brown, M. C. (2023). *Ebony towers in higher education: The evolution, mission, and presidency of historically black colleges and universities.* Routledge Publishing.

Rosenberg, J. S. (2021). Affirmative action: RIP or release 3.0?. *Academic Questions, 34*(2), 46–56.

Stein, S. (2022). *Unsettling the university: Confronting the colonial foundations of US higher education.* Johns Hopkins University Press.

Thelin, J. R. (2019). *A history of American higher education.* Johns Hopkins University Press.

United States Department of Agriculture. (2023, September 18). *Secretaries of education, agriculture call on governors to equitably fund land-grant HBCUs.* USDA.gov.

U.S. Department of Commerce, Bureau of the Census. (1790). *The social and economic status of the Black Populations in the United States: An historical view, 1790–1978* Series P-23, No. 80 (p. 11). U. S. Government Printing Office.

Watkins, S. (2024). The state of South Carolina vs. South Carolina State University: The underfunding of a Black land grant university. *The Macksey Journal, 4*(1). Article 28.

Wilder, C. S. (2013). *Ebony and ivy: Race, slavery, and the troubled history of America's universities.* Bloomsbury.

Wilder, C. S. (2019). Sons from the Southward & some from the West Indies": The academy and slavery in revolutionary America. In L. M. Harris, J. T. Campbell, & A. Brophy (Eds.), *Slavery and the university: Histories and legacies* (pp. 21–45). University of Georgia Press.

Williams, H. A. (2007). *Self-taught: African American education in slavery and freedom.* University of North Carolina Press.

Williams, J., & Ashley, D. (2004). *I'll find a way or make one: A tribute to historically Black colleges and universities.* HarperCollins.

Williamson, J. A. (2013). *Black power on campus: The University of Illinois* (Vols. 1965–75). University of Illinois Press.

Wilson, J. K. (1995). The myth of reverse discrimination in higher education. *The Journal of Blacks in Higher Education*, (10), 88–93.

Work, M. N. (1919). The life of Charles B. Ray. *The Journal of Negro History, 4*(4), 361–371.

Additional Reading

Lorde, A. (2007). *Sister outsider: Essays and speeches.* Crossing Press.

CHAPTER 2

EBONY TOWERS: THE MISSIONS AND RELEVANCE OF HBCUs

ABSTRACT

Historically Black Colleges and Universities (HBCUs) were born out of resistance to systemic injustice, serving as spaces where academic rigor, cultural affirmation, and social empowerment converge. African American leaders and committed advocates founded these institutions with a clear mission to educator its students and equip them to uplift their communities. While HBCUs share this foundational goal, they are not monolithic. Whether public or private, religiously affiliated, or serving single-sex populations, each institution expresses its mission in ways shaped by its history, context, and community needs.

Chapter 2 explores the evolving missions and continued relevance of HBCUs emphasizing their foundational role in shaping educational, cultural, and musical life for African Americans. This chapter further examines the historical debates surrounding vocational versus liberal arts education, most notably through the philosophies of Booker T. Washington and W. E. B. Du Bois. The chapter also investigates the unique missions of historically Black women's colleges, emphasizing their role in advancing intersectional empowerment. With particular attention to music education, the chapter argues that aligning music programs with institutional missions is key to delivering culturally relevant and socially meaningful instruction. In a post-affirmative action era, HBCUs remain vital as transformative educational spaces committed to identity formation, artistic excellence, and educational justice.

In a 2018 interview at Georgetown University, Spelman College President Emerita Johnetta Cole aptly described Historically Black Colleges and Universities (HBCUs) as "special mission institutions where what they do and what they provide is what we hope is a great education" (Friedman, 2018). Her distinction is well-founded. HBCUs are not ordinary institutions; they have a unique mission centered on uplifting those who have been systematically oppressed. Like other American colleges and universities, HBCUs are committed to providing a quality education that equips students with the skills they need to succeed. While they share a common mission, each HBCU has its own distinct culture, which reflects the diversity within the African American community. Just as we are not monolithic, neither are HBCUs.

The need for HBCUs arose from the fundamental belief that education is a right, not a privilege, and that every individual deserves access to it. Beyond academics, HBCUs foster a supportive and affirming environment. In these Ebony Towers,[1] faculty, staff, and students find a space where their identities are valued, and their humanity is never questioned. This nurturing atmosphere is essential to the realization of HBCUs' missions. While HBCUs share a common historical mission to educate Black students, it has evolved over time. Each institution, although rooted in this shared legacy, has developed its own purpose, goals, and philosophy that guide its unique approach to education.

Unity Amidst Diversity

Every college and university is guided by a mission statement that outlines its roles, purposes, and functions. For many years, HBCUs operated with a shared a common mission born from years of profound adversity: the commitment to providing a better education for African Americans. This shared mission became the foundation upon which these institutions were built, evolved, and later officially defined. The Higher Education Act of 1965, as amended, defines an HBCU as

> any historically black college or university that was established prior to 1964, whose principal mission was, and is, the education of black Americans, and that is accredited by a nationally recognized accrediting agency or association determined by the Secretary [of Education] to be a reliable authority as to

the quality of training offered or is, according to such an agency or association, making reasonable progress toward accreditation. (Higher Education Act of, 1965)

While the original purpose of HBCUs was to educate African Americans, this definition offers limited insight into the specific objectives of each institution (Ricard & Brown, 2008). HBCUs are not monolithic, and their missions are based on the diverse contexts in which they operate—public or private, located in rural, urban, or suburban settings, religious affiliation, or focused on serving single-sex populations. Understanding the unique missions of HBCUs is essential to effectively discuss teaching music teaching in these institutions, because it illuminates how music is integrated into the broader academic experience for HBCU students.

The evolution of HBCUs reflects the dynamic nature of their missions over time, often significantly shaped by their founders and social contexts. For instance, two of the three HBCUs formed before the Civil War, Cheyney University (1837) and Lincoln University (1854), both in Pennsylvania, were founded in direct opposition to prevailing racist beliefs that African Americans were incapable of academic achievement. Cheyney University was established through a $10,000 bequest from Richard Humphreys, a Quaker philanthropist, to educate African Americans and train them as teachers. Similarly, Lincoln University (initially called Ashmun Institute) was founded by Presbyterian minister John Dickey and his wife, Sarah Cresson, an abolitionist Quaker. They aimed to prepare young African American men with a classical, scientific, and theological education primarily to serve as missionaries in Africa. In contrast, the third school, Wilberforce University, located in Ohio, was founded in 1856 by African American leaders from the African Methodist Episcopal Church, and is one of the few HBCUs created and operated by African Americans. Its mission centered on providing classical education and training teachers to educate and uplift the Black community.

From Reconstruction through the Jim Crow Era, Christian denominations and religious organizations founded the majority of private HBCUs with missions that reflected Christian ideals (e.g., biblical training, morality, and acts of service). Many HBCUs, including Bethune-Cookman University in Florida, Claflin University in South Carolina, and Clark Atlanta University in Georgia, are affiliated with the United Methodist Church. Xavier University of Louisiana holds the distinction as the only historically Black Catholic University, established by Mother Katherine Drexel who dedicated her life to the needs of Native Americans and African Americans. Oakwood University located in Alabama, established by the Seventh-day Adventist Church, is the sole HBCU founded and operated by this denomination. The American Baptist Home Mission Society, along with its women's arm, played a significant role in founding institutions such as Benedict College in South

Carolina, Morehouse College in Georgia, Shaw University in North Carolina, Spelman College in Georgia, and Virginia Union University in Virginia.

Many of these schools started in church spaces, using those areas for classes until permanent buildings could be secured. Interestingly, several HBCU institutions began in church basements, including Morehouse College, Rust College, and Spelman College. Morehouse started as the Augusta Institute in 1867 in the Springfield Baptist Church in Georgia. Rust College was founded a year earlier in Holly Springs, Mississippi, at Ashbury Methodist Episcopal Church. Spelman College began its first classes in the basement of Friendship Baptist Church in Atlanta, and Georgia and Bennett College began in the basement of Wernersville Methodist Episcopal Church (now St. Matthews United Methodist Church) in Greensboro, North Carolina.

Approximately half of all HBCUs were established by Christian organizations that received significant funding from private philanthropists. Men and women affiliated with these organizations had been sympathetic to the abolitionist cause now saw the social uplift of freedmen as a crucial part of their work. Scholars have examined the underlying motives of these Christian groups in founding these institutions (Fleming, 1983; Singleton, 2022; Woodson, 1998). Historically, religion and education have been used as instruments to exert control over systematically oppressed groups. For example, Cohen and Kisker (2010) point out that William and Mary, Harvard, and Dartmouth were partly founded with the mission of Christianizing and 'civilizing indigenous and Black populations, a mindset that persisted in the founders of HBCUs in the mid-to-late 19th century. Missionaries often perceived Blacks as hapless victims of a corrupt and immoral system that inculcated values antithetical to civilization. They viewed their God-given task as both to civilize and educate the freedmen, and in so doing to ensure the survival of American society (Allen & Jewell, 2002). In *The Education of Blacks in the South*, Anderson (1988) argues that while the intentions of these White religious groups and missionary philanthropists in funding several private HBCUs were ostensibly well-meaning, they were not devoid of racist, supremacist, and self-interested overtones.

> Missionary philanthropists held that slavery had generated pathological religious and cultural practices in the black community. Slavery, not race, kept blacks from acquiring the important moral and social values of thrift, industry, frugality, and sobriety, all of which were necessary to live a sustained Christian life. In turn, these missing morals and values prevented the development of a stable family life among Afro-Americans. Therefore, missionaries argued, it was essential for education to introduce the ex-slaves to the values and rules of modern society. Without education, they concluded, blacks would rapidly degenerate and become a national menace to American civilization. (p. 242)

The use of religion and education as tools of control, despite intentions sometimes marred by racism and self-interest, inadvertently catalyzed a response in the African American community. Motivated by a desire for self-determination and with the aid of White abolitionists, African American preachers and community leaders took the initiative to establish their own educational institutions (Lovett, 2015). These institutions, founded by and for African Americans, represented a pivotal shift toward autonomy. The African Methodist Episcopal Church played a crucial role in this movement, founding and maintaining institutions such as Allen University in South Carolina, Morris Brown College in Georgia, Wilberforce College in Ohio, Paul Quinn College in Texas, Edward Waters College in Florida, Kittrell College in North Carolina, and Shorter College in Arkansas. Unlike their counterparts founded by White benefactors, these schools were focused on the social uplift of African Americans. They developed their educational missions independently, free from the control of White religious benefactors. This approach allowed them to tailor their missions to the specific needs and aspirations of the African American community (Watkins, 2000).

The passage of the Morrill Act of 1890 led to a surge in the establishment of land-grant HBCUs. The initial mission of these land-grant HBCUs were to educate students in agricultural, vocational training, mechanical and industrial arts to enable them to become viable in the labor work force. This federally supported model of vocational education, although attractive to some African Americans, inadvertently promoted the idea that they were intellectually less capable than Whites and should be offered a separate and lower-caliber education (Anderson, 1988; Davis, 1998).

Roebuck and Murty (1993) posit that public HBCUs were created for the following reasons: "To get millions of dollars in federal funds for the development of white land-grant universities, to limit African American education to vocational training, and to prevent African Americans from attending white land-grant colleges" (p. 27). Some African Americans protested vocational education, noting the indignity that slavery added to labor. Although students with this mindset protested the initial mission of early Black land-grant colleges, they ultimately felt that, in a segregated society, they would be better off financially if they pursued a practical education in vocational training rather than liberal arts and sciences.

In the landscape of higher education, Black women play a pivotal and transformative role that cannot be overlooked. Their journey through academia has been shaped by historical systems of oppression, making their voices crucial in reshaping educational spaces (Watkins, 2009). Thus, Black women have a distinctive standpoint from which to understand the missions of HBCUs specifically created for them. Women's colleges have long been prominent in women's education. Many women's colleges, including the Seven Sisters, which offered the equivalent of an Ivy League education, did not automatically open their doors to Black women. At a time when coeducational institutions of higher learning were increasingly admitting Black men, many women's colleges actively discouraged Black women from applying.

In response to this situation, abolitionists, religious organizations, and other advocates recognized the need to create institutions specifically designed to meet the unique needs of Black women. While the missions of White women's colleges focus primarily on gender issues, the missions of historically Black women's colleges emphasize the intersection of both race and gender, recognizing how these factors uniquely impact the lives of Black women. Two of these institutions—Spelman College, located in Atlanta, Georgia, and Bennett College, in Greensboro, North Carolina—are the only Black women's colleges that still exist.

Spelman College was founded in 1881 as the Atlanta Baptist Female Seminary. Founders Sophia B. Packard and Harriet E. Giles, two White teacher-missionaries from New England, traveled to Georgia with a mission to create educational opportunities for Black women. Packard and Giles were leading pioneers in the fight for women's education and taught women the rudiments of reading, writing, and arithmetic. They accomplished this goal with few teaching resources, enduring unforgiving classroom settings. Undaunted by such challenges, the two women persevered, slowly working up from these rudimentary lessons to the highest levels of an arts and science program (Lefever, 2005). Bennett College in North Carolina was originally established in 1873 by the Freedmen's Aid Society as a coeducational normal school, aimed at training both men and women to become teachers. When many of the men were drafted to serve in World War I, however, opportunities for women expanded, creating a greater demand for women to pursue higher education. In 1926, the Women's Home Missionary Society of the Methodist Episcopal Church established an all-female institution of higher learning and was offered to do so on the site of Bennett College. Consequently, in 1926, Bennett transitioned into a historically Black, four-year liberal arts college exclusively for women.

The basis for educating women in the United States differed primarily along the lines of race, particularly during the early 1900s. For most White, middle-class young women, education was a critical component to maintain a social and class identity. Education was used to train young Black women to become refined ladies and to uplift the Black race (Collins, 2001). Educating Black women was crucial to the liberation of an entire race, and the mission of historically Black womens' colleges reflected this view. Coleman-Burns (1989) provides an explanation for this belief:

> Historically for the Black child, it was first the mother who determined the status. The education of Black women, it was reasoned, would raise the status of the Black child. Second, community emphasis was on Black women's education because the type of employment that she could gain beyond being a domestic would more likely be of a higher and more prestigious character than that of the Black male. Third, Black women, like all women, have been viewed as the carriers of the culture. Schooling was socially a "finishing" process for women, preparing them for society and the transmission of culture to their children. However, the goals and aspirations of Black women went far beyond those of Whites. An educated woman was viewed by the Black community as an asset. (p. 153)

It was believed that educating Black women, from some perspectives more than Black men, could launch avenues for wealth, respectability, and economic development in the Black community, opportunities that would last for decades.

Whether public or private, religiously affiliated, or serving single-sex populations, the core mission of HBCUs has always been to provide higher education opportunities for African Americans. Each institution originally pursued a distinct mission, such as training teachers, tradesmen, or offering a liberal arts education, but these missions have evolved over time. Despite what the term historically Black might imply, HBCUs were never excluded non-Black students. Founded during a time when African Americans were legally and socially barred from most postsecondary opportunities, HBCUs were race-based by custom rather than by policy (Wilson, 2023). There was never a policy forbidding any racial group from attending these institutions. This commitment to inclusivity underscores the unique role of HBCUs in the broader educational landscape. Their missions remain vital today, as they continue to address the educational needs of historically oppressed groups, providing an opportunity to students from diverse backgrounds.

Two Paths, One Destination

As HBCUs evolved, a debate emerged regarding the ultimate mission of education for Blacks. The question arose, What exactly is the goal of these institutions? Philanthropists, administration, and Black leaders posed several suggestions on how the curriculum should reflect the mission. Public land-grant colleges were not receiving a fair distribution of federal funding, and resources had diminished for many of the small, private religious-funded HBCUs. Industrial philanthropists such as Andrew Carnegie and John D. Rockefeller offered their support to HBCUs as a sign of their belief in Black higher education, but with their own personal gain in mind. Their efforts were intertwined with their ambitions to promote their own industries by leveraging Black labor (Gasman & Esters, 2024). By 1915, these philanthropists had begun to direct their financial support to Black colleges that boasted a liberal arts curriculum.

An ongoing debate questioned whether Christian education, trades and manual labor, teacher-education training, or liberal arts should dominate the mission of HBCUs (Lovett, 2015). The debate over a vocational education, advocated by Booker T. Washington, versus a liberal arts education, championed by W. E. B. Du Bois, was central in shaping the educational missions of HBCUs. Washington promoted vocational training as a practical means to achieve economic self-sufficiency and immediate employment opportunities, while Du Bois argued for a classical education that would develop the intellectual and leadership capacities of African Americans. This debate ultimately influenced the differing missions adopted by HBCUs, reflecting a blend of both approaches to cater to the varying needs of their students.

A Need for Something More

Educator, scholar, and orator Booker T. Washington (1856–1915) is considered one of the most influential African Americans in the early 20th century. Born a slave on a farm in West Virginia, Washington overcame his dire circumstances to gain an education at Hampton Normal and Agricultural Institute (Hampton University) in Virginia, where he studied both agriculture and academics. Driven by his belief in the power of education, Washington founded the Tuskegee Institute (now Tuskegee University). He advocated for an education that included both academics and vocational training. Contrary to popular belief at the time, his mission was not merely to produce farmers and tradesmen, but to educate entrepreneurs and teachers who could impart these skills across the South's new schools for African Americans.

Washington's philosophy was popular among White constituents. Bell (2005) noted, "Whites welcomed Washington's conciliatory, non-confrontational policy, and deemed it sufficient self-acceptance for the society's involuntary subordination of Blacks in every area of life" (p. 86). Washington accepted the status quo of segregation and believed that the Black population could achieve significant societal advancements and economic independence through skilled labor (Washington, 1901/2020). Many contemporaries, including W. E. B. Du Bois and Anna Julia Cooper, were critical of Washington's philosophy, often labeling him a compromiser and an accommodationist (Hudson, 2024). Wilson (2023), however, advocates for a more nuanced examination of Washington and urges scholars to consider the personal experiences that shaped his mission for the Tuskegee Institute.

Born into slavery, Washington spent his early years working on a plantation until he was 9 years old. During his childhood, he witnessed the inhumane treatment of Black people, including close family members who were whipped and beaten. Even after working his way through college, Washington could not escape the threat of anti-Black violence. One of his classmates at Hampton narrowly avoided being lynched by the Ku Klux Klan simply for teaching Black children. These harrowing experiences profoundly influenced Washington's belief that economic independence was essential for African Americans.

By the time he graduated from Hampton in 1875, Washington was convinced that financial self-sufficiency was the key to overcoming the systemic barriers imposed by segregation. Despite the dangers associated with educating Black people, particularly in the South where Washington sought to establish Tuskegee, he remained steadfast in his goal to create a program that would equip Southern Blacks with the skills necessary to achieve economic freedom. Drawing on his experiences at Hampton Institute, Washington set out to create his own industrial school: the Tuskegee Institute.

When Washington arrived in Tuskegee, Alabama, he found himself in one of the most hostile regions of the country. The segregationist era was rising, and anti-Black terrorism, including lynching, voter suppression, political disenfranchisement, and targeted attacks on Black education, had become disturbingly common. Just a decade before Tuskegee's first class convened in 1881, the alarming increase in these violent acts prompted a special investigation by a Joint Select Committee of the US Congress. Given this harsh reality, Washington was more inclined to accept segregation as a fact of life and often advocated working within its constraints to advance Black education. Many HBCUs, including Tuskegee, had no choice but to navigate within a system they did not create in order to gain academic legitimacy, secure employment opportunities for their students, and raise the necessary funds to sustain their institutions (Koch & Swinton, 2022).

Heavily influenced by Washington's philosophy, northern philanthropists Andrew Carnegie and John D. Rockefeller directed substantial financial support to developing institutions modeled after Tuskegee. Between 1900 and 1910, Carnegie devoted his entire budget for Black education to supporting Tuskegee and Hampton. By 1915, philanthropic contributions to industrial schools like these far exceeded those to liberal arts colleges. That year, Hampton Institute's endowment reached $2.7 million and Tuskegee's grew to $1.9 million, together accounting for more than half of the total endowment of private Black colleges in the United States (Dennis, 2001). Regardless of one's view of Washington's philosophical motives, his business acumen and conciliatory approach to civil rights made him adept at fundraising. In his 34 year tenure, Washington grew the one-room classroom into one of the largest, most successful institutions in the South and secured a sizable endowment few colleges could boast of at the time.

An avid singer and pianist, Washington had a profound appreciation for music and valued music education as a tool for cultural expression, community building, and the preservation of African American heritage. In *The Story of the Negro* (2005), Washington documents the history of African Americans before and after slavery. He expresses his personal views of Black music and its value to American society.

> I have heard musical critics, whose judgment the world respects, say that the old plantation hymns and songs were among the most original contributions that America has made, not only to music but to any one of the so-called fine arts. . . . For myself, though it has been my privilege to hear some of the best music both in Europe and America, I would rather hear the jubilee or plantation songs of my race than the finest chorus from the works of Handel or any other of the great composers that I have heard. Besides, this music is the form in which the sorrows and aspirations of the Negro people, all that they suffered, loved, and hoped for, in short their whole spiritual life, found its first adequate and satisfying expression. For that reason, if for no other, it should be preserved. (pp. 12–13)

His mission centered on practical education and vocational training, Washington approached formal music education for African Americans with a nuanced perspective. He championed a balanced approach, advocating for music programs that not only fostered artistic expression but also incorporated practical skills leading to jobs. Washington believed in tailoring education to address the specific needs of African Americans, recognizing that their unique experiences called for a distinct educational approach. Long before culturally relevant teaching became a defined pedagogical practice, Washington emphasized the necessity of understanding the unique lived experiences of African Americans and providing them with the education that best served their needs, even if it differed from what was offered to other races. For Washington, these differences were not inherent or racial; rather, they stemmed from the centuries of unequal opportunities that African Americans had endured. In *The Future of the American Negro* (1899), he wrote,

> One of the saddest sights I ever saw was the placing of a three hundred dollar rosewood piano in a country school in the South that was located in the midst of the "Black Belt." Am I arguing against the teaching of instrumental music to the Negroes in that community? Not at all; only I should have deferred those music lessons about twenty-five years. There are numbers of such pianos in thousands of New England homes. But behind the piano in the New England home there are one hundred years of toil, sacrifice, and economy; there is the small manufacturing industry, started several years ago

by hand power, now grown into a great business; there is ownership in land, a comfortable home, free from debt, and a bank account. In this "Black Belt" community where this piano went, four-fifths of the people owned no land, many lived in rented one-room cabins, many were in debt for food supplies, many mortgaged their crops for the food on which to live, and not one had a bank account. Someone may be tempted to ask, Has not the negro boy or girl as good a right to study a French grammar and instrumental music as the white youth? I answer, Yes, but in the present condition of the negro race in this country there is need of something more. (pp. 25–26)

That "something more" Washington spoke of was the practical application of education to real-world economic opportunities. Moreover, he believed that music education for African Americans should not only enrich cultural identity, but also equip students with the skills necessary to thrive economically. Although he valued formal music training as part of a college education, he had reservations about the *priority of* such instruction in the lives of young African Americans, a sentiment that many parents and students share today.

Music as Cultural Advancement

William Edward Burghardt Du Bois (1868–1963) was a sociologist and reformer, widely regarded as the most important Black leader of the 20th century who considered higher education a tool for Black struggle and liberation (Allen & Jewell, 2002). Born in an integrated community in Massachusetts, Du Bois attended Fisk University in Tennessee before studying at Harvard University, where he earned two degrees in history and a doctorate. He believed that higher education was crucial for the full emancipation of Black people. In his notable work *The Souls of Black Folk*, Du Bois (1903/2014) referred to HBCUs as social settlements in which freedmen not only accessed higher education, but also began integrating into civic life.

Du Bois is perhaps best known for the concept of the talented tenth, advocating that full citizenship and equal rights for African Americans would be achieved through the efforts of an intellectual elite. Du Bois argued that HBCUs should promote a liberal arts curriculum to foster critical thinking skills, a stance that many White people opposed as they feared it would lead to rebellion (Anderson, 1988; Gasman, 2025; Ricard & Brown, 2008). In theory, HBCUs would help cultivate this talented tenth, the most highly educated and skilled Black people who would then be able to uplift all Black people through their achievements, including musical achievements.

Like Washington, Du Bois's personal experiences greatly influenced his views on Black education. Du Bois's upbringing, however starkly contrasted that of Washington. Born of bi-racial descent—his father was Franco-Haitian, his mother Black—Du Bois was raised by his mother in a both racially and socioeconomically integrated neighborhood in Great Barrington, Massachusetts. He was afforded some of the best educational opportunities available, surpassing those accessible to many Whites at the time. After graduating as valedictorian of his racially integrated high school, Du Bois set off for Fisk University in Nashville, Tennessee. Despite concerns from his family and friends about venturing into the South, Du Bois eagerly anticipated attending college with peers he could relate to.

Du Bois continued the classical education he had begun in high school when he enrolled at Fisk University, an institution heavily influenced by White philanthropists and instructors who were heirs to New England and Western Reserve (Ohio) abolitionism. Fisk was one of the nation's foremost "factories of uplift suasion and assimilationist ideas" (Kendi, 2016, p. 267). Du Bois's time at Fisk, however, also exposed him to the harsh realities of Southern racism as well as to the rich cultural heritage of African Americans. These provided him with a deeper understanding of both the challenges and the strengths in his community. Although Du Bois had glimpses of racial differences while in Massachusetts, in Tennessee he witnessed extreme forms of bigotry, hostility, and oppression directed at Blacks. After graduating from Fisk University in 1888, Du Bois returned to the North, where he earned another Bachelor of Arts degree at Harvard in 1890, a master's degree in 1891, and in 1895, became the first African American to earn a PhD from the institution. His dissertation, "The Suppression of the African Slave Trade to the United States of America, 1638–1870" (1896), was one of the earliest scholarly works on the subject. Du Bois remained determined to lift up Black Americans from oppression and poverty, focusing on how the intellectual, rather than vocational, skills of the Black professional class could be harnessed to achieve this goal.

Du Bois began his teaching career at Wilberforce University of Ohio in 1894 while completing his doctoral studies at Harvard. Although he was highly qualified to teach and continue his research on African Americans and race at any of the leading White research institutions, faculty positions at these major colleges and universities were not open to Black scholars. In 1897, Horace Bumstead, then president of Atlanta University (now Clark Atlanta University), invited Du Bois to join his faculty. Despite being a well-traveled scholar and having spent time in Europe and other major US cities, Du Bois was particularly drawn to Atlanta University. It was one of the few major Black universities at the time, located in a city with a diverse population, and had already established a center for the study of African Americans (Morris, 2017). After careful consideration, Du Bois accepted the position and devoted 23 years of service to the institution.

Atlanta University proved to be an ideal match for his scholarly interests, and his time there became one of the most productive periods of his career in both scholarship and activism. At Atlanta that Du Bois wrote several of his best-known works, including *The Souls of Black Folk*, *Dusk of Dawn*, and *Black Reconstruction*. He also established *Phylon*, a journal dedicated to the African American experience. In 1909, Du Bois co-founded the National Association for the Advancement of Colored People (NAACP) with other Black intellectuals, an organization that remains active in the Civil Rights Movement today. One of Du Bois's most significant contributions during his tenure at Atlanta University was the establishment of its sociology department. Instrumental in shaping the curriculum, he played a pivotal role in teaching students to become leaders, to conduct rigorous research, to collect and analyze data, and to critically engage with scholarly work.

Du Bois's deep appreciation for music, particularly Negro spirituals, and their broader cultural significance is profoundly evident in his seminal work *The Souls of Black* Folk (1903, 2014). Like Washington and many other Black intellectuals of the early 20th century, Du Bois held Negro spirituals in high regard, famously writing, "There is no true American music but the wild sweet melodies of the Negro slave" (p. 15). His admiration for spirituals, both as a musical form and a cultural expression, is intricately woven into the structure of *The Souls of Black Folk*. Each chapter begins with a text or poem, typically by a White poet, followed by an excerpt of a musical score from a spiritual, deliberately presented without lyrics. Edwards and Du Bois (2007) suggests that Du Bois may have withheld the lyrics to create a deliberate barrier for the reader, implying that Black culture—life "within the veil"—remains inaccessible to White audiences. Du Bois dedicates an entire chapter, entitled "Of the Sorrow Songs," to Black music, in which he underscores the importance of preserving spirituals and recognizing their contribution to American culture. He writes:

> [T]he Negro folk-song—the rhythmic cry of the slave—stands today not simply as the sole American music, but as the most beautiful expression of human experience born this side of the seas. It has been neglected, it has been, and is, half despised, and above all, it has been persistently mistaken and misunderstood; but notwithstanding, it still remains as the singular spiritual heritage of the nation and the greatest gift of the Negro people. (p. 190)

This profound reverence for spirituals underscores Du Bois's belief in their enduring cultural and artistic value; he positions them as an essential component of America's musical heritage and a testament to the resilience and creativity of the Black community.

Du Bois's philosophy of assimilation in relation to Black music became increasingly evident during the New Negro Movement that emerged from the Harlem Renaissance. Along with philosopher Alain Locke and poet James Weldon Johnson, Du Bois emphasized the arts as a means of achieving equality with Whites. These leaders believed that showcasing the mastery of classical techniques by Black writers, painters, and composers could help dismantle racial oppression and segregation. They had hoped this artistic approach would challenge and ultimately eliminate the myth of Black inferiority (Lovett, 2015).

Du Bois's push for racial equality through cultural assimilation, however, presented a dilemma. The only path to acceptance seemed to lie in conforming to culturally prestigious forms of art, often defined by European standards. The works most celebrated by intellectuals like Du Bois were those that reflected Black heritage but did so within these esteemed forms. Composers such as James Weldon Johnson and William Grant Still, who adhered to this vision, became exemplars of Du Bois's efforts. While Du Bois championed the musical excellence of spirituals and Black classical music, he rarely discussed Black popular music (e.g., blues and jazz) as a musical art form despite its popularity. His omission reflected a broader trend within HBCU music programs, particularly those with liberal arts missions that prioritized Classical music over jazz. As a result, jazz, although a significant Black cultural force, was often overlooked in several HBCUs, a trend that, unfortunately, lasted for decades.

Common Ground

By the early 20th century, Washington and Du Bois were the two most influential Black men in the country and became pivotal figures in shaping strategies in the struggle for educational rights for African Americans. Over time, each came to appreciate the other's perspective on the mission of educating Blacks, particularly at HBCUs. Whereas Washington was able to carry out his educational initiatives within a segregationist system, Du Bois initially embraced some assimilationist ideals, seeing higher education for Blacks as the antidote to racialized problems. Initially a proponent of vocational training, Washington eventually embraced a more comprehensive approach that included liberal arts, stating, "So that, having learned practical and theoretical house-building at Tuskegee, they would be able to go out and build for themselves decent homes, and teach our people how to do the same thing" (Washington, 1902, p. 34). This integration of practical skills with broader educational objectives aligned with Du Bois's advocacy for an education that uplifted the race as a whole.

Conversely, Du Bois, often mistakenly seen as solely a proponent of a classical liberal arts education, later denounced certain aspects of his talented 10th and recognized the value in vocational training. Over time, he became more disillusioned with America, particularly the Black elite—the group that he dubbed as the Black upper class—believing that they had failed in their obligation to lead the masses of African Americans out of retrograde circumstances (Johnson & Watson, 2004). He emphasized the importance of technical education, even for those who had received a college education, asserting, "After we have sent our most promising to college, then not only the rest, but the college men too, need training in technical school for the actual technique" (Du Bois, 1906a, 1906b). Despite their initial differences, Washington and Du Bois demonstrated that the mission of HBCUs at the turn of the 20th century was not monolithic, but they were unified by a common goal: to educate African Americans and uplift their race (Gasman & McMickens, 2010). This shared vision underscored the complexity and richness of the educational missions that continue to shape HBUCs today.

Although not always explicitly stated, many HBCUs still reflect the philosophies of Washington and Du Bois in their approach to education. By incorporating these two frameworks, HBCUs can continue to align their music programs in ways that reflect their institutions' missions. Washington might advocate for substantial investment in areas in which African American students and other oppressed groups see themselves already successfully represented, such as music technology, music production, popular music performance, and entrepreneurship. This approach would not only deepen students' appreciation of the cultural significance of African American music, but also provide them with the practical skills needed to succeed in the modern industry. Washington would likely support music education programs that align with his broader philosophy of self-reliance, community uplift, and practical knowledge.

Du Bois, on the other hand, would likely encourage HBCUs to focus on cultivating composers and scholars of color, particularly in fields like musicology and theory, in which non-White representation is traditionally lacking. He would urge music administrators to develop programs that prepare student performers for advanced graduate studies, equipping them to break racial barriers in predominantly White orchestras. Du Bois would advocate for nurturing music advocates who could take on leadership roles in accreditation boards, positioning HBCUs to earn the same respect and recognition as White institutions. Du Bois would support music programs that align with his broader philosophy of intellectual excellence, cultural elevation, and the pursuit of equality through the arts. Whatever the direction, aligning HBCU music programs with these foundational philosophies ensures that they advance both the institution's mission and the broader cultural goals.

HBCUs Still Matter

Since the inception of HBCUs, questions of their relevance have persisted. Some critics imply that race-based institutions of higher education are no longer needed in a post-racial society (McWhorter, 2000; Steele, 1990; Thernstrom & Thernstrom, 2009). Whereas the initial mission of HBCUs was to educate African Americans, HBCUs have always been open to all students. HBCUs are not monolithic. Although many similarities exist among all HBCUS (i.e., culturally inclusive environments, family-like atmosphere, and transformative learning spaces), each HBCU has its own identity and its own culture. Those either unfamiliar with HBCU culture or have received misleading information may incorrectly assume that these institutions lack diversity and consist entirely of Blacks. HBCUs feature a diverse student body, encompassing a wide range of racial and ethnic backgrounds, religions, socioeconomic statuses, genders, sexual orientations, and countries of origin (Gasman, 2025; Gasman & Esters, 2024; Palmer & Williams, 2023). Although HBCUs were originally founded to educate Black students, people of all racial and ethnic backgrounds have always been welcomed.[2]

In *Hope and Healing: Black Colleges and the Future of Democracy* (2023) former Morehouse College President John S. Wilson, Jr. writes: "No HBCU ever established any policies forbidding access to any racial group. Only the predominantly white institutions were segregated, and quite literally and deliberately for centuries. As a result, Black colleges were race-based by custom, not rule" (p. 6). Today, HBCUs play critical roles in the expansion of access to higher education not only for African Americans, but all oppressed groups. HBCUs serve mostly first-generation college-goers, economically poor, or with weak academic backgrounds, or who have suffered discrimination (Gasman & Esters, 2024). HBCUs have continued to provide quality education for non-traditional as well as systematically oppressed students. Because HBCUs are committed to upholding the historic mission of providing educational opportunities to underrepresented populations, they take students from where they are at the point of entry and nurture their talents toward academic success (Gasman, 2025; Schexnider, 2008). Critics continue to question the relevance, rationale, and mission of HBCUs in the 21st century. Albritton (2012) argues that HBCUs should move beyond their historical mission and adopt innovative strategies to address the changing demographics and societal conditions they face. Boland and Gasman (2014) emphasize the need for HBCUs to expand their missions and develop programs that broaden their student recruitment efforts. According to the National Center for Education Statistics (2019), 30% of students enrolled at HBCUs in 2022 were not African Americans. Some suggest that the increasing presence of White students at predominantly Black institutions has influenced the character and identity of these schools (Ricard & Brown, 2008). Other critics claim that the historical mission of HBCUs is outdated. As their demographics shift, these institutions continue to play a crucial role in higher education (Johnson et al., 2017). Despite the growing diversity in their student populations, HBCUs remain committed to their unique historical mission.

HBCUs have long fulfilled a distinct social contract by acting as social equalizers, providing social capital and opportunities for success to students from underserved communities (Brown & Davis, 2001). The recent Supreme Court decision in *Students for Fair Admissions v. Harvard* (2023), which limits affirmative action in college admissions, further underscores the importance of HBCUs. With reduced opportunities for talented students of color to gain entry into other institutions, HBCUs are well-positioned to fill this gap by offering quality education in a supportive environment.

The mission of HBCUs to empower students from underrepresented communities and promote racial diversity in higher education is more vital now than ever. HBCU music students need academic environments in which they are prepared to deal with community and global issues from a centered perspective (Bryan & Stewart, 2016). This means recognizing music students as central to the teaching and learning process and creating environments where music serves as a tool for shaping identity and social awareness, both locally and globally. When music programs are closely aligned with their institution's mission, they are better equipped to meet the needs of students (Oliver, 2022). As HBCUs evolve, it is necessary for their music programs to align with these new missions.

Despite relentless efforts to undermine their legitimacy, HBCUs have not only survived, but thrived in many ways. Since the turn of the 21st century, HBCUs have faced challenges similar to those of predominantly White institutions, including maintaining a robust enrollment, boosting endowment funds, and managing the escalating costs (Wilson, 2023). HBCUs have a distinct advantage in their long history and mission to provide a quality education despite these hurdles. Nearly all of the existing 100 HBCUs (See Appendix A) have emerged from modest origins, persevering through historical, social, and academic obstacles such as Jim Crow laws, insufficient funding, deferred maintenance, and accreditation challenges,—all the while, producing Americans best music teachers, performers, and scholars. The entire history of higher education has been a series of obstacles created for African Americans and people of color. Nonetheless, HBCUs remain as Ebony Towers, pillars of educational resilience,—a space for intellectual growth for those historically excluded, underestimated, and marginalized by mainstream academic institutions.

Despite persistent attempts to challenge their legitimacy, HBCUs have persevered, demonstrating a profound resilience. If a question arises as to the relevance of HBCUs, look at who and what HBCUs have produced.[3] Although HBCUs make up only 3% of the country's colleges and universities, they enroll 10% of all African American students and produce almost 20% of all African American graduates (Palmer & Wood, 2012). HBCUs are responsible for producing approximately 33% of Black graduates with bachelor's degrees, 75% of all Black PhDs, 46% of all business executives, 50%

of all Black engineers, 80% of Black federal judges, 70% of all Black doctors and dentists, 57% of Black STEM graduates, 40% of Black congressmen and women and 50% of all Black attorneys, 13% of Black CEOs, 50% of Black professors at non-HBCUs and nearly a 30% of all Black music education graduates (United Negro College Fund, 2023). HBCUs not only produce the overwhelming majority of Black college graduates in the country, they have produced some of the most accomplished.

Notes

1. Ebony Towers is often used to describe HBCU's educational institutions, a play on Ivory Towers, which refers to predominantly White college and university systems.
2. In 2020, 73.8% of undergraduate students at HBCUs were Black, 11.4% were White, 5.1% were Hispanic or Latino, and 9.7% were from other backgrounds. These data reveal a growing trend of non-Black students attending HBCUs.
3. North Carolina A&T State University is the nation's top producer of Black undergraduate engineering degree holders. Nine of the top ten colleges that graduate the most African Americans who go on to earn PhDs are HBCUs. Spelman College and Bennett College together produce over half the nation's African American women doctorates in all science fields. Xavier University is ranked first nationally for the number of African American graduates who enroll in medical school. Among the graduates of HBCUs are civil rights leader Martin Luther King, Jr., United States Supreme Court Justice Thurgood Marshall, and United States Vice President Kamala Harris.

References

Albritton, T. J. (2012). Educating our own: The historical legacy of HBCUs and their relevance for educating a new generation of leaders. *The Urban Review, 44*(3), 311–331. https://doi.org/10.1007/s11256-012-0202-9

Allen, W. R., & Jewell, J. O. (2002). A backward glance forward: Past, present and future perspectives on historically Black colleges and universities. *The Review of Higher Education, 25*(3), 241–261.

Anderson, J. D. (1988). *The education of Blacks in the south, 1860–1935*. University of North Carolina Press.

Bell, D. A. (2005). Racial realism. In R. Delgado & J. Stefancic (Eds.), *The Derrick Bell reader* (pp. 55–96). New York University Press.

Boland, W. C., & Gasman, M. (2014). *America's public HBCUs: A four-state comparison of institutional capacity and state funding priorities*. Center for Minority Serving Institutions. cmsi.gse.rutgers.edu.

Brown, M. C., & Davis, J. E. (2001). The historically Black college as social contract, social capital, and social equalizer. *Peabody Journal of Education, 76*(1), 31–49. https://doi.org/10.1207/S15327930PJE7601_03

Bryan, D. M., & Stewart, F. R. (2016). Valuing the history, missions and traditions of HBCUs: Back to the basics. In C. B. Prince & R. L. Ford (Eds.), *Administrative challenges and organizational leadership in historically Black colleges and universities* (pp. 1–24). IGI Global.

Cohen, A. M., & Kisker, C. B. (2010). *The shaping of American higher education: Emergence and growth of the contemporary system.* John Wiley & Sons.

Coleman-Burns, P. (1989). African American women—Education for what? *Sex Roles, 21*(1–2), 145–160. https://doi.org/10.1007/BF00289733

Collins, A. C. (2001). *Socialization at two black women's colleges: Bennett college and Spelman college.* Publication No. 249993735 Doctoral dissertation. University of Pittsburg. ProQuest Dissertation & Theses.

Davis, J. E. (1998). Cultural capital and the role of historically Black colleges and universities in educational reproduction. In K. Freeman (Ed.), *African American culture and heritage in higher education research and practice* (pp. 143–153). Praeger.

Dennis, M. (2001). *Lessons in progress: State universities and progressivism in the new south, 1880–1920.* University of Illinois Press.

Du Bois, W. E. B. (1903). *The souls of Black folk.* A. C. McClurg & Company. (reprinted by Dover 1994)

Du Bois, W. E. B. (1906a). Commencement speech at Hampton Institute. In C. D. Wintz (Ed.). (1995) *African American political thought, 1890-1930: Washington, Du Bois, Garvey, and Randolph.* M.E. Sharpe. Routledge.

Du Bois, W. E. B. (1906b). Commencement speech at Hampton Institute. In C. D. Wintz (Ed.), (1995) *African American political thought, 1890-1930: Washington, Du Bois, Garvey, and Randolph.* M.E.

Edwards, B. H., & Du Bois, W. E. B. (2007). *The souls of Black folk.* Oxford University Press.

Fleming, C. G. (1983). The effect of higher education on black tennesseans after the civil war. *Phylon, 44*(3), 209–216. https://doi.org/10.2307/274933

Friedman, J. (2018, October 19). Former Spelman president: Universities must combat racism. *The Hoya.* https://thehoya.com/news/former-spelman-president-universities-must-combat-racism/

Gasman, M. (2025). *Why historically black colleges and universities natter: 25 years of historical research for justice.* Teachers College Press.

Gasman, M., & Esters, L. T. (2024). *HBCU: The power of Historically Black Colleges and Universities.* Johns Hopkins University Press.

Gasman, M., & McMickens, T. L. (2010). Liberal or professional education? The missions of public black colleges and universities and their impact on the future of African Americans. *Souls, 12*(3), 286–305.

Higher Education Act of (1965), *Title III, §* Vol. 322(2).

Hudson, J. E. (2024). What purpose education? Anna Julia Cooper's and Booker T. Washington's differing views on education. *Freedom Schools: A Journal of Democracy and Community, 1*(1), 35–51.

Johnson, G. S., Gray, V., Gray, L. D., Richardson, N. L., Rainey-Brown, S. A., Triplett, K. L., & Bowman, L. E. (2017). Historically Black colleges and universities (HBCUs) in the twenty-first century: An exploratory case study analysis of their mission. *Race, Gender & Class, 24*(3–4), 44–67.

Johnson, K. V., & Watson, E. (2004). The WEB DuBois and Booker T. Washington debate. *Journal of Technology Studies, 30*(4), 65–70.

Kendi, I. (2016). *Stamped from the beginning: The definitive history of racist ideas in America*. Bold Type Books.

Koch, J. V., & Swinton, O. H. (2022). *Vital and valuable: The relevance of HBCUs to American life and education*. Columbia University Press.

Lefever, H. G. (2005). The early origins of Spelman College. *The Journal of Blacks in Higher Education, 47*, 60–63. https://doi.org/10.2307/25073174

Lovett, B. L. (2015). *America's historically black colleges & universities: A narrative history from the nineteenth century into the twenty-first century*. Mercer University Press.

McWhorter, J. H. (2000). *Losing the race: Self-sabotage in black America*. Simon and Schuster.

Morris, A. (2017). *The scholar denied: W.E.B. Du Bois and the birth of modern sociology*. University of California Press.

National Center for Education Statistics. (2019). *Historically Black colleges and universities*. https://nces.ed.gov/fastfacts/display.asp?id=667

Oliver, W. (2022). *The influence of isomorphism on HBCU music (Performance and teacher training) programs and the alignment of broader institutional mission*. Publication No. 2700382697 Doctoral dissertation. Pennsylvania State University. ProQuest Dissertation & Theses.

Palmer, R. T., & Williams, J. L. (2023). "Peeling back the layers": A deeper look at the diversity among black students at historically black colleges and universities. *Journal of Diversity in Higher Education, 16*(4), 447.

Palmer, R. T., & Wood, J. L. (Eds.). (2012). *Black men in college: Implications for HBCUs and beyond*. Routledge.

Ricard, R. B., & Brown, M. C. (2008). *Ebony towers in higher education: The evolution, mission, and presidency of historically Black colleges and universities*. Stylus Publishing.

Roebuck, J. B., & Murty, K. S. (1993). *Historically Black colleges and universities: Their place in American higher education*. Praeger Publishers.

Schexnider, A. J. (2008). Executive leadership: Securing the future of Black colleges and universities. *International Journal of Organization Theory and Behavior, 11*(4), 496–517. https://doi.org/10.1108/IJOTB-11-04-2008-B003

Singleton, H. (2022). Faith goes to college: The religious factor in the founding and development of HBCUs. In A. Bagasra, A. M. C. Letchie, & J. Wesley (Eds.), *Contributions of historically Black colleges and universities in the 21st century* (pp. 1a–20). IGI Global.

Steele, S. (1990). *The content of our character: A new vision of race in America*. St. Martin's Press.

Thernstrom, S., & Thernstrom, A. (2009). *America in black and white: One nation, indivisible*. Simon and Schuster.

Washington, B. T. (1899). *The future of the American Negro*. Small, Maynard.

Washington, B. T. (1902, September). Problems in education. *The Cosmopolitan, 33*(3), 30–36.

Washington, B. T. (2005). *The story of the Negro*. University of Pennsylvania Press. (originally published 1909)

Watkins, W. H. (2000). Curriculum, culture, and power. In C. C. Yeakey & R. D. Henderson (Eds.), *Surmounting all odds: Education, opportunity, and society in the new millennium* (pp. 31–50). Information Age Publishing.

Watkins, A. P. (2009). *Sisters of hope, looking back, stepping forward: The educational experiences of African-American women*. Peter Lang.

Wilson, J. S. (2023). *Hope and healing: Black colleges and the future of American democracy*. Harvard Education Press.

Woodson, C. G. (1998). *The mis-education of the Negro*. Africa World Press. (originally published in 1933)

Additional Readings

Edwards-Ingram, Y. (2019). Scholars, lawyers, and their slaves: St. George and Nathaniel Beverly Tucker in the college town of Williamsburg. In L. M. Harris, J. T. Campbell, & A. Brophy (Eds.), *Slavery and the university: Histories and legacies* (pp. 211–231). University of Georgia Press.

CHAPTER 3

ECHOES OF HERITAGE: THE MUSICAL TRADITIONS OF HBCUs

ABSTRACT

Music at HBCUs is more than entertainment. Their musical traditions shapes identity, honors heritage, and challenges exclusion. HBCUs have cultivated vibrant musical traditions that serve as instruments of cultural expression, social resistance, and educational transformation. By centering the voices of students, faculty, and historical figures, the chapter explores how these institutions build and sustain choral programs, gospel ensembles, marching bands, jazz studies, orchestras, and music education programs.

Chapter 3 begins by examining the role of spirituals and the legacy of choirs such as the Fisk Jubilee Singers, whose global impact reframed African American music as a serious art form. The chapter then explores how gospel choirs and marching bands became cultural cornerstones on Historically Black Colleges and University (HBCU) campuses, blending artistry with activism and forging community through performance. The chapter highlights the pioneering, but often the overlooked, contributions of HBCUs to jazz education, as well as the ongoing struggle to maintain orchestral programs and music education degrees amid systemic inequities.

HBCU music programs have preserved and reimagined Black musical traditions, resisting marginalization in mainstream academia. By aligning musical practice with institutional missions discussed in previous chapters, HBCUs affirm cultural pride, foster student agency, and shape the broader musical landscape. These echoes of heritage continue to inspire, educate, and challenge dominant narratives in American music education.

In his writings, including those about music, Baldwin often highlights a crucial paradox—the simultaneous construction of race and the lived consequences of this construction (Friedberg, 2023). This concept is particularly relevant when examining the musical traditions at HBCUs, which are not merely random musical practices, but have been constructed over time through deliberate efforts, cultural influences, and the collective lived experiences of the African American community. These musical traditions serve the specific social, cultural, and educational purposes evident today. We need to explore these traditions to understand how they have contributed to the broader cultural and educational landscape, as well as how they continue to shape the experiences of students at HBCUs today.

HBCUs have been pivotal not only in training generations of African American musicians, composers, scholars, and educators but also in advancing American music and influencing global cultural phenomena (Price et al., 2011). Since the 19th century, HBCUs have served as conservatories of Black musical talent, playing a crucial role in the musical development of African Americans (Williams & Ashley, 2004). HBCU faculty and students have actively contributed to the arts by teaching, leading arts organizations, establishing schools of music, publishing, composing, and performing. Despite such significant cultural contributions, the academic programs that support these musical traditions have received relatively limited scholarly attention.

HBCUs have a rich musical history, serving as educational, cultural, and musical hubs since the 19th century. Exploring these institutions reveals the profound ways in which Black music both shapes and is shaped by these communities (Hadley, 2023). The music created, studied, and performed on HBCU campuses has not only enriched the African American culture, but has also extended its influence, to impact the broader culture.

Music at HBCUs has played a pivotal role in transforming American culture and influencing global culture (Lovett, 2015). The international dissemination of spirituals, the worldwide cultural influence of HBCU marching bands, and the globalization of jazz all stem from the musical traditions nurtured at HBCUs. Although these styles have deep connections to HBCU musical traditions, it is equally important to examine other musical practices that, while once central to HBCU musical traditions, have struggled to maintain their relevance in recent years.

"Steal Away": Preserving and Disseminating Spirituals

Fisk University offers a notable example of how vocal music has played a crucial role in the musical development of HBCUs, one that continues to be embraced by many HBCUs today. The original Fisk Jubilee Singers, formed in 1871, played a pivotal role in preserving what were then known as slave songs and now recognized as Negro spirituals. These efforts were orchestrated by George L. White, a Northern abolitionist who provided informal extracurricular music lessons on campus. He enlisted an extraordinarily talented student, Ella Shepherd, who had arrived at Fisk in 1868. Already an accomplished pianist and singer at 16, Shepherd became White's musical assistant and Fisk's first Black instructor a year later. Together, they taught students a variety of genres, including sacred anthems, abolitionist hymns, patriotic songs, and even entire cantatas.

To secure funding for the newly established Fisk University, White, who also served as the institution's treasurer, organized a series of choral concerts across Tennessee. Widespread uncertainty prevailed about how a Black performing ensemble would be received in a formal concert setting, especially without engaging in the stereotypical minstrel show elements of dancing and joke-telling (Southern, 1997). These concerns proved valid as some audiences were initially surprised by the appearance of the college singers, who differed greatly from the exaggerated caricatures commonly seen on the minstrel stage (Anderson, 2010). It became clear that the group needed to distinguish themselves from the stereotypes of minstrelsy to avoid public confusion about their mission to raise funds to prevent the school's closure.

After hearing Fisk students sing songs passed down by their ancestors, White decided to incorporate them into the concert program. With the help of Shepherd, White arranged spirituals, adapting them to appeal to White audiences' preferences for the European concert style (Ward, 2000). White replaced the traditional heterophonic singing with four-part Soprano, Alto, Tenor, Bass harmony, and removed spontaneous vocal improvisations, clapping, and other body percussion. As Fisk graduate, composer and musicologist John W. Work, noted, White "eliminated every element that detracted from the pure emotion of the song. Finish, precision, and sincerity were demanded by this leader. Mr. White strove for an art presentation" (Work, 1998, p. 15). Despite such changes, fundamental elements of the folk spiritual tradition remained.

The new concert program maintained the standard repertoire but now ended with spirituals, eliciting mixed reactions. Audiences greeted the hymns, patriotic songs, and parlor music with indifference but responded with enthusiasm to the spirituals. For many Northerners, minstrel troupes had been their only frame of reference for African American performances, so the authenticity and emotion of the Fisk Jubilee Singers' renditions were compelling (Anderson, 2010). The reputation and prestige of the singers quickly spread nationally and internationally. Their fame reached new heights when President Ulysses S. Grant invited them to perform at the White House in 1872, and they later embarked on an international tour, including a performance for Queen Victoria in 1873.

The success of Fisk Jubilee Singers inspired other HBCUs to follow suit. After hearing the Fisk Jubilee Singers perform in Boston, General Samuel Chapman Armstrong, then superintendent of Hampton Normal and Agricultural Institute (now Hampton University), created a similar group at Hampton. Thomas Fenner, Hampton's first music instructor, formed a choir of 17 singers, and by 1873, the chorus began touring, performing in some of the same cities and churches as had the Fisk Jubilee Singers. Unlike White's European-style arrangements, however, the Hampton singers performed in a folkloric style, introducing White concertgoers to new perceptions of authenticity (Thurman, 2021). Fenner also allowed for a flexible approach to pitch characteristic of folk traditions, kept much of the natural dialect, and featured a shouter—a soloist who inspired enthusiasm among both the singers and the audience (Shipley, 2011). These elements reflected Fenner's commitment to maintaining the spirituals' folkloric essence while introducing them to new audiences.

The HBCU choral tradition is recognized as the primary force preserving and disseminating spirituals. If not for choirs from institutions such as Fisk, Hampton, and Tuskegee, the global acceptance of Negro spirituals might not have occurred (Lovett, 2015) and could have been lost. Some of the nation's most esteemed composers led HBCU choirs, continuing the legacy of choral excellence and spiritual preservation.

Canadian-born composer R. Nathaniel Dett (1882–1943), for example, published essays on African American music as well as two volumes of over 100 spirituals arranged for choir. During his 19-year tenure at Hampton, Dett led the choir to international acclaim, touring extensively across Europe and performing at venues such as Carnegie Hall and before President Calvin Coolidge. Similarly, composer William Dawson (1899–1990), known for his spiritual arrangements, organized and headed the School of Music at Tuskegee University. Under his conductorship, from 1931 to 1955, Dawson transformed the Tuskegee Institute Choir into an internationally renowned ensemble. Dett and Dawson were catalysts in an era of HBCU choral directors who bridged the past with the 20th century.[1]

Today, many HBCU choirs continue the tradition established by the Fisk Jubilee Singers and the Hampton Institute, touring nationally and internationally, bringing acclaim to their institutions, and raising funds for scholarships. This practice has become a standard, as well as the expectation, for HBCU choral programs. Central to this tradition is the preservation of spirituals as a core component of the HBCU choral canon. By maintaining spirituals in their repertoire, HBCU choirs play a crucial role in preserving and honoring the rich heritage of African American music. By continuing to perform concert spirituals, HBCU choirs help preserve the performance practice of this traditional African American art form, ensuring its relevance in the modern era (Reed-Walker, 2008; Simmons, 2023). These performances offer a window into the history and culture of their times and serve as a powerful teaching tool for American musical history.

Gospel Choirs

Almost every HBCU has at least one gospel choir, a group that has become integral to campus life. The first HBCU gospel choir was founded in the fall of 1968 at Howard University by Melanie Russell (Lee) and Rosalind Thompkins (Lynch). Shortly afterward, other HBCU gospel choirs began to emerge, including the Hampton University Gospel Choir, established in 1969 with 50 singers under the name His Chosen Sounds, and the Southern University Gospel Choir, also founded in 1969. The emergence of gospel choirs at HBCUs mirrored the modern gospel era, which began in the 1970s and was dominated by artists such as Andrae Crouch, Tremaine Hawkins, Walter Hawkins, Sandra Crouch, Richard Smallwood, Bobby Jones, Raymond Wise, and the Clark Sisters. The choirs were primarily student-led and operated as extracurricular clubs. By the late 1990s, the influence of Black gospel music in HBCUs highlighted a dynamic shift in social-cultural norms, peer relations, and educational activities across America (Beard, 2021). Today, HBCU gospel choirs continue to thrive, offering a blend of traditional and contemporary gospel music, including works by artists like Kirk Franklin, Hezekiah Walker, and Tye Tribbett.

Despite their significance, most HBCU gospel choirs remain ancillary ensembles, often considered nontraditional or specialty choirs. Emerging research suggests a need to develop pedagogical techniques for music educators to effectively lead gospel choirs. A growing advocacy has arisen to include these ensembles as part of the HBCU core music curriculum (Shaffer, 2018). At institutions at which the gospel choir has been elevated to a curricular inclusion—such as becoming an approved ensemble in a music performance or music education program—the gospel choir serves as a pedagogical tool for a broader group of students preparing for careers in music. The proven longevity of HBCU gospel choirs and growing interest from both students and the community shows an increasing acceptance of gospel music in the core music curriculum. This shift signifies a broader recognition of gospel music's cultural and educational value in HBCU schools.

Marching Bands: The Musical Heartbeat of the HBCU

Historically Black Colleges and Universities' marching bands are the most recognizable and most celebrated musical expressions at HBCUs. Not long after many of the 1890 land grant HBCUs were established, marching bands emerged. Virginia State University, Tuskegee University, and Alabama A&M University were among the first HBCUs to have documented marching bands (Whitehead, 2023). W. C. Handy, known as the Father of the Blues, began leading the band at Alabama State Normal and Industrial School (now Alabama A&M), becoming the first band director at a Black college to introduce Black popular songs into band performances. Handy could achieve this because he was the first Black professional musician hired at an HBCU with experience in both military and minstrel bands. Before Handy, these bands had primarily performed traditional marches, but Handy's innovative approach to music selection quickly spread among Black college bands, including bands at predominantly White institutions (Whitehead, 2023). Florida A&M University's followed Alabama A&M's template and established their band in 1892. Established in 1895, Tuskegee Institute is believed to have the oldest continually active marching band at an HBCU (Clark, 2019).

HBCU college marching bands developed significantly between 1944 and 1946. After World War II, many Black veterans took advantage of the GI Bill to pursue higher education, which led to increased enrollment at HBCUs because Blacks were not allowed to attend White schools. This surge in enrollment, combined with the rising popularity of football and intercollegiate sports, contributed to the growth of HBCU marching bands. The modern HBCU marching band style dates to June 1, 1946, with the creation of the Marching 100 at Florida A&M College. The band's longest-tenured director, and the only fourth director in its history, William P. Foster, is seen as a pioneer in the HBCU marching band movement for his incorporation of popular music and dance movements into traditional military precision-style drills. In *Band Pageantry: A Guide for the Marching Band* (1968), Foster lists more than Florida A&M30 innovations to marching band techniques (he called this pageantry) that occurred at the university, such as double-quick marching and high-stepping. Foster's vision for the school's Marching 100 combined traditional techniques with interpretations of Black popular music and dance and influenced college bands around the country, including Southern University's Human Jukebox, Jackson State University's Sonic Boom of the South, Grambling State University's World Famed Marching Band, North Carolina A&T University's Blue and Gold Marching Machine, and the Tennessee State University Aristocrat of Bands.

These marching bands have differentiated themselves from other band programs in the US and abroad by their diverse repertoire, the distinct quality of their sound, and their entertaining performances. The diverse musical repertoire of HBCU bands and their dynamic movements, resonate deeply with both performers and audiences. While these bands perform classical and traditional marching music, they also draw from the rich tradition of African American contemporary music, incorporating genres such as jazz, gospel, funk, soul, rhythm and blues, pop, R&B, and hip-hop (Lewis & Wilson, 2011). During a football halftime show, one may hear marches of composers such as John Philip Sousa and Karl King to the music of Stevie Wonder, Usher, or Kendrick Lamar. HBCU bands such as the one at Southern University have recently gained the reputation of presenting gospel shows in which they play the popular gospel tunes "Order My Steps" and Richard Smallwood's "Total Praise" to contemporary gospel of Tye Tribbett—all with a vocalists and crowd participation.

In addition to playing diverse repertoire of both traditional and popular music, HBCU marching bands have a distinctive sound rooted in African American influences. These factors include self-training, conceptual models of ensemble sonority, and an emphasis on volume and bright tone (Clark, 2019). Musical enculturation, in which informal learning and cultural influence shape musical styles, plays a significant role in the combining these factors that development of the HBCU sound (Whitehead, 2023). Mimicking the vocal sounds of blues and jazz singers was a common practice by African American horn players of the New Orleans jazz era. Blue notes as well as slides, scoops, and growls became common performance practice in Black music performed by these players (Southern, 1997). The emulation of vocal qualities, along with the preference for bright, intense sounds of jazz big bands, became the hallmarks of HBCU marching bands.

While the brightness of tone and intensity of volume are often highlighted as defining features of the HBCU sound, several HBCU bands have maintained a program deeply rooted in the symphonic band tradition. Antron D. Mahoney (2021) points out that not all HBCU marching bands sound the same, emphasizing that each has its own unique style and identity. Foster, from Florida Agricultural and Mechanical University (FAMU), greatly admired the sound of the University of Michigan's band, particularly the arrangements by Jerry Bilick (Rowley, 2013). As a result, Richard Powers, a former Bilick student, was hired as FAMU's chief arranger. Foster credits Powers with shaping the distinctive FAMU sound, which blended many of Bilick's techniques with textural elements from Wagner's compositions. Elsa's Procession into the Cathedral from Wagner's *Lohengrin* became a signature piece for the band (Rowley, 2013).

Due to historical stereotypes of Black band programs, especially those from HBCUs called "show bands," the impact these ensembles have had on the larger wind band community often goes unnoticed or is not taken seriously. HBCU-style marching bands have often been criticized by mainstream music educators and adjudicators for lacking musicianship and technical precision, a bias often reflected in evaluations and assessments at competitions (Reid, 2020). Ironically, and at the same time, the traditions of HBCU marching bands are increasingly visible in American musical culture. HBCU bands have influenced many predominately White university programs and competitive drum and bugle corps who look to HBCUs for performance practices and creative influences. Nationally recognized programs like the University of Michigan, University of Southern California, Madison Scouts, Blue Devils have adopted several of the innovative concepts that HBCU band programs have been known for since the 1940s, such as flashy dance choreography, creative drum line cadences, and intense rhythmic complexity (Rowley, 2013, p. 4).

HBCU marching bands have not only influenced the marching bands at White schools, but also greatly impact popular culture. In addition to appearing in movies and television shows such as "Drumline" (2002) "The Quad" (2017) that introduced broader audiences to HBCU culture, HBCU marching bands are catching the attention of popular events. In 2018, when Beyoncé became the first Black woman to headline the Coachella music festival, she drew directly from the rich traditions of HBCU marching bands and their distinctive style in her own homecoming (Mahoney, 2021). The popular sports network ESPN televised the first of its annual HBCU Band of the Year National Championship in 2023 with the "Blue and Gold Marching Machine" of North Carolina A&T receiving first place in the competition. HBCU band culture received international recognition when Jackson State University's Sonic Boom of the South was featured in the 2024 Super Bowl halftime show along with headliner Usher. In 2023, Tennessee State University's Aristocrat of Bands made history as the first collegiate band to win two Grammy awards. Making them the first college marching band to achieve this distinction. They won a Grammy for their album *The Urban Hymnal*, in the Best Roots Gospel Album category, and for their contribution to J. Ivy's *The Poet Who Sat by the Door* in the Best Spoken Word Album category.

The HBCU marching band culture has significantly influenced school-based music programs beyond the school setting. HBCU marching bands often offer more scholarships than do other ensembles to attract talented students who wish to pursue music as a major or to enrich their college experience. The marching bands' ability to recruit students and represent schools is essential to these institutions' overall operation. This band culture is so powerful that some HBCUs have marching bands but no football team. They are necessary to the HBCU experience.

In addition to their significant enhancement to the HBCU experience, HBCU marching bands are integral to the greater Black community as a source of cultural pride. Their performances consist of more than a show.

They are seen as treasured hallmarks of the community, even by those who did not attend college. Lewis and Wilson (2011) write:

> Marching band performances become celebrations of African American aesthetics, featuring foregrounded percussion. . . . Deeply emblematic of diaspora expressive traditions, HBCU band performances unfold as bold public declarations of what it means to be African American today. Through their musical choices; their dance routines; their treatment of public space; their commitment to evaluation; and their penchant for pageantry, competition, originality, adaptability, rhythmic complexity, and performer-audience conversations, HBCU marching bands embody aesthetics that transcend band membership and embrace values belonging to time-honored traditions of African American expressivity. (p. 146)

HBCU bands are a vital part of the Black culture. They showcase Black American music traditions and cultural relevance both through music education and by a display of cultural presentation. As part of the HBCU band not only do students receive a culturally relevant musical experience, but they do so embraced in the HBCU culture.

Jazz—Not Serious Enough?

A serious gap exists in the history of America's college jazz education (Goodrich, 2001). Before the New School of Social Research in New York became the first institution of higher learning to offer jazz history for academic credit, in 1941, and before the University of North Texas offered the first college degree in jazz in 1947,[2] college jazz programs had already begun at HBCUs in the form of jazz or stage bands. Tuskegee established a band by 1890 and Florida A&M by 1892 that played ragtime and jazz. William C. Handy had also established a marching band that also played ragtime and blues at Alabama A&M State College in 1900. The earliest documented sanctioned collegiate jazz ensemble was the Tuskegee Institute's Syncopated Band, initiated in 1919 by the renowned educator and bandleader Len Bowden. Andy Goodrich, administrator, musician, scholar and jazz educator, an alumnus of Tennessee State University, reminds us that

> [People] don't know the role that black colleges played in getting jazz acknowledged in the educational curriculum, and how the efforts of great jazz players while they were students at these schools helped get the music respected and recognized academically on campus. . . The black college jazz movement enabled musicians to get undergraduate and graduate degrees in the field, but too many people don't know this story. (paraphrased in Wynn, 2003)

Beginning as early as the 1900s, many African American students on campuses of HBCUs were among the first to perform jazz in institutions of higher education.

Between the mid-1920s and the mid-1950s, approximately 38 HBCUs had jazz bands, sometimes called dance orchestras. These student-led groups played for a variety of social and academic events, including student dances, faculty and administration functions, and campus recruitment drives. Among the most notable were The Fisk Collegians of Fisk University, which featured Jimmie (James Melvin) Lunceford. Clark Atlanta's Collegian Rambles was one of the first touring jazz bands and the Bama State Collegians of Alabama State University. Tennessee A&I College's (Tennessee State University) jazz group The Collegians was voted the top college jazz band in the country by the *Pittsburgh Courier*. Duke Ellington, Count Basie, Ray Charles, Louis Armstrong, and others recruited members from these jazz bands, many of whom became historical figures in the field of jazz.[3]

From the mid-1950s on, the popularity and acceptance of jazz in American culture paved the way for the establishment of jazz studies degree programs largely in the music departments at predominantly White colleges and universities. Moreover, following the *Brown* ruling these colleges began recruiting Black talent and established jazz bands larger and better funded than the ones at HBCUs. Meanwhile, the debate about the academic legitimacy of jazz, along with concerns about the stability and viability of careers in jazz, created uncertainty around its place within the formal music curricula at HBCUs. The Black middle-class's efforts to improve its status through assimilation often involved distancing themselves from certain aspects of Black music, including jazz. Music critic Henry Pleasants (1969) provided his perspective:

> The circumstances of its origin in the Negro slums of New Orleans and the back country of the American South and the banality of its earliest diffusion throughout the white community in the Dixieland and white dance bands of the 1920's prompted the spokesmen of serious music—composers, performers, critics and educators—to dismiss it as juvenile and inferior and, consequently, to ignore it, or at best to patronize it as an indigenous urban folk music. (p. 118)

Many HBCU music faculty viewed themselves as "spokesmen of serious music" for their race. Their anti-jazz attitudes stemmed from an ingrained sense of cultural inferiority felt toward the genre. Some HBCUs were so adamant about maintaining a reputation of only studying serious music that student musicians were punished if they used practice rooms to rehearse jazz.[4]

During the 1960s, along with civil, social, and racial unrest that involved both Black and White college student protests across the nation. Along with this unrest was a renaissance of a Black culture that encouraged racial pride among Black youths. HBCUs and White schools began to reevaluate their curricula. A historic 1968 protest at Howard University included over

2,000 students who held a sit-in at the Administration Building and demanded that the university's curriculum offer more Afro-centric courses. The protests resulted in the creation of the Department of African Studies and ultimately of the Jazz Department, making Howard the first HBCU to offer a Bachelor of Music in Jazz Studies (Barrie et al., 2024). In 1974, Fred Irby III joined the music faculty and formed the internationally acclaimed Howard University Jazz Ensemble in 1975, and he served as the director of the ensemble for over 50 years. Under Irby's influence Howard University's jazz program has evolved to include multiple instrumental and vocal ensembles, as well as offered a Master of Music degree in Jazz Studies.

Other HBCUs recognized the potential of the Howard's jazz program and followed suit. Gene Strassler, then the head of North Carolina Central University's Music Department, contacted Donald Byrd, who had established Howard's jazz studies program, to inquire about assistance in organizing a jazz series consisting of lectures, performances, and workshops. The positive responses from students and faculty led to the formation of a jazz program. In 1977, North Carolina Central University became the first university in North Carolina to offer the Bachelor of Music degree in Jazz Studies. Their Jazz Studies program has since included a comprehensive vocal jazz component and the Master of Music degree in Jazz Composition and Jazz Performance. Spelman College's Jazz Ensemble was founded in 1983 by saxophonist and jazz pedagogue Joe Jennings. At that time, Spelman College boasted of having one of the country's few jazz ensembles at a women's college, a rarity in the heavily male-dominated artistic field. Jennings developed a women's ensemble that would perform at venues such as the New Orleans Jazz Festival and The Schomburg in Harlem.

In *Jazz Educated, Man* (1973), jazz critic Allen Scott asked the pertinent question, "Where are the Black jazz players in jazz education?" Many HBCU jazz educators are still asking this today. Given that jazz has historically been the music of the Black community, one might have expected predominantly HBCUs to have led the charge in jazz education. The opposite, however, is true. When London Branch conducted research on jazz education in HBCUs in 1975, 23 HBCUs had jazz programs. Since then, many HBCUs have phased out their jazz programs. Even Spelman College, which once boasted the only jazz program of its kind, phased out its jazz ensemble in 2017 shortly after Joe Jennings 30-year tenure at the College came to an end. According to Jennings, "With the cost of Spelman, most African-American families were not going to send their daughters to college to study jazz" (NPR, Pellegrinelli, 2018). Today, approximately 10 of the 101 HBCUs have an academic jazz program. Unfortunately, the many decades of seeing jazz as peripheral in the HBCU music curricula, and the lack of financial support for the student talent, have resulted in a cultural void in the very art form inherent to Black music.

Silent Strings: The Struggle to Maintain Orchestras at HBCUs

Orchestras and chamber music on HBCU campuses have existed in some capacity for over 100 years, as early as the 1900s. Today, however, orchestras and chamber music ensembles are probably the *least* visible entities at HBCUs. Of the 28 HBCUs accredited by the National Association of Schools of Music (NASM) (See Appendix B), the accrediting body for college music programs, approximately half have chamber music or an orchestra ensemble as part of their music program (NASM, 2024). This decrease was not a coincidence, due to the fact that African Americans have been participants in orchestras since the 19th century. During the 19th century, when White orchestra refused to admit African American musicians, Black musicians formed their own orchestras.[5] This omission leads to the belief that the African American community did not,—and still do not—have orchestral ensembles (Lundy, 2015), even that they were incapable of playing or appreciating orchestral music.

Demeaning beliefs regarding a supposed African American incapacity to play European instruments to participate in orchestras, coupled with 19th- and 20th-century socio-cultural norms, have continued to perpetuate exclusionary practices in America's professional orchestras. These beliefs and practices continue to impact our lives today in often subtle ways. Flagg (2020) notes,

> In the case of orchestras, there is a documented history of conscious exclusion, harassment, and discrimination that includes segregated unions; hostile groups of musicians, staff, and board leaders; and bifurcated access to gatekeepers and mentors. This history, like all history, has a present-day impact: a legacy embedded in the routine processes of life that we may not even see. (p. 31)

Indeed, one of these subtle impacts is the noticeable absence of orchestras at many HBCUs, contributing to the broader underrepresentation of African Americans in orchestras.

DeLorenzo (2012) highlighted the lack of African American participation in orchestras, which shows up in K–12 schools and extends to the university level. Because of this phenomenon, HBCUs have a small pool of orchestra students from which to recruit. Even more challenging is the fact that top music students often choose White schools' music programs or conservatories that can provide them with scholarships and other financial assistance (Floyd, 2021). Lundy (2015) examined the experiences of orchestra directors at HBCUs and found that shortage of funding for scholarships and resources was one of the main challenges faced by orchestra directors trying to build their orchestra programs. One participant in the study indicated that, although ample youth orchestras were located in the HBCU region where he teaches, he is still unable able to recruit students because his HBCU lacks sufficient orchestra scholarships.

> I couldn't even count the number of students who've come in, played good auditions, and then, well, they get a full ride somewhere else. So, well, that's something that I think unfortunately [happens]. I think until the higher administrations at the [HBCU] schools really recognize the value of the orchestra as an ambassador; that having a touring orchestra, and is willing to back [it], that's not going to happen just by accident and completely organically. It has to be kick-started, and the kick-starter is really money; that's what it comes down to. (John, personal communication, April 23, 2024)

Offering scholarships to orchestral studies students is only one aspect of addressing the issue of the absence of orchestras at HBCUs. In an era of rising college costs, families are increasingly focused on the tangible return on investment, especially when orchestral careers appear elusive given the fact that Black musicians comprise only 2.4% of musicians in surveyed orchestras (League of American Orchestras, 2023). This lack of representation not only limits visibility but also reinforces the belief that the orchestral world has no place for Black students.

Acknowledging the absence of orchestras at HBCUs is a necessary first step toward dismantling the ideologies that have marginalized Black concert musicians. Acknowledgment alone is, however, not sufficient. We must interrogate the structural barriers that sustain this underrepresentation. As DeLorenzo (2012), Elpus and Abril (2011), and Ladson-Billings (2004) argue, the exclusion of Black musicians from orchestral spaces is not merely a musical issue: it is a matter of social justice. In this light, HBCUs are uniquely positioned to form a bridge between the African American community and the world of orchestral music, helping to reshape the narrative and create pathways for Black excellence in concert music.

HBCUs provide a community for its students—giving them a sense of belonging, opportunities to perform culturally relevant repertoire, and chances to connect with others who look like them—a climate often absent from college orchestras. The lack of orchestras at HBCUs not only limits opportunities for students to perform this repertoire but also perpetuates the historical exclusion of Black voices from the Classical music narrative. Without institutional support, financial resources for recruitments, and infrastructure to maintain HBCU orchestra students have fewer platforms to cultivate their talents, learn, and showcase their contributions to concert music in environments that celebrate diverse composers and genres. This situation could be detrimental to professional orchestras' quest for diversity; it cuts off a pipeline of potential musicians. Building these ensembles at

HBCUs could be a key to diversifying orchestras worldwide and offer a path toward greater representation in the global music scene.

Music Education—Untapped Potential

HBCUs have long designed their music programs with the goal of preparing students to pursue professional careers as music educators, should they choose that path. Central to this mission is the belief that these educators would not only be skilled practitioners, but also transformative figures, catalysts for change in their communities and for the students they served.

Given the historical barriers Black Americans faced in achieving an education, teaching was an accessible and respected career path in the 20th century. As a result, the teaching profession became a powerful site of community uplift and intellectual advancement, leading to an increase of the number of college-educated Black teachers (Fairclough, 2000; Madkins, 2011). There emerged a need for Black music educators, individuals formally trained in the musical arts who could return to Black communities to provide structured, rigorous music instruction that expanded beyond the informal or community-based learning experiences many Black students had previously encountered (Shipley, 2011). By 1950, approximately half of all Black professionals in the United States were employed as teachers (Gordon, 2000; Perkins, 1989), a significant portion of whom were music educators. Many of these educators were graduates of HBCUs and held advanced degrees, which reflected the role these institutions played in producing highly qualified Black teachers (Siddle Walker, 2000).

The large number of music teachers HBCUs once produced has drastically declined. The National Association of Schools of Music conducted a national report that indicated a disproportionate percentage of music education and performance graduates according to race, with Black students graduating at 6.6% of all music education graduates (McKoy, 2012). The state of Georgia boasts of its status as having the third highest number of HBCUs, eight. The majority of these institutions, however, no longer offer music education degree programs (Thompson, 2022). Only two Georgia HBCUs offer music education degrees, Albany State University and Savannah State University. As Georgia remains a significant hub for HBCU education, the diminished presence of music education programs raises significant questions about access, representation, and the long-term vitality of culturally responsive music instruction in Black communities.

The few HBCUs offering music education degrees is deeply concerning, especially given the low number of Black students completing undergraduate degrees in music education (Elpus, 2015) and the scarcity of Black educators in classrooms (DeLorenzo & Silverman, 2016). This situation did not arise by chance. Several historical events and racially discriminatory policies have contributed to the current dilemma. For example, the 1954 *Brown vs. Board of Education* ruling led to a dramatic decline in the number of Black educators; their numbers dropped from 82,000 to 38,000, primarily in southern states (Tillman, 2004). Despite being highly regarded and often more qualified than their White counterparts—that is with a higher likelihood of holding bachelor's degrees and advanced teacher licensure—many Black teachers were outright fired as states used the ruling as a pretext to purge Black educators (Barnes-Johnson, 2011; Milner & Howard, 2004). These displaced teachers were barred from seeking employment at White schools, further exacerbating the decline in the number of Black educators. These decisions have had a lasting, detrimental impact on the field and led to the current shortage of Black music teachers and the diminished presence of music education programs at HBCUs.

The mass removal of Black educators from the field of education was compounded by the introduction of standardized tests, which further hindered the recruitment of Black teachers. Between the late 1970s and early 1990s, teacher certification exams led to the elimination of nearly 100,000 minority teachers across 35 states (Oakley et al., 2009; Tillman, 2004), a trend that continues. Many Black teacher candidates at HBCUs struggle to pass the Praxis Series Examination on their first attempt (Brock, 2020), a significant barrier to increasing the number of Black educators, particularly in music education (Elpus, 2015; Koza, 2002). The difficulty in passing these high-stakes exams not only deters Black students from teaching at HBCUs but from entering the teaching profession.

The lower pass rates among Black candidates should not be misconstrued as a reflection of their academic abilities. Despite the focus on exam failures, a notable lack of research addresses the challenges faced by inadequately prepared music teachers in K–12 schools serving minority communities (Elpus, 2015; Elpus & Abril, 2019). Policymakers and HBCU leadership must address the inequities in entry-level requirements and certification benchmarks, such as the Praxis/GACE exams, that disproportionately impact Black students (Fenwick, 2021). HBCU music administrators must also recognize their own role when questioning why their students struggle to pass these exams and take proactive steps to support them.

Despite these challenges, HBCUs play a critical role in maintaining a pipeline of Black music educators unmatched by predominantly White institutions. During the latter half of the 20th century, a significant number of African American students began enrolling in predominantly white institutions rather than HBCUs. Despite this shift, DeAngelis (2022) found that out of 29,869 students who graduated with bachelor's degrees in music education between 2011 and 2018, 81% were White, 7% were Hispanic/Latino, 4% were Black/African American, 2% were Asian, 0.5% were American

Indian/Native Alaskan, 0.1% were Native Hawaiian/Pacific Islander, and 2% identified as two or more races. DeAngelis's study revealed that HBCUs comprised only 5% of schools in this data set, yet accounted for nearly a third of all Black music education graduates. This statistic underscores the significant, yet disproportionate role that HBCUs play in music education and highlights their importance in nurturing future Black music educators.

Diversifying the landscape of music education will continue as an uphill battle if HBCUs are not considered as key figures. Because of the declining rate of college students pursuing music as a profession, it is imperative to include HBCUs in discussions about diversifying music education. The gradual phasing out of music education degree programs from HBCU curricula has created a significant gap in the teacher pipeline. Given the proportion of Black music education graduates from HBCUs, these institutions are vital to increasing diversity in music education. Before proposing solutions to this dilemma, we must listen to the voices of those who have been marginalized, and HBCUs must be central in these discussions. The continued removal of music education programs from HBCU curricula not only harms students of color but also risks losing valuable opportunities for many Black students, which could then significantly impact American schools. Despite these challenges, HBCUs are in a unique position to fulfill the need for more music educators. They hold immense, untapped potential to nurture and develop future Black music educators.

Notes

1. Wendell Whalum of the Morehouse Glee Club from 1953 to 1987; Roland Carter, known as the "great, modern Hampton maestro," served at Hampton from 1965 to 1989; Nathan Carter of Morgan State University served from 1970 to 2004; and Roland Allison served Spelman College as director of the Glee Club from 1967 to 1990.
2. The University of North Texas was the first university in the world to offer a degree in Jazz Studies, specifically with a major in Dance Band or dance music. At that time, the school chose to use the term *dance band* instead of *jazz band* because they did not want to risk the program being viewed negatively or not being taken seriously. The term *jazz* was often associated with certain stereotypes, so the term *dance band* helped the program gain broader acceptance and avoid potential stigma.
3. They included Lil Harding Armstrong of Fisk University, Cannonball Adderly and Nat Adderly of Florida A&M Collegians, Una Mae Carlisle and Nancy WIlson of Wilberforce Collegians, Morris Ellis and Bill Hughes of the Howard University Swingmasters, Alvin Baptiste of Southern University Collegians, Jimmy Blanton, Erskine Hawkins, and Hank Crawford of the Tennessee State Collegians.

4. In "The Story of Jazz" (Wynn, 2003), Andy Goodrich recounts a conversation with saxophonist Benny Golson. "Benny Golson told me that when he was at Howard during the late 1940s, he had to practice in the Home Economics building because the music department wouldn't allow jazz players to use their facilities." For his entrance audition, Golden could not play his saxophone, only the clarinet and piano.
5. One of the earliest known all Black African American orchestras was the Negro Philharmonic Society, founded in New Orleans in the 1830s and had over 100 members. The Symphony of the New World existed from 1964 to 1976 as a fully integrated professional orchestra in New York. The Symphony of the New World was a support program channeling instrumentalists of color to perform with professional mainstream orchestras.

References

Anderson, T. P. (2010). *"Tell them we are singing for Jesus": The original Fisk Jubilee Singers and Christian reconstruction, 1871–1878.* Mercer University Press.

Barnes-Johnson, J. M. (2011). *Efficacy-related beliefs and practices about equitable science teaching: A case study in an urban elementary school.* Publication No. 874289510 Doctoral dissertation. Temple University. ProQuest Dissertations & Theses.

Barrie, A., Byrd, B., Pearson, V., Spencer, E., Prandy, Z., Morgan, B., Warren, C., & Lyman, M. (2024, February 5). Jazz band born at Howard celebrates 50th anniversary at the Howard Theatre. *Hilltop.* https://thehilltoponline.com/2024/02/05/jazz-band-born-at-howard-celebrates-50th-anniversary-at-the-howard-theatre/

Beard, A. D. (2021). *Trends in the gospel music ensemble experience: Establishing the precedent and need for inclusion of gospel choir ensemble experience and pedagogy into the collegiate level music curriculum.* Publication No. 3027 Doctoral dissertation, Liberty University. Doctoral Dissertations and Projects.

Branch, L. G. (1975). *Jazz education in predominantly Black colleges.* Publication No. 302805333 Doctoral dissertation, Southern Illinois University at Carbondale. ProQuest Dissertation & Theses.

Brock, T. P. (2020). *Black music teacher candidates' preparation and performance on the praxis music examination.* University of North Carolina at Greensboro]. ProQuest Dissertation & Theses. Publication No. 2431792105 Doctoral dissertation.

Clark, R. H. (2019). A narrative history of African American marching band: Toward a historicultural understanding. *Journal of Historical Research in Music Education, 41*(1), 5–32. https://doi.org/10.1177/1536600619847933

DeAngelis, D. R. (2022). Recent college graduates with bachelor's degrees in music education: A demographic profile. *Journal of Music Teacher Education, 32*(1), 25–37.

DeLorenzo, L. C. (2012). Missing faces from the orchestra: An issue of social justice? *Music Educators Journal, 98*(4), 39–46.

DeLorenzo, L. C., & Silverman, M. (2016). From the margins: The underrepresentation of Black and Latino students/teachers in music education. *Visions of Research in Music Education, 27*(1), 3.

Elpus, K. (2015). Music teacher licensure candidates in the United States: A demographic profile and analysis of licensure examination scores. *Journal of Research in Music Education, 63*(3), 314–335.

Elpus, K., & Abril, C. R. (2011). High school music ensemble students in the United States: A demographic profile. *Journal of Research in Music Education, 59*(2), 128–145. https://doi.org/10.1177/0022429411405207

Elpus, K., & Abril, C. R. (2019). Who enrolls in high school music? A national profile of US students, 2009-2013. *Journal of Research in Music Education, 67*(3), 323–338. https://doi-org.ezproxy.bu.edu/10.1177/00224294198628

Fairclough, A. (2000). "Being in the field of education and also being a Negro . . . seems . . . tragic": Black teachers in the Jim Crow south. *Journal of American History, 87*(1), 65–91.

Fenwick, L. (2021). *The history, current use, and impact of entrance and licensure examinations cut scores on the teacher of color pipeline: A structural racism analysis.* American Association of Colleges for Teacher Education. https://aacte.org/wp-content/uploads/201/10/CREA-v2.pdf

Flagg, A. (2020, August 13). *Anti-Black discrimination in American orchestras.* Symphony. https://symphony.org/features/anti-black-discrimination-in-american-orchestras/

Foster, W. P. (1968). *Band pageantry: A guide for the marching band.* Hal Leonard Music.

Friedberg, J. (2023, June 19). James Baldwin digs into the roots of American music. *PopMatters.* https://www.popmatters.com/james-baldwin-american-music

Goodrich, A. L. (2001). Jazz in historically Black colleges. *Jazz Education Journal, 34*(3), 54–58.

Gordon, J. (2000). *The color of teaching.* Routledge.

Hadley, F. M. (2023). The world we make: Black colleges and Black music studies. *American Music, 41*(2), 205–210.

Koza, J. E. (2002). Corporate profit at equity's expense: Codified standards and high-stakes assessment in music teacher preparation. *Bulletin of the Council for Research in Music Education, 152,* 1–16.

Ladson-Billings, G. (2004). Landing on the wrong note: The price we paid for Brown. *Educational Researcher, 33*(7), 3–13. https://doi.org/10.3102/0013189X033007003

League of American Orchestras. (2023). *Impact report.* https://americanorchestras.org/2023-impact-report/

Lewis, W., & Wilson, C. R. (2011). Marching bands, HBCU. In H. H. Jackson (Ed.), *The new encyclopedia of southern culture: Volume 16: Sports and recreation* (pp. 145–147). University of North Carolina Press.

Lovett, B. L. (2015). *America's historically black colleges & universities: A narrative history from the nineteenth century into the twenty-first century.* Mercer University Press.

Lundy, G. (2015). *An ethnographic case study of orchestra directors at historically Black colleges and universities.* Publication No. 1773953027 Doctoral dissertation. University of Houston. ProQuest Dissertation & Theses.

Madkins, T. C. (2011). The Black teacher shortage: A literature review of historical and contemporary trends. *The Journal of Negro Education, 80*(3), 417–427.

Mahoney, A. D. (2021). Reclaiming the beat: The sweet subversive sounds of HBCU marching bands. *Southern Cultures, 27*(4), 78–97.

McKoy, C. L. (2012). Effects of selected demographic variables on music student teachers' self-reported cross-cultural competence. *Journal of Research in Music Education, 60*(4), 375–394. https://doi.org/10.1177/0022429412463398

Milner, H. R., & Howard, T. C. (2004). Black teachers, Black students, Black communities, and Brown: Perspectives and insights from experts. *The Journal of Negro Education, 73*(3), 285–297. https://doi.org/10.2307/4129612

National Association of Schools of Music. (2024). *Accredited institutions.* http://nasm.arts-accredit.org/

Oakley, D., Stowell, J., & Logan, J. R. (2009). The impact of desegregation on Black teachers in the metropolis, 1970–2000. *Ethnic and Racial Studies, 32*(9), 1576–1598. https://doi.org/10.1080/01419870902780997

Pellegrinelli, L. (2018, May 15). *Spelman College quietly eliminates one of the country's few jazz programs for women.* NPR. https://www.npr.org/sections/therecord/2018/05/15/611280239/spelman-college-quietly-eliminates-one-of-the-countrys-few-jazz-programs-for-wom. Accessed on April 20, 2025.

Perkins, L. M. (1989). The history of Blacks in teaching: Growth and decline within the profession. In D. Warren (Ed.), *American teachers: Histories of a profession at work* (pp. 344–369). American Educational Research Association.

Pleasants, H. (1969). *Serious music, and all that jazz: An adventure in music criticism.* Simon & Schuster.

Price, E. G., Kernodle, T. L., & Maxile, H. J. (Eds.). (2011). *Encyclopedia of African American music.* Greenwood.

Reed-Walker, R. P. (2008). *Preserving the Negro spiritual: An examination of contemporary practices.* ProQuest. Publication No. 304839344 Doctoral dissertation. Wilmington University. ProQuest Dissertation & Theses.

Reid Sr, J. E. (2020). *Marching sound machines: An autoethnography of a director of bands at an historically Black college and university.* Publication No. 2451425625 Doctoral dissertation. Boston University. ProQuest Dissertation & Theses.

Rowley, S. L. (2013). *William Patrick Foster and his impact on African American wind band conductors.* Publication No. 1346185120 Doctoral dissertation. Columbia University. ProQuest Dissertation & Theses.

Scott, A. (1973). *Jazz educated, man: A sound foundation.* American International Publishers.

Shaffer, D. M. (2018). *An introductory pedagogy for gospel music for the choral conductor.* Publication No. 10749240 Doctoral dissertation. University of South Carolina. ProQuest Dissertation & Theses.

Shipley, L. (2011). Music education at Hampton Institute, 1868–1913. *Journal of Historical Research in Music Education, 32*(2), 96–121.

Siddle Walker, V. (2000). Valued segregated schools for African American children in the South, 1935–1969: A review of common themes and characteristics. *Review of Educational Research, 70*(3), 253–285. https://doi.org/10.2307/1170784

Simmons, T. L. (2023). *HBCUs unhushed: Transformative spiritual resilience within the life histories of African American graduates of historically Black colleges and universities.* Publication No. 2798983820 Doctoral dissertation. University of Wisconsin at Madison. ProQuest Dissertation & Theses

Southern, E. (1997). *The music of Black Americans: A history.* W. W. Norton & Co.

Thompson, J. E. (2022). *The effects of limited music education offerings in Georgia HBCUs: Undergraduate school choice for African American music students in the state of Georgia.* Publication No. 2685448358 Doctoral dissertation. University of Georgia. ProQuest Dissertation & Theses.

Thurman, K. (2021). *Singing like Germans: Black musicians in the land of Bach, Beethoven, and Brahms.* Cornell University Press.

Tillman, L. C. (2004). (Un)intended consequences? The impact of the Brown v. Board of education decision on the employment status of Black educators. *Education and Urban Society, 36*(3), 280–303. https://doi.org/10.1177/0013124504264360

Ward, A. (2000). *Dark midnight when I rise: The story of the Jubilee Singers, who introduced the world to the music of Black America.* Farrar, Straus, and Giroux.

Whitehead, T. L. (2023). *A comparative study of the marching bands at four historically Black colleges and universities.* Publication No. 2825103019 Doctoral dissertation. Liberty University. ProQuest Dissertation & Theses.

Williams, J., & Ashley, D. (2004). *I'll find a way or make one: A tribute to historically Black colleges and universities.* HarperCollins.

Work, J. W. (1998). *American Negro songs: 230 folk songs and spirituals, religious and secular.* Dover Publications. (originally published in 1940)

Wynn, R. (2003, April 10). The story of jazz TSU alum Andy Goodrich, respected jazz veteran, returns to town to take part in a daylong celebration of the music. *Nashville Scene.* https://www.nashvillescene.com/arts_culture/the-story-of-jazz/article_b30fcb1f-b5a4-5c32-baba-942fd6dd5ee7.html

Floyd, J. J. (2021). *Perceptions of African American students regarding their experiences in high school orchestra.* Publication No. 262498681 Doctoral dissertation. University of Georgia. ProQuest Dissertation & Theses.

Additional Readings

Freeman, K. (2012). *African Americans and college choice: The influence of family and school.* State University of New York Press.

Maultsby, P. K., Burnim, M. V., Epstein, D. J., Oehler, S., DjeDje, J. C., Evans, D., Riis, T., & Koskoff, E. (2005). African American musical cultures. In E. Koskoff (Ed.), *Music cultures in the United States* (1st ed., pp. 185–242). Routledge. https://doi.org/10.4324/9780203997161-9

CHAPTER 4

ENTWINED REALITIES: CURRICULUM, COMMUNITY, CHALLENGES

ABSTRACT

Facilitating transformative music education at HBCUs requires more than revising curriculum, it demands intentional engagement with community, culture, and historical context. Chapter 4 examines how music education at HBCUs reflects a deeply entwined relationship between cultural preservation, academic rigor, and student empowerment. This convergence, while powerful, also presents tensions. Centering African American musical traditions and communal experiences not only challenge Eurocentric norms in music education, but can also generate conflicts when institutional standards conflict with culturally responsive practice. Teaching in affirming environments empowers students, yet risks institutional resistance when curricula reject dominant frameworks.

Historically Black Colleges and University (HBCU) music programs navigate a complex dual imperative: maintaining historical mission while adapting to 21st-century student needs. Educators must manage demands for technological fluency and industry relevance alongside calls for curricular decolonization. At the same time, holistic admissions and inclusive pedagogy broaden access but invite critique from traditional gatekeepers. Efforts to align with professional benchmarks may unintentionally marginalize gospel, jazz, or vernacular styles. Meanwhile, faculty must uphold artistic standards while fostering student identity development in the face of systemic inequities.

This chapter argues that thoughtful, context-driven curriculum reform is essential to sustain the cultural, social, and musical vitality of HBCU programs. By honoring community-rooted traditions while embracing innovation, HBCUs can empower a music education that supports student belonging, artistic expression, and academic excellence without reproducing exclusionary norms.

While the global community often hears the powerful product of HBCU music education—from the stirring presentation of spirituals by choral ensembles to the electrifying performance of marching bands—what remains largely unseen is the environment in which this music is created. The broader world experiences the sound but not the soil, that is the community, culture, and context that give rise to such musical excellence. As the character Ma Rainey reminds us in August Wilson's play, *Ma Rainey's Black Bottom* (1982), to witness the cultural richness of a people without understanding its origins or the lived experiences that shape it is easy. For Rainey, the blues, more than entertainment, was a profound expression of truth, a way to process life's pain and joy, and a deeply rooted cultural practice born from the community. Similarly, HBCU musical traditions cannot be fully understood apart from the social spaces that nurture them.

Research into music education has focused on the individual achievement of musical ability and neglected the dynamics of community contexts (Carter, 2013). Scholars often focus on the performance, the spectacle, rather than on the context in which music is taught and learned. There remains an urgent need to expand the scholarly lens to include not only the musical output of HBCUs but the educational systems that produce it. As discussed in the Chapter 3, understanding HBCU musical traditions is not solely about content, but about the convergence of curriculum, community, and cultural identity. These components do not function autonomously. Rather, they exist in a mutually dependent and co-constructive relationship. In this cohesive environment positive learning outcomes take root and flourish. Deeply grounded in African American history and resilience, HBCU music programs are designed not only to preserve cultural legacies but to propel them forward. Such preservation, however, does not occur in a vacuum. It happens in academic structures and communal spaces where the experiences of students are centered, affirmed, and celebrated. While this is deeply empowering, it also brings unique challenges that HBCUs continue to navigate.

Praxial and Esthetic Philosophies

Historically Black Colleges and Universities are as diverse as their music programs. An institution's location, religious affiliation, accreditation, and public or private status all influence their music curricula. Certain commonalities can be observed across these programs, however. While not always explicitly acknowledged, the notion of HBCU music as a social and cultural construct plays a significant role in shaping how the curricula has evolved. The music curricula at HBCUs are deeply intertwined with both praxial (Elliott, 1995, 2012) and esthetic (Reimer, 2003) philosophies.

The praxial philosophy particularly resonates at HBCUs, as music education extends beyond technical proficiency to encompass performances, community involvement, and the use of music as a vital form of social commentary and cultural expression. Simultaneously, HBCUs enrich the esthetic philosophy of music education, which emphasizes the beauty and expression of music, particularly music of the African American experience. The esthetic experience at HBCUs is profoundly connected to African American heritage and history, offering students a deeper appreciation of music as an expression of collective memory and resilience.

This dual focus between praxial and esthetic is exemplified in the curriculum in which various genres are studied not only for their artistic qualities but also as essential elements of Black creativity. HBCU music programs reflect a dynamic synthesis of tradition and innovation, one rooted in cultural identity while responding to contemporary realities. As the musical landscape continues to shift, HBCU curricula likewise evolve to meet the needs of their students and ensure they are not only culturally grounded but also well prepared for the demands of the ever-changing field of music.

Vocational Versus Classical

Whether HBCUs stressed either vocational or classical education, teaching music was a vital part of the college curricula. For example, at Fisk, from the time the school opened both teachers and students demonstrated considerable interest in music. In their leisure hours, students gathered and sang songs learned when still enslaved (Richardson, 1980). Only weeks after establishing Spelman College in 1881, founders Harriet B. Giles and Sophia B. Packard hired their first teacher, a music teacher named E. H. Kruger, who gave voice lessons (Grissom-Broughton, 2020). When Booker T. Washington founded Tuskegee in 1881, he made communal singing a part of daily activities. Washington established a musical tradition during chapel worship that promoted the congregational singing of a mixture of standard hymns and plantation melodies (Malone, 2023).

HBCUs that stressed a vocational education often constructed their music curricula that not only positioned their students for employment, but also enhanced their skills as educators. For instance, before Cheyney University received its charter, it functioned as normal college, Cheyney Training School for Teachers. To receive teaching certificates, students were required to take music courses as extended work to make them well-rounded educators. According to the course catalog:

> The modern school must do more than give to its students a reasonable acquaintance with books, methods, and processes. It must make itself felt in the life of the community which it serves. The Cheney Training School for Teachers endeavors to respond intelligently to this demand. [Music] students will be able to help in the neighboring colored churches, and frequently groups of students trained by our teacher of music go to the towns and villages nearby and help in many good causes by providing wholesome and instructive entertainment and good music, especially Negro melodies.

At Historically Black Colleges and Universities that emphasized liberal arts the music curricula often balanced the need for formal instruction in the canons of Western music with experience in Black vernacular traditions (Prouty, 2011). Students received musical training in private and group lessons in voice, piano, and violin and course work in music theory and music history. Courses for credit were offered, and vocal and instrumental music lessons made available to all students.

Howard University, for example, reorganized its curriculum into eleven departments just seven years later after its founding in 1867 one of which was the music department. In addition to music theory and history courses, Howard's music curriculum also required students to take three years of private piano instruction, two years of private organ and vocal music, and one year of harmonium (Logan, Academic Catalog). The rigorous music programs ensured that students were well-prepared and exceptionally capable of competing with their peers from music programs elsewhere.

At Historically Black Women's Colleges such as Spelman College and Bennett College, the curriculum reflected a liberal arts classical model. Musical training at these specialized institutions differed from other liberal arts HBCUs, because the mission of these institutions specifically addressed the needs of Black women. At Black women's colleges, musical training was meant to foster the development of what they called a well-rounded Black woman, capable of leadership and prepared to lift up the Black race. Simultaneously, collegiate music training served as a tool to improve the Black woman's femininity in a society that tended to stereotype them with degrading characterizations and misogynistic depictions (Grissom-Broughton, 2020). At White colleges for women, music was considered an ornamental subject designed to foster social refinement and elegance. For Black women, music became a vocational area of study along with domestic sciences, nursing, and missionary training (Watson & Gregory, 2023). Black women who received musical training at HBCUs provided cultural enrichment for the Black community through solo recitals, choirs, small musical groups, and as visiting artists. Ultimately, music training for Black women served to improve their economic status through whatever musical employment a racist and sexist society afforded them.

Evolving With the Moment

Between 1900 and 1920, several HBCUs established music departments, but the curricula varied depending on whether the institution was public or private. Many private HBCUs, founded by White Christians and abolitionists, saw their music and arts programs shaped by the cultural values of White instructors. As most of the music faculty were graduates of predominantly White institutions (PWIs), they modeled their curricula after those institutions. Consequently, these curricula often did not fully represent the cultural heritage of African Americans. The need to prepare Black students for postgraduate study and professional careers led to a music curriculum that prioritized Western Classical music over music rooted in the Black experience. This shift occurred as predominantly White colleges with graduate programs began slowly admitting African Americans as in addition to growing demand for teachers in Black public schools. As a result, the curriculum aligned with Western Classical traditions to better equip students for these opportunities, but at the expense of the rich musical heritage of the Black experience.

From the 1920s to 1940s, the music curricula at HBCUs began to diversify, offering more opportunities for the general student population to engage with ensembles that featured music from the African American heritage. This evolution was closely tied to the changing demographics of the faculty. Oberlin College played a significant role in this transformation. One of the first institutions to provide African American students access to both undergraduate and graduate music studies, Oberlin became a key source of Black music educators.

Since traditionally White colleges and universities were slow to hire African American music professors, many of Oberlin's first Black graduates began their music teaching careers at HBCUs. These pioneering educators significantly influenced the music curriculum by diversifying course content, particularly by incorporating music that reflected the African American experience. Notable figures include composer and director R. Nathaniel Dett, the first Black double-major graduate from Oberlin Conservatory in piano and composition, who became the first African American director of music at Hampton University. Violinist Clarence Cameron White, an Oberlin graduate, taught at West Virginia State University. Camille Nickerson, another graduate, taught at Howard University, where she established the Junior Preparatory Department, a program that nurtured talents such as Pulitzer Prize-winning composer George Walker, who later earned his undergraduate degree from Oberlin.

During the 1940s and 1950s, the HBCU music curricula evolved rapidly. Courses in music theory and music history became standard in most HBCU music curricula. HBCU faculty developed a robust music curriculum that could compete with those at White institutions. Some HBCUs sought accreditation from the National Association of Schools of Music[1] for legitimacy and proof that their music program could meet specific rigorous standards (Haughton, 2011). The first four HBCUs to attain accreditation for their music programs were Howard University in 1944, Lincoln University in 1951, Fisk University in 1952, and Virginia State University in 1954. Other HBCUs would obtain accreditation, but not all desired to be accredited.

These robust HBCU music programs during the 1940s and 1950s, at the height of Jim Crow, did not occur by chance. This success was largely due to the increasing number of Black music faculty members who gained access to graduate studies and earned terminal degrees from institutions outside of the South, such as Oberlin College and Northwestern University. In the South, where most HBCUs were located, African Americans were denied opportunities for higher education beyond the bachelor's degree.[2] All the states of the former Confederacy, as well as border states, declined to establish postbaccalaureate programs at their Black colleges. As a result, African Americans in the South seeking master's or doctoral degrees migrated to schools elsewhere. Sanders (2024) describes this as the forgotten migration.

> During pre-*Brown v. Board of Education*, and in some cases, African American college graduates were awarded "segregation scholarships" by states in the US South to Black students seeking graduate education. Under the *Plessy v. Ferguson* decision, decades earlier, southern states could provide graduate opportunities for African Americans by creating separate but equal graduate programs at tax-supported Black colleges or by admitting Black students to historically white institutions. Most did neither and instead paid to send Black students out of state for graduate education.

Spelman College music professor and organist Joyce Johnson, a graduate of Fisk University, recalls:

> When I came to Spelman the following summer [in 1953], I immediately began my masters work at Northwestern University, attending Northwestern every summer for four summers and coming back to teach during the school year and then later taking a leave of absence to complete my doctorate. Why did I choose Northwestern? Because of segregation. It is not widely known

that African Americans were not even permitted to enter Southern universities for graduate study; students of color were sent out of state, including to major institutions, with expenses paid by the respective Southern states. That accounts for my graduate study at Northwestern University in Illinois, from which I earned the Master of Music and the Doctor of Music degrees, both in piano.[3] The State of Georgia actually paid all my expenses for my education at Northwestern University those four summers. (Spelman College, 2024)

Segregation scholarships continued from the 1940s to 1960. Like Johnson, many Black musicians and educators pursued graduate studies through these scholarships at predominantly White institutions. While these schools were quick to accept the financial resources that came with these scholarships, they were often hostile to African American students. Many HBCU music faculty who chose to further their education at these institutions endured severe racism and oppressive treatment while earning advanced degrees. Despite these challenges, they returned to the Jim Crow South, armed with new knowledge and a deep determination to strengthen their communities and HBCUs.

During the 1960s, civil, social, and racial unrest involved both Black and White student protesters across the nation. Accompanying this unrest, a renaissance of a Black culture that brought about racial pride among Black youths. Thousands of Black students demonstrated on campuses across the country, and among their demands were the inclusion of Black history, literature, and humanities courses (Williams & Ashley, 2004). Black students demanded that music courses reflect African American genres. Courses such as History of Jazz and History of African American Music were offered at many HBCUs. Although the music curricula were still Eurocentric, courses that emphasized Black music became impactful. The inclusion of such courses, along with more students attending HBUCs, resulted in an increase of music graduates from HBCUs.

As HBCUs have evolved to meet the demands of the 21st century, so too have their music curricula. By the early 2000s, many institutions had expanded their offerings to include music technology, contemporary popular music, production, and music business. This ensured that their programs remained competitive with PWIs and prepared students for a rapidly changing industry. Yet, the high cost of staying current with technological advancements has posed challenges, particularly for HBCUs with limited funding. Despite such financial hurdles, several HBCUs have successfully positioned these modern concentrations as defining features of their music departments, drawing students eager to gain industry-relevant skills while studying in culturally affirming environments. HBCU music programs continue to celebrate the African American musical heritage while preparing students to become transformative musicians, educators, and scholars, equipped to shape the future of music.

Nurturing and Belonging Spaces

The arts have long been a vital aspect of Black cultural expression at HBCUs, offering students a community to express themselves artistically, politically, and socially. Of all the arts, music has consistently garnered the highest level of student participation. Just as HBCU music programs are not monolithic, neither are its music students. What truly sets music education at HBCUs apart is the inclusive and diverse community that students become a part of. Whether they have had years of private piano lessons, participated in band since elementary school, or gained their musical experience playing in church, these students from various socio-economic backgrounds learn side by side. At HBCUs, students are welcomed to the music programs, embraced for who they are, and recognized for their potential as musicians, scholars, and educators. Not confined to the narrow expectation to become professional Classical musicians, they are encouraged to develop their unique musical identities. These affirming environments go beyond technical skill-building, they empower students to shape their own artistic paths, while immersing them in Black musical traditions.

Our Doors Are Open

Only a small amount of research examines the experiences of African Americans in music programs in higher education (Bradley, 2007). Particularly in White schools, where the curricula do not reflect diverse culture, audition requirements may possibly play a role in the low enrollment and engagement of minority students (Koza, 2010). Palmer (2011) provides a compelling perspective on this significant issue by citing that low expectations for students of color can adversely affect their college auditions. He notes that these students not only struggle gaining access to higher education, but also face hurdles in the music admission process, such as the bias toward Western Classical music in audition requirements.

This mismatch between students' musical backgrounds and the expectations of academic institutions can create barriers, as Abramo and Bernard (2020) point out. They argue that the values and musical experiences of students of color do not always align with traditional performance-based auditions. Auditions are used to predict future musical study achievement and vocational success (Jørgensen, 2009). Several authors have noted that the traditional performance-based audition can serve to exclude prospective students who do not exhibit outstanding musicality in the Western European traditions (Abramo & Bernard, 2020; Bradley, 2007; Fitzpatrick et al., 2014; Kaschub, 2024; Kaschub & Smith, 2014; Koza, 2010).

Although the audition requirements for many music programs at HBCUs largely mirror those of White schools (i.e., technical assessments, standard instrument repertoires, sight-reading), HBCUs generally evaluate music elements such as singing or playing by ear and proficiency in gospel and jazz, genres deeply rooted in many of these institutions. These extraordinary talents are not always valued at White schools. HBCUs are also known for their open admission policies, which strive to democratize access to education, and especially benefits students of color by providing a nurturing and culturally inclusive learning environment (Brooks & Starks, 2011). Several HBCUs adopt a more holistic approach to their auditions by considering prospective students' leadership qualities and community involvement in addition to their academic and musical achievements This approach recognizes the social contributions of students, not only their musical abilities. HBCUs accept music students based on their potential as both scholars and musicians regardless of their prior musical background.

The value of HBCU music programs extends far beyond the technical skills and musical talent of their members and benefits not only the students but also the wider community. These programs foster a strong sense of community, provide vital avenues for cultural expression, promote personal growth, and serve as platforms for social and political engagement. Well beyond the realm of musical performance, they contribute to the development of individuals and enrich the broader community. According to Haughton (2011), many African American students who faced racial barriers in accessing music opportunities turned to HBCUs for these essential experiences. These programs have supplied young musicians to communities, filled vital roles in church music ministries, and acted as leaders in community music organizations.

Making music at HBCUs transcends conventional barriers in music education, cultivating an environment rich in diversity and inclusivity. Utilizing Milner's (2012) opportunity gap framework to discover systematic inequalities of college access, Abramo and Bernard (2020), researchers from the University of Connecticut, examined the representation of students of color in their school of music. Their study revealed that high school students of color showed low interest in Classical music literature, largely due to lack of exposure through private lessons, and often inaccessible due to financial, transportation, and time constraints. HBCUs effectively bridge this gap by welcoming students of various musical skill levels and backgrounds, providing them with opportunities to engage in music making of diverse styles and genres within a supportive community in which they are valued while held to high standards.

The supportive community of a diverse music faculty is a key but frequently underestimated factor. HBCUs typically boast music faculty who not only reflect the racial and cultural backgrounds of their students but also bring a wide range of musical traditions and pedagogies. Faculty members at HBCUs play an integral role, not only in education but as part of a rich cultural legacy. They engage deeply with the ethos, history, and resilience of Black communities, enriching the educational experience (HatcherPuzzo et al., 2023). Research highlights the critical support that HBCU faculty provide by offering substantial care and guidance to their students (Koch & Swinton, 2022). The combination of cultural immersion and dedicated support defines the unique contribution of HBCU faculty. This alignment significantly enhances the learning experience, providing a sense of belonging rare at PWIs.

HBCU's faculty and music staff enjoy a reputation for maintaining high musical standards across all genres, not only Classical music. They offer dynamic opportunities to create music that include a range of culturally relevant musical styles such as jazz, gospel, R&B, and hip-hop, as well as Classical music. This diverse musical exposure ensures that students not only enhance their technical skills but also deepen their cultural understanding. Through ensemble playing and community-based events, HBCUs foster a sense of belonging among students, emphasizing music as an inclusive activity that celebrates all students' rich musical heritage.

Affirming Environments

Historically Black Colleges and Universities have long been pivotal in nurturing the academic and personal growth of African American students. HBCUs have consistently graduated more African American undergraduates than PWIs (Boykin et al., 2017) and have excelled at providing culturally responsive learning environments (Carter, 2013). Research indicates that the choice to attend an HBCU often extends beyond financial or academic considerations. Johnson and McGowan (2017) and Van Camp et al. (2010) found that students are frequently drawn to HBCUs for their racial composition and historical mission. Additionally, the interracial diversity within HBCUs fosters deeper identity development among students (Squire & Mobley, 2015). This nurturing atmosphere coupled with a student-centered mission not only makes students feel at safe, but also encourages them to explore various areas in the university, thereby enhancing their integration into its traditions and boosting academic success.

The high achievement rates of Black students at HBCUs can be attributed to several factors, including a nurturing environment, culturally relevant curricula, and the absence of racial stereotype threats (Palmer & Young, 2011; Williams et al., 2022). By providing an affirming space in which students can explore their aspirations without fear of judgment, HBCUs cultivate the conditions necessary for students to thrive personally, academically, and musically.

One may assume that because of the universal esthetic of music, African American music students at PWIs do not experience, or experience less racial stressors. Brower and Ketterhagen (2004) found that Black music students at White institutions experience an "inherent mismatch" (p. 96). In many cases, music programs at White schools are merely microcosmoses of their campus-wide learning environments. Black music students often feel isolated (Anderson, 2018; McCall, 2015; Robinson & Hendricks, 2018), and devalued, both musically and academically by White peers and professors. Moreover, Black music students often find it difficult to connect with instructors unfamiliar with their unique cultural experiences (Parker, 2024). In contrast, HBCUs offer culturally affirming environments that not only recognizes, but support the holistic development of its music students.

Despite facing resource constraints and enrolling a high percentage of students from lower socioeconomic backgrounds, HBCUs create supportive socio-psychological environments that promote student retention and completion more effectively than White institutions (Palmer and Young, 2011). These institutions have proven effective in a landscape in which African American students continue to experience greater social isolation and overt racism at predominantly White colleges (Rothstein & Rothstein, 2023). This sense of isolation is compounded in educational settings that lack diversity in faculty and pedagogical approaches, which often leaves students feeling alienated. Today, African American students are more isolated than they were over 40 years ago, while most education policymakers and reformers have abandoned integration as a cause (Rothstein, 2013). Students of color, especially those in mostly White schools in which their teachers are also White, often feel isolated, self-conscious, alienated, undervalued, and disconnected. As a result, these students find it difficult to engage with or challenge teaching that reflect Eurocentric approaches, ultimately leaving them feeling unheard or excluded in learning environments.

The tenacity it takes to become a Black composer, performer, or music educator, particularly in higher education, is regularly instilled in students. Maintaining the HBCU musical legacy means not merely upholding musical excellence. It means becoming a leader, a change agent. Grambling University Choral Director Cordara Harper mentions this situation in his own research (2023).

As an undergraduate music student at a HBCU, I had my first experiences with culturally relevant leadership in an ensemble setting. My voice teacher and choir director charged all of us to preserve the Negro Spiritual and to perform all music with intense focus, honor, and respect. My voice teacher also encouraged me to "give myself permission" to be both Black and excellent when all I previously heard was that being Black equated to being bad.

In the context of my one-on-one conversations with my choir director, to give oneself permission means to get out of one's own way to achieve success. Her words inspired me to want to become an agent of change (pp. 2, 3).

In the wake of the Black Lives Matter movement, intensified by the events of 2020 including the killings of George Floyd and Breonna Taylor, a renewed interest has arisen in Historically Black Colleges and Universities among college-bound Black students. Many Black families, having witnessed both the racial disparities in health outcomes during the coronavirus pandemic and the eruption of protests over police brutality, began to prioritize safety and cultural relevancy for their children. Furthermore, given the recent Supreme Court ruling in *Students for Fair Admissions v. Harvard* (2023) banning race-conscious admissions policies, students are increasingly seeking institutions that affirm their identities. This has led them to seek spaces where they are seen, welcomed, and affirmed, a quality that HBCUs have historically provided (McLean, 2024). This backdrop makes the HBCU environment especially enticing for music students, where the rich cultural heritage integral to these institutions can be fully embraced and explored.

Although limited empirical data on rates of avocational music participation at HBCUs is available, qualitative research affirms that these institutions provide deeply affirming learning musical environments for Black students. Marching bands (Carter, 2013) and choirs (Simmonds, 2005) hold cultural and social significance and offer students not only opportunities for musical growth but also peer respect. These ensembles serve as more than performance outlets; they are dynamic cultural spaces in which students connect to history, community, and each other.

HBCU music programs emphasize the community in shaping both student identity and success. Many students enter college with a rich foundation in Black musical traditions—gospel, jazz, blues—cultivated through family, church, and community engagement. HBCU curricula build upon this knowledge and teach technical proficiency while affirming the legitimacy of Black musical expression. Faculty members play a central role in this process, helping students understand that their creativity is part of a long-standing legacy of Black excellence. Being a member of an HBCU music ensemble means being part of a cultural legacy, an intergenerational community rooted in Black ethos, history, and resilience (HatcherPuzzo et al., 2023). These musical spaces not only elevate institutional visibility but also nurture the students' untapped talent. In doing so, they foster inclusive, empowering environments in which students can thrive musically without feeling the weight of racial marginalization.

Balancing Tradition and Innovation

Music programs at HBCUs are a key feature of the schools' relevance, serving as powerful expressions of cultural identity, historical legacy, and community pride. Challenges exist, however, in aligning the music programs with those of the HBCU, primarily because the music curriculum continues to reflect a Eurocentric bias. A friction arises between the music department and the institution; this misalignment can hinder the effectiveness of the music programs in fulfilling the institutions' missions (Ba, 2022; Walker, 2020). Cordona-Mejia et al. (2020) suggest that pressures to conform to mainstream academic standards can lead HBCUs to stray from their original objectives. Despite these challenges, a study by Oliver (2022) demonstrates that music programs, as well as programs in the arts, do indeed align with the mission of HBCUs. The bigger question remains, however: how do HBCU music programs continue the historic mission of the institution while also adapting to the changing circumstances of today's musical landscape?

Between 1936 and 1942, numerous African American musicians pursued careers in popular music due to the limited professional opportunities available in academia. This trend made a lasting impact on Black students studying music at HBCUs. The Eurocentric curriculum often left students feeling confined to traditional roles such as orchestral performers, conductors, opera singers, or college music professors, with few seeing themselves in careers outside these paths. Without a proper balance, HBCUs may find it difficult to develop innovative music programs that serve students effectively.

Tucker (2011) posits that the current music education curricula in higher education do not meet the needs of 21st-century students; many curricula are primarily designed to fulfill antiquated requirements. Because of this, Bergee and Demorset (2003) suggested that the cultural disconnect and subsequent attrition of minority music students beginning secondary music programs is due to the transmission of a repertoire that reinforces the Western European Classical music model. Although HBCUs promote learning environments that reflect its student population, they often replicate a Eurocentric music curriculum to validate their music education programs and to remain relevant within traditional norms. If in an effort to remain relevant HBCUs continue to follow PWIs as a template, they will risk their students' interest in studying music in college.

Today, students who seek HBCUs to further their study in music are increasingly drawn to programs that offer degrees in popular music and to nontraditional courses with practical applications for the careers, many of which are not offered by HBCUs. Clements (2009) notes that such programs could expand students' career choices and provide them with opportunities beyond the conventional paths in Classical music. This shift reflects a growing recognition of the need to diversify the music curriculum. As Nelms (2010) explains, "the future of HBCUs will rely upon their competitiveness, responsiveness, and relevance" (p. 17). HBCUs need to review their curriculum to make certain it reflects students' interests as well as their societal needs.

In many HBCU music programs the marching band serves as the central ensemble. Groups such as choirs, jazz bands, and orchestras have lower visibility and student participation. McCall's study (2015) found that these programs tend to prioritize marching bands as primary recruitment tools as the flagship of their departments. This emphasis can marginalize other areas of student music making. While the curriculum itself often reflects Eurocentric content, the cultural heart of many HBCU music programs revolves around the prestige, visibility, and time demands associated with marching bands.

This disproportionate focus is reinforced by the broader popular culture, which also tends to spotlight HBCU marching bands over other ensembles. For example, in 2003, the American Honda Motor Company launched the Honda Battle of the Bands, an annual showcase that brings together eight HBCU bands to compete for monetary awards. This event regularly attracts more than 50,000 fans. Similarly, in 2021, during the Southwestern Athletic Conference Championship, PepsiCo debuted a national advertising campaign honoring HBCU marching bands. The campaign featured Jackson State University's Sonic Boom of the South and Florida A&M University's Marching 100 and celebrated their influence beyond the football field. While this attention elevates the cultural significance of HBCU marching bands, it also suggests that ensembles such as jazz bands or orchestras are less relevant.

Although HBCU's highly visible music programs attract student participation, particularly in marching bands, many institutions enroll relatively few students majoring in music compared with other academic disciplines. We have little quantitative research data that investigates the HBCUs music majors' (BA or BM) graduation rates. The data we do have is reported through the NASM Higher Education Arts Data Services (HEADS) survey. This number, however, does not give a true picture of the number of music graduates from HBCUs because only 28 of the 103 HBCUs institutions are accredited through NASM (see Appendix C for list of HBCUs accredited by the NASM). This low percentage of nonaccredited music programs does not indicate that HBCUs have no quality music programs (Koza, 2010). Several HBCUs are not accredited, but have a reputation of producing top music graduates who became educators, scholars, and performers. HBCUs may not be well served by the push to adopt norms set by White institutions (Oliver, 2022).

HBCU music programs will require taking decisive actions—steps that would address its challenges. Issues such as unprepared students due to inadequate secondary school funding, students' varying socio-economic backgrounds, and diverse enrollments are often cited as obstacles facing HBCU music programs (Mixon, 2005). Such challenges however, are merely symptoms of a profound problem. They stem from complex social justice issues and systemic, long-standing inequities. Just as chronic underfunding has hindered HBCUs from reaching their full potential, similar long-term inequities perpetuated by the dominant culture have shaped music education. Eurocentric practices have dominated music curricula, the standards for music education, professional ensembles, music theory, and other areas leading to a lack of diversity. Addressing these systemic barriers is essential for HBCUs to continue to make a significant impact on society.

HBCUs serve a critical function beyond that of an educational institution; they are vital cultural and economic pillars in their communities, providing unique educational opportunities for Black students and contributing to the diversity of American culture. The potential disappearance of HBCUs music programs would result in significant losses, not only to Black students and but also to the broader cultural fabric of the nation. If the objective is to increase diversity in the fields of music, then strengthening HBCUs should be a priority. This support is essential not only to preserve the rich heritage of these institutions but to ensure a diverse academic landscape. If we are serious about having more people of color in our academic fields, classrooms, and orchestras, then we must promote and support HBCUs.

Notes

1. Founded in 1924, the National Association of Schools of Music (NASM) is an organization of schools, conservatories, colleges, and universities with approximately 628 accredited institutional members. It establishes national standards for undergraduate and graduate degrees and other credentials for music and music-related disciplines and provides assistance to institutions and individuals engaged in artistic, scholarly, educational, and other music-related endeavors. As of 2025, 28 HBCUs are accredited by NASM.
2. As of 2024, seven HBCUs offer music degrees in graduate studies.
3. Johnson would become the first Black woman to earn a doctorate in piano from Northwestern University, in 1971.

References

Abramo, J. M., & Bernard, C. F. (2020). Barriers to access and university schools of music: A collective case study of urban high school students of color and their teachers. *Bulletin of the Council for Research in Music Education, 226*(226), 7–26. https://doi.org/10.5406/bulcouresmusedu.226.0007

Anderson, S. (2018). *A qualitative study of black doctoral music students' and graduates' management of identity stereotypes*. [Unpublished doctoral dissertation]. Georgia State University.

Ba, O. (2022). When teaching is impossible: A pandemic pedagogy of care. In A. W. Szarejko (Ed.), *Pandemic pedagogy: Teaching international relations amid COVID-19* (pp. 113–125). Palgrave Macmillan.

Bergee, M. J., & Demorset, S. M. (2003). Developing tomorrow's music teachers today. *Music Educators Journal*, 89(4), 17–20. https://doi.org/10.2307/3399899

Boykin, T. F., Hilton, A., & Palmer, R. (Eds.). (2017). *Profession education at historically Black colleges and universities: Past trends and future outcomes*. Routledge.

Bradley, D. (2007). The sounds of silence: Talking race in music education. *Action, Criticism and Theory for Music Education*, 6(4), 132–162.

Brooks, F. E., & Starks, G. L. (2011). *Historically Black colleges and universities: An encyclopedia*. Bloomsbury.

Brower, A. M., & Ketterhagen, A. (2004). Is there an inherent mismatch between how Black and White students expect to succeed in college and what their colleges expect from them? *Journal of Social Issues*, 60(1), 95–116. https://doi-org.ezproxy.bu.edu/10.1111/j.0022-4537.2004.00101.x

Carter, B. A. (2013). "Nothing better or worse than being Black, gay, and in the band": A qualitative examination of gay undergraduates participating in historically Black college or university marching bands. *Journal of Research in Music Education*, 61(1), 26–43.

Clements, A. (2009). Minority students and faculty in higher music education. *Music Educators Journal*, 95(3), 53–56. https://doi.org/10.1177/0027432108330862

Cordona-Mejia, L. M., Pardo del Val, M., & Dasi Coscollar, M. D. S. (2020). The institutional isomorphism in the context of organizational changes in higher education institutions. *International Journal of Research in Education and Science*, 6(1), 61–73.

Elliott, D. J. (1995). *Music matters: A new philosophy of music education*. Oxford University Press.

Elliott, D. J. (2012). Music education philosophy. In G. E. McPherson & G. F. Welch (Eds.), *The Oxford handbook of music education*, (volume 1, pp. 63–88). Oxford University Press.

Fitzpatrick, K. R., Henninger, J. C., & Taylor, D. M. (2014). Access and retention of marginalized populations within undergraduate music education degree programs. *Journal of Research in Music Education*, 62(2), 105–127.

Grissom-Broughton, P. A. (2020). A matter of race and gender: An examination of an undergraduate music program through the lens of feminist pedagogy and Black feminist pedagogy. *Research Studies in Music Education*, 42(2), 160–176. https://doi.org/10.1177/1321103X19863250

Harper, C. Q. (2023). *Exploring the ways Black choral conductors negotiate racism and nonculturally relevant leadership in choral music spaces in the United States*. Publication No. 2845346149 Doctoral dissertation. University of Memphis. ProQuest Dissertation & Theses.

HatcherPuzzo, A., Martin, S., Payton, D., & Virelles, A. (2023). The creative spaces at HBCUs. In K. Schupp (Ed.), *Futures of performance: The responsibilities of performing arts in higher education* (pp. 89–105).

Haughton, E. N. (2011). Historically Black colleges and universities. In E. G. Price, T. L. Kernodle, & H. J. Maxile (Eds.), *Encyclopedia of African American music* (pp. 309–320). Greenwood.

Johnson, J. M., & McGowan, B. L. (2017). Untold stories: The gendered experiences of high achieving African American male alumni of Historically Black Colleges and Universities. *Journal of African American Males in Education, 8*(1), 23–44.

Jørgensen, H. (2009). *Research into higher music education: An overview from a quality improvement perspective.* Novus.

Kaschub, M. (2024). Marginalized no more: Composition in music education. In M. Kaschub (Ed.), *The Oxford handbook of music composition pedagogy* (pp. 3–24). Oxford University Press.

Kaschub, M., & Smith, J. (Eds.). (2014). *Music teacher education in transition, promising practices in 21st century music teacher education.* Oxford University Press.

Koch, J. V., & Swinton, O. H. (2022). *Vital and valuable: The relevance of HBCUs to American life and education.* Columbia University Press.

Koza, J. (2010). Listening for whiteness: Hearing racial politics in undergraduate school music. In T. A. Regelski & T. J. Gates (Eds.), *Music education in changing times: Guiding visions for practice* (pp. 85–95). Springer.

Malone, M. H. (2023). *William Levi Dawson: American music educator.* University Press of Mississippi.

McCall, J. M. (2015). *Degree perseverance among African Americans transitioning from historically Black colleges and universities (HBCUs) to predominantly white institution (PWIs).* Publication No. 1682266271 Doctoral dissertation. Arizona State University. ProQuest Dissertation & Theses.

McLean, D. (2024, March 19). Some HBCUs are seeing enrollment surge. Here's why. *HigherEd Dive.* https://www.highereddive.com/news/hbcus-enrollment-surge-why/710494/

Milner, H. R. (2012). Beyond a test score: Explaining opportunity gaps in education practice. *Journal of Black Studies, 43*(6), 693–718.

Mixon, K. (2005). Building your instrumental music program in an urban school. *Music Educators Journal, 91*(3), 15–23. https://doi.org/10.2307/3400071

Nelms, C. (2010). HBCU reconstruction. *The Presidency, 13*(1), 14–19.

Oliver, W. (2022). *The influence of isomorphism on HBCU music (performance and teacher training) programs and the alignment of broader institutional mission.* Publication No. 2700382697 Doctoral dissertation. Pennsylvania State University. ProQuest Dissertation & Theses.

Palmer, C. M. (2011). Challenges of access to post-secondary music education programs for people of color. *Visions of Research in Music Education, 18*(1), 7.

Palmer, R. T., & Young, E. (2011). The uniqueness of an HBCU environment. In T. L. Strayhorn & M. C. Terrell (Eds.), *The evolving challenges of Black college students: New insights for policy, practice, and research* (pp. 138–160). Routledge.

Parker, Q. D. (2024). We wear the mask: The lived experiences of Black undergraduate music education students in predominantly white schools of music. *Journal of Research in Music Education, 72*(2), 203–224.

Prouty, K. (2011). Educators, schools, colleges, and universities. In E. G. Price, T. L. Kernodle, & H. J. Maxile (Eds.), *Encyclopedia of African American music* (Vol. 1, pp. 309–320).

Reimer, B. (2003). *A philosophy of music education: Advancing the vision* (3rd ed.). Prentice Hall.

Richardson, J. M. (1980). *A history of Fisk University, 1865–1946.* University of Alabama Press.

Robinson, D., & Hendricks, K. S. (2018). Black keys on a white piano: A Negro narrative of double-consciousness in American music education. In B. C. Talbot (Ed.), *Marginalized voices in music education* (pp. 28–45). Routledge.

Rothstein, R. (2013, May). Why our schools are segregated. *Educational Leadership*, *70*(8), 50–55.

Rothstein, L., & Rothstein, R. (2023). *Just action: How to challenge segregation enacted under the color of law*. Liveright.

Sanders, C. R. (2024). *A forgotten migration: Black southerners, segregation scholarships, and the debt owed to public HBCUs*. University of North Carolina Press.

Simmonds, K. M. (2005). *Jubilee: The place of Negro spirituals as perceived by choir directors at historically Black colleges and universities*. Publication No. 305415224 Doctoral dissertation. University of South Carolina. ProQuest Dissertation & Theses.

Spelman College Office of Research, Innovation, and Collaboration. (2024, March 12). *Dr. Joyce Johnson gives Spelman and the world the gift of music*. https://oricspelman.com/blog_details/21

Squire, D. D., & Mobley, S. D. Jr. (2015). Negotiating race and sexual orientation in the college choice process of Black gay males. *The Urban Review*, *47*(3), 466–491. https://doi-org.ezproxy.bu.edu/10.1007/s11256-014-0316-3

Tucker, M. S. (2011). *Standing on the shoulders of giants: An American agenda for education reform*. National Center on Education and the Economy (NJ3).

Van Camp, D., Barden, J., & Sloan, L. R. (2010). Predictors of Black students' race-related reasons for choosing an HBCU and intentions to engage in racial identity—Relevant behaviors. *Journal of Black Psychology*, *36*(2), 226–250. https://doi-org.ezproxy.bu.edu/10.1177/0095798409344082

Walker, A. (2020). Traditional white spaces: Why all-inclusive representation matters. *Journal of Dance Education*, *20*(3), 157–167.

Watson, Y. L., & Gregory, S. T. (2023). *Daring to educate: The legacy of the early Spelman College presidents*. Taylor & Francis.

Williams, J., & Ashley, D. (2004). *I'll find a way or make one: A tribute to historically Black colleges and universities*. HarperCollins.

Williams, K. L., Mobley Jr, S. D., Campbell, E., & Jowers, R. (2022). Meeting at the margins: Culturally affirming practices at HBCUs for underserved populations. *Higher Education*, *84*(5), 1067–1087.

Wilson, A. (1982). *Ma Rainey's black bottom*. Plume.

Additional Readings

Koza, J. E. (2002). Corporate profit at equity's expense: Codified standards and high-stakes assessment in music teacher preparation. *Bulletin of the Council for Research in Music Education*, *152*, 1–16.

Simmons, T. L. (2023). *HBCUs unhushed: Transformative spiritual resilience within the life histories of African American graduates of historically Black colleges and universities*. Publication No. 2798983820 Doctoral dissertation. University of Wisconsin at Madison. ProQuest Dissertation & Theses.

Walker, R. (2007). *Music education: Cultural values, social change and innovation*. Charles C. Thomas Publishing.

CHAPTER 5

MUSIC AT HBCUS: CONSCIOUSNESS AND CULTURAL EMPOWERMENT PEDAGOGY

ABSTRACT

Consciousness and cultural empowerment is my term for a pedagogical approach grounded at the intersection of three foundational theories: W.E.B. Du Bois's double consciousness, Tara Yosso's community cultural wealth, and Barbara Omolade's Black feminist pedagogy. Chapter 5 explores how this framework empowers music educators to affirm identity, value cultural assets, and cultivate transformative empowerment through culturally rooted instruction. While these pedagogical moves promote liberation and belonging, they also carry complex tensions. Emphasizing Black musical traditions within Western-dominated curricula can create tensions between cultural authenticity and institutional conformity. Centering lived experiences may invite transformative reflection, yet risks being reduced to performative inclusion without structural change.

This chapter argues that implementing consciousness and cultural empowerment requires more than diversifying course content. The approach demands a sustained commitment to reshaping the learning environment itself. Historically Black Colleges and University (HBCU) music programs exemplify this practice by cultivating student identity, honoring communal knowledge, and preparing learners to resist and reimagine oppressive systems. Still, educators must remain attentive to the pitfalls of tokenism, ideological rigidity, or shallow representation that obscure true empowerment. By grounding music education in consciousness and cultural empowerment, educators create spaces in which students do not merely adapt to the system, but gain the tools to transform it.

In academia, questions are routinely asked about teaching music to systematically oppressed groups of students. I use the term *systematically oppressed groups* rather than *marginalized groups* to bring attention to historical, institutional, and system-based policies that have isolated groups such as African Americans from economic, educational, and socio-political participation. When exploring the educational practices unique to HBCUs, one must ask these critical questions: "Which content is most relevant to teach in these spaces?" "Who should be teaching (and learning) this content?" "How do cultural and historical factors influence pedagogical practices?" and "What is the academic and musical transformation that takes place in these institutions, and how is it exemplified in the lives of students and the broader community?"

The answers can be found by examining the foundational values that drive educational spaces committed to self-actualization and liberation. Martin Luther King, Jr. reminds us that before realizing any academic (and musical) achievement each individual must recognize their inherent dignity and value. In his speech to teens in 1967 at Barratt Junior High School in Philadelphia, King used the word *somebodiness* as a term of resistance to the systems that have devalued Black lives. In other words, self-worth is not granted by others, but is cultivated from already deeply rooted aspects of oneself. *Somebodiness* is a celebration of human worth and dignity and serves as the foundation for agency, resilience, and empowerment. HBCUs have long nurtured this *somebodiness* through the transformative pedagogical approach I call consciousness and cultural empowerment.

Consciousness and cultural empowerment is my term for a transformative pedagogical approach grounded at the intersection of three foundational theories: W. E. B. Du Bois's concept of double consciousness (1903), Tara Yosso's community cultural wealth (2005), and Barbara Omolade's Black feminist pedagogy (1987). Together, these frameworks provide a holistic lens to understand empowerment, identity, and resistance in systematically oppressed communities. This approach enables students to navigate the complexities of their dual identities (double consciousness), draw strength from their cultural heritage (community cultural wealth), and engage in critical resistance that fosters both personal and collective empowerment (Black feminist pedagogy). This type of empowerment emphasizes creating an educational environment in which students' multifaceted identities are not only recognized but celebrated, their cultural knowledge is valued as a vital asset, and they are equipped to dismantle oppressive structures (see Figure 5.1).

When examining transformative music teaching at HBCUs, my critical framework goes beyond a historical or socio-cultural analysis of these institutions. It centers on how HBCU music programs navigate multiple narratives, preserve cultural integrity, resist systemic oppression, and leverage their unique strengths in academic, social, and musical contexts. This pedagogical approach underscores the importance of valuing

Figure 5.1

Consciousness and Cultural Empowerment Converging Points.

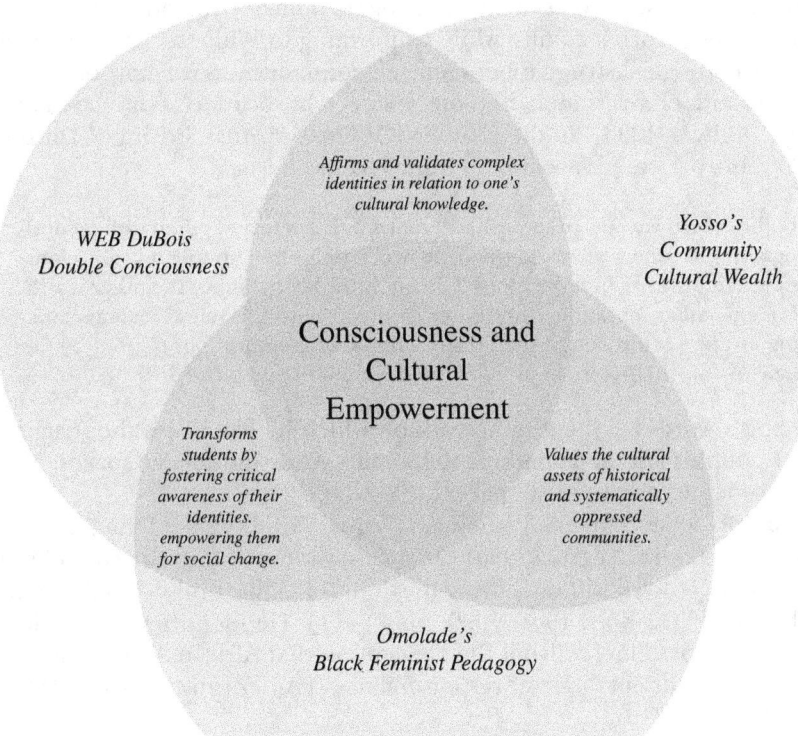

Source: Author's own.

the knowledge and experiences of systematically oppressed groups and advocating for an inclusive and empowering education, one deeply rooted in cultural pride. It equips educators and students to become change agents.

To fully grasp the significance of consciousness and cultural empowerment, we must revisit the elements of its tripartite foundation—double consciousness, community cultural wealth, and Black feminist pedagogy—and explore how they intersect with music education at HBCUs. By doing so, we can better understand how this framework helps to foster a transformative educational experience that honors cultural identity, promotes resistance to oppression, and empowers students.

Double Consciousness

Coined by W. E. B. Du Bois in *The Souls of Black Folk* (1903), double consciousness is described as the inner struggle of many African Americans to remain true to Black culture while conforming to White society. It consists of a psychological struggle between self-consciousness, or how one views oneself, and self-realization, how one is viewed by society (Ciccariello-Maher, 2009; Du Bois, 1903). In the chapter "Of Our Spiritual Strivings," Du Bois (1903) introduces his account of double consciousness.

> [T]he Negro is a sort of seventh son, born with a veil, and gifted with second-sight in this American world—a world which yields him no true self-consciousness, but only lets him see himself through the revelation of the other world. It is a peculiar sensation, this double-consciousness, this sense of always looking at one's self through the eyes of others, of measuring one's soul by the tape of a world that looks on in amused contempt and pity. (p. 9)

Du Bois's words lay the groundwork on which he elucidates the struggles Black people faced and continue to face in a White-dominated spaces, physical, academic, and musical spaces.

Du Bois states that "the [American Negro] simply wishes to make it possible to be both a Negro and an American, without being cursed and spat upon by his fellows, without having the doors of Opportunity closed roughly in his face" (Du Bois, 1903/1999, pp. 10–11). He identifies how societal incongruencies emerge from the conception that African Americans have fewer civil rights but no fewer responsibilities of American citizenship (Meer and Du Bois, 2019).

In the context of music education at HBCUs, this conflict underscores the paradox that while African American students may not possess the same cultural privileges as their White counterparts, they are still expected to acquire the same musical proficiency in Western Classical music that has historically marginalized them. Just as African Americans were expected to fulfill the responsibilities of citizenship despite systemic oppression, HBCU students are required to master a musical tradition that may not fully reflect their cultural heritage but is still seen as essential for their success. This expectation can create a tension in which students must conform to dominant cultural norms to be seen as legitimate musicians, even while their own musical traditions—central to their identity—are undervalued. This paradox reflects the broader theme of double consciousness, in which African American students navigate the internal conflict of excelling in a system that does not fully recognize their cultural contributions.

Du Bois's concept of double consciousness addresses the internal conflict often experienced by Black men. This phenomenon undermines the Black women's commitment to a hypermasculine Black culture by conforming to White patriarchal society and adhering to White feminist spaces. What does this mean for Black women, who must not only navigate their Black musical experiences in White spaces but simultaneously navigate gendered roles in spaces that value maleness over the contributions and experiences of women? Despite some assumptions about HBCUs, particularly HBCUs for women, these spaces are just as vulnerable to the ills of racism, classism, and sexism as are other institutions of higher learning (Turpin, 2007).

Inspired by W. E. B. Du Bois's identification of double consciousness, Welang (2018) developed the triple consciousness theory, according to which Black woman's experiences are refracted through three lenses: America, Blackness, and womanhood. Although data would show that Black women students at HBCUs have higher cultural alignment and life satisfaction ratings than Black women students at White institutions (Constantine & Watt, 2002; Gasman, 2009), HBCUs' historical emphasis on the struggle against racism has obscured efforts to explicate gender-related issues (Bonner, 2001). Many Black women enrolled in coed HBCU music programs encounter biases similar to those plaguing women music students in predominantly White institutions (e.g., sexual harassment, rehearsing and performing in hostile environments, discriminatory practices of ensemble leadership roles, etc.). Nevertheless, music training on HBCU campuses, particularly at HBCUs for women, gives Black women opportunities to satisfy the need for self-realization through creative outlets and musical programs that expand their cultural experiences.

Du Bois addresses the profound feelings of isolation that result from double consciousness. These emotions are often echoed by Black music students navigating predominantly White music spaces. McCall (2015) explored the experiences of eight African American males who attended an HBCU for music studies before transitioning to a predominantly White school of music for graduate study. McCall's research revealed that these students' experiences were significantly shaped by encounters with racism in their graduate schools. Along with the loneliness common among Black students at predominantly White institutions, the participants had their competence, intelligence, and musical abilities questioned due to their HBCU background. This led to feelings of rejection and devaluation by White peers and professors. While this research offers critical insights into the experiences of Black graduate students, further work is needed to understand how students of color navigate double consciousness in their own schools.

While double consciousness is often associated with Blacks navigating predominantly White spaces, it can also explain the cognitive dissonance experienced when teaching and learning Western art music in institutions designed for underrepresented students. Since their inception, HBCUs have embraced a dual responsibility of preparing students for future success. Black colleges must meet the same music standards as predominantly White institutions while also providing African Americans with a culturally relevant education (Ricard & Brown, 2008). Students must know the music of Bach, Beethoven, and Wagner. HBCU music programs, however, emphasize the music of William Dawson, Harry Burliegh, Margaret Bonds, and other canonic Black composers. The pressure to prepare Black HBCU students for postgraduate study or professional careers—and to remain relevant in predominantly White music schools—has resulted in curricula that prioritize Western Classical music over music rooted in the Black experience. This emphasis on Western art music can intensify students' struggle to balance their Black cultural traditions against the presumed superiority of White musical traditions.

Although HBCUs celebrate African American history and culture, its music programs that focus on Western Classical traditions lead some students to feel that their own cultural musical forms are undervalued. As a result, students may experience tension between embracing their personal identities and conforming to the standards of Western Classical music seen as the benchmark for musical excellence. This conflict can make it difficult for students to validate their cultural identity while trying to meet the high expectations of a predominantly Eurocentric curriculum.

Other HBCU music students are more apt to accept a predominantly Western Classical music curriculum, but not as an elevated form of music. They can do this because this music is situated in an HBCU, a larger, macrocommunity of cultural empowerment. Because of this, they are able to excel as Classical musicians, performers, and composers. They can study the nuances of Classical music without needing to disassociate from their cultural heritage. They are equipped to resist the erasure of their cultural heritage and navigate their dual musical identity.

Double consciousness does not necessarily result in a negative experience. Du Bois (1903) had commented on a double consciousness; it was "dogged strength" to possess "two souls, two thoughts, two unreconciled strivings, two warring ideals" (p. 9). He writes of being of "the Negro is a sort of seventh son." (In folklore, the seventh son has special powers.) Building on Du Bois's insight and on 20th-century feminist writing, Collins (1986) coined the phrase *outsiders within* to describe the possibilities of double consciousness.

> Theorizing from outsider-within locations reflects the multiplicity of being on the margins within intersecting systems of race, class, gender, sexual, and national oppression, even as such theory remains grounded in and attentive to real differences in power. This, to me, is what distinguishes oppositional knowledges developed in outsider-within locations both from elite knowledges (social theory developed from within systems of power such as whiteness, maleness, heterosexuality, class privilege, or citizenship) and from knowledge developed in oppositional locations where groups resist only one form of oppression (e.g., a patriarchal Black cultural nationalism, a racist feminism, or a raceless, genderless class analysis). In other words, theorizing from outsider-within locations can produce distinctive oppositional knowledges that embrace multiplicity yet remain cognizant of power. (p. 8)

Even when HBCU music graduates lack technical skills that required musical aptitude, they have used "dogged strength" and the special (em)power(ment) of a form of resilience to not only break racial barriers in the field of music, but to also to represent how one can forge multiple cultural bridges between Western art music and music of the Black tradition.

Double consciousness, once thought to primarily affect African Americans, now extends to various ethnic groups that grapple with merging their unique cultural heritages with dominant White values. This internal conflict is felt deeply by students caught between embracing their cultural identities and conforming to the Western (and often White) musical traditions. Du Bois scholars such as Paul Gilroy (2000) and feminist scholar Linda Alcoff (2006) acknowledge the shifting color line, suggesting that thinking solely in terms of Black and White no longer suffices when referring to double consciousness. Alcoff notes, "If W. E. B. Du Bois were alive today, he would probably tell us that the problem of the twenty-first century will be the lines between communities of color and the questions of cross-ethnic relations" (p. 247). Music education must address the challenges of cultural diversity and inclusion by creating space for multiple musical traditions and by acknowledging the unique experiences of students from different ethnic backgrounds navigating this double consciousness.

Community Cultural Wealth

For several decades, *cultural capital* has been used to explain how differences in educational attainment, career opportunities, and social status are influenced by one's cultural background and upbringing (Lareau & Weininger, 1973, 2003). The concept was first introduced by French sociologist Pierre Bourdieu in his seminal essay, "Cultural Reproduction and Social Reproduction" (1973). In the late 1960s and 1970s, Bourdieu studied inequalities in educational outcomes among children and young adults; he concluded that wealth alone did not account for the advantages of the upper class. Instead, *cultural assets*—including knowledge, behavior, taste, and communication abilities—contributed to one's social standing. Bourdieu argued that cultural knowledge serves as currency that helps individuals navigate society. These non-tangible assets, such as professional skills, personal demeanor, and social communication, are crucial to attain social power and class distinction. Cultural capital is as important as economic capital in determining social mobility (Bourdieu & Passeron, 1990).

Bourdieu's findings suggests that access to formal musical training, especially in Classical music, confers cultural capital, providing students with entry into elite professional networks. Those with years of Classical music training are more likely to be accepted into prestigious music schools, orchestras, and other elite institutions than those trained in less prestigious musical genres. As a result, students with access to Classical music training from an early age are better positioned to gain cultural capital and move up the social hierarchy (Orr, 2003).

Bourdieu and Passeron (1990) defined cultural capital as familiarity with society's dominant cultural codes. This familiarity, he argued, is often mistaken for academic brilliance and disproportionately rewarded in educational institutions. Children from high socioeconomic status backgrounds typically possess more cultural capital than those from low-status backgrounds, which gives them an advantage in the educational system and reproduces their privileged social positions (Bourdieu & Passeron, 1990). The dominant class benefits from this cultural capital by entering the education system already well-prepared to succeed. Individuals outside the dominant class face barriers in accessing these forms of capital.

While Bourdieu's cultural capital theory has been widely applied to investigate student achievement (e.g., Roscigno & Ainsworth-Darnell, 1999; Strayhorn, 2010), contemporary scholars have critiqued its limitations. Some have called for expanding the concept to include diverse forms of capital that reflect the experiences of historically marginalized groups (Carter, 2003; Yosso, 2005). For instance, Carter argues that Bourdieu's framework privileges Western, White, male perspectives and fails to account for the cultural wealth of nondominant groups. This critique is particularly relevant in music education, in which Western European Classical traditions have long been dominant. European dominance in music education reinforces the notion that Classical music is superior, further entrenches social hierarchies, and limits opportunities for students.

Using critical race theory to challenge traditional interpretations of cultural capital, Yosso (2005) developed the notion of community cultural wealth to provide value to cultural knowledge, skills, abilities, and contacts possessed by people of color. Yosso posits that marginalized groups possess their own highly valuable forms of capital, and judging them only by the standards of the dominant culture fails to acknowledge their unique strengths. Those whose culture is subordinate must employ strategies to access dominant cultural capital. According to Yosso,

> Therefore, while Bourdieu's work sought to provide a structural critique of social and cultural reproduction, his theory of cultural capital has been used to assert that some communities are culturally wealthy while others are culturally poor. This interpretation of Bourdieu exposes White, middle class culture as the standard, and therefore all other forms and expressions of "culture" are judged in comparison to this "norm." In other words, cultural capital is not just inherited or possessed by the middle class, but rather it refers to an accumulation of specific forms of knowledge, skills and abilities that are valued by privileged groups in society. (p. 76)

Music education privileges White, middle-class culture embodied in the norm of Western Classical music. All other musical forms, especially those rooted in African American, Indigenous, or non-Western traditions, are measured against this standard and often devalued. Specific abilities elevated in music programs, such as proficiency in Classical Western music, are valued by the dominant, privileged groups in society. This situation creates a system in which students from marginalized backgrounds, who may excel in other musical traditions, are seen as lacking in cultural capital, which then perpetuates inequality in music education.

Yosso (2005) identifies six types of cultural capital: aspirational, navigational, social, linguistic, familial, and resistant. Yosso uses several sources to describe each form of capital. These six forms of capital are not mutually exclusive, but rather dynamic processes that build on each other.

Aspirational Capital

"Aspirational capital refers to the ability to maintain hopes and dreams for the future, even in the face of real and perceived barriers" (Yosso, 2005, p. 78). HBCUs foster an environment in which both institutions and students envision possibilities beyond their current circumstances and despite limited resources (Preston & Palmer, 2018). Faculty and administrators at HBCUs often recognize the unique challenges their students face, such as underfunded high school music programs, limited access to Classical music training, or to support systems that empower students to overcome these barriers. Through mentorship, performance opportunities, and tailored curricula that emphasize both Western Classical traditions and African American musical heritage, HBCUs create environments in which students can build the confidence and skills needed to pursue ambitious careers.

Linguistic Capital

"Linguistic capital includes the intellectual and social skills attained through communication experiences in more than one language and/or style" (Yosso, 2005, p. 78). Linguistic capital reflects the idea that Black students arrive at school with multiple communication skills. In HBCU music programs, this manifests through students' ability to switch among different musical genres such as gospel, jazz, blues, hip-hop, and Classical music. Students also use various modes of musical expression, including oral traditions, rote learning, and storytelling, to convey messages and emotions. Such musical versatility enables HBCU students to thrive in both performance and educational settings by drawing upon their diverse linguistic and cultural backgrounds.

Familial Capital

"Familial capital refers to those cultural knowledges nurtured among familia (kin) that carry a sense of community history, memory and cultural intuition" (Yosso, 2005, p. 79). HBCUs are known for creating familial atmospheres shaped by an ethic of care, in which faculty and administrators encourage cultural advancement through moral responsibility (Hirt et al., 2008). Familial capital, highly valued in HBCU music programs, often includes early exposure to music through family, church, and community. Whether singing in church choirs, performing at community events, or learning instruments from family members, these informal musical experiences ground students in their cultural roots and keep them connected to their heritage.

Social Capital

"Social capital can be understood as networks of people and community resources" (Yosso, 2005, p. 79). Black intellectuals and professionals on HBCUs' alumni, faculty, and staff serve as primary producers of social capital for Black students (Preston & Palmer, 2018). HBCUs play a pivotal role in creating these networks for Black students, particularly in the music industry. Drawing from local musicians and church leaders as well as from prominent figures in jazz, gospel, and classical music, HBCU music programs emphasize networking and connections. These relationships provide valuable mentorship, internships, and career pathways. Alumni networks offer ongoing support to current students, helping them to navigate the professional music world.

Navigational Capital

"Navigational capital refers to skills of maneuvering through social institutions" (Yosso, 2005, p. 80). HBCU faculty often provide students with personalized guidance, instill institutional pride, and equip them with tools necessary for success (Berger & Milem, 2000; Palmer & Gasman, 2008). Studies show that HBCU faculty not only offer active support but also express a higher level of confidence in their students' abilities compared with faculty at predominantly White institutions (Guiffrida, 2004). In HBCU music programs, navigational capital is especially important to help students overcome barriers in the music industry and academia. HBCUs often teach students how to use their unique experiences to equip them with the skills to navigate these environments with confidence. Students learn how to thrive in spaces in which they are underrepresented (such as orchestras, conservatories, and academic conferences) while staying true to their cultural identity.

Resistant Capital

"Resistant capital refers those knowledges and skills fostered through oppositional behavior that challenges inequality" (Yosso, 2005, p. 80). The mission of HBCUs is to empower Black students to succeed in hostile environments (Brown et al., 2001). Music programs at HBCUs provide students with the tools to resist dominant narratives in the Classical music industry. By incorporating African American musical forms into the curriculum, HBCUs empower students to challenge the dominance of Western Classical music. Resistant capital also allows students to use music as a tool for social activism, whether by performing protest songs, composing works that address injustice, or organizing events that celebrate African American culture.

Community cultural wealth is especially relevant to music programs at HBCUs because it emphasizes the overlooked strengths that African American students bring to their education, These diverse forms of capital, such as cultural knowledge, resilience, and community support, collectively enrich the learning experience at HBCUs. Recognizing that students' success in music extends beyond formal instruction, HBCUs integrate these assets into their curriculum, teaching approaches, and community-building initiatives. This holistic approach empowers students to excel both academically and professionally, ensuring their education is about both mastering technical skills and leveraging their cultural backgrounds.

Black Feminist Pedagogy

While Black women were participants in the earliest feminist movement (1848–1920), the emergence of the Black feminist movement stemmed from the exclusion of Black women from the goals of White feminism. During the birth of the feminist movement, White feminists assumed that the experiences of White women were universal and that the same strategies would work for all women. At the 1848 Seneca Falls Convention, the first women's rights convention in the United States, the Declaration of Sentiments outlined their demands but did not mention the challenges faced by Black women. At the same convention, Sojourner's Truth confronted the declaration in her famous speech "Ain't I a Woman." Truth opposed the idea that only White women were entitled to the rights of citizenship. She argued that Black women were just as capable as White women and deserved the same opportunities.

Just as the First Wave of feminism was linked to women's suffrage, the Second Wave was connected to the Civil Rights Movement. Black feminists such as Angela Davis, Audre Lord, Fannie Lou Hamer, and Dorothy Height contended that the earlier movements, led by White middle-class women, failed to consider race and class when it came to the oppression of all women. Black feminists have repeatedly pointed out that White feminists have disregarded or misrepresented the range of feminist practices, especially by women of color, working-class and poor women, and women in grassroots organizations (Vogel, 2000). Audre Lorde (1984) argued that White women failed feminism in their "refusal to recognize differences and to examine the distortions which result from misnaming them" (p. 115). Angela Davis (1983) once believed that feminism was only for White women. She realized later that the feminism she knew was based on White feminism, which did not resonate with her because she identified as a Black revolutionary rather than a White woman. King, M. L., Jr. (1967, October).

The exclusion of Black women continued in the walls of academia. While colleges and universities were establishing programs for women's studies, Black feminist scholars noted the exclusion of issues concerning Black women. Black feminist scholars such as Patricia Hill-Collins, Beverly Guy-Sheftall, bell hooks, Audre Lorde, Alice Walker, Gloria Joseph were among those leading a distinctive African American women's literary tradition and establishing Black women's studies. Black women's studies as an autonomous discipline began to emerge in the late 1970s, and interest increased rapidly evolved in the 1980s due, in part, to further scholarship on topics relating to Black women. As such publications surfaced, the need for pedagogical tools for this subject became apparent. The result was Black feminist pedagogy, which challenged the White patriarchal education system by teaching students from historically marginalized groups about their own cultures from critical perspectives.

Barbara Omolade (1987) first used the term *Black feminist pedagogy* to describe "teaching and learning strategies informed by Black women's historical experiences with race/gender/class biases and their consequences of marginality and isolation" (p. 32). Black feminist pedagogy posits a specialized approach to teaching women of color. Omolade's comprehensive view of Black feminist pedagogy centers on the Black woman's unique experience.

> A Black feminist pedagogy is not merely concerned with the principles of instruction of Black women by Black women and about Black women; it also sets forth learning strategies informed by Black women's historical experiences with race/gender/class bias and the consequences of marginality and isolation. Black feminist pedagogy aims to develop a mindset of intellectual inclusion and expansion that stands in contradiction to the Western intellectual tradition of exclusivity and chauvinism. It offers the student, instructor, and institution a methodology for promoting equality and multiple visions and perspectives that parallel Black women's attempts to be and become recognized as human beings and citizens rather than as objects and victims. (p. 31)

Since Black women's experiences and scholarship are seldom placed in the larger scope of traditional scholarship, this specialized pedagogical approach builds on feminist pedagogy, which is based on social constructivism and critical theory and offers an alternative approach for teaching music. By critiquing the traditional, patriarchal ways of teaching music, Black feminist pedagogy calls for inclusion and expansion rather than exclusiveness and chauvinism.

Often overlooked in pedagogical approaches, Black feminist pedagogy bases its theoretical principles on Black feminist thought, which critiques Western education. In the Black feminist landmark book, *Black Feminist Thought*, Collins (2000) describes five major themes that construct Black feminist thought summarized here.

1. Experiences and positionality of Black women: Black feminist thought centers the perspectives of Black women as a starting point for analysis. It highlights the unique ways in which Black women navigate intersecting forms of discrimination and inequality.

2. Solidarity and coalition-building: Black feminist thought emphasizes the need for solidarity and coalition-building among marginalized groups. It recognizes the interconnectedness of struggles against various forms of oppression and advocates for collective action to challenge systemic inequities.
3. Challenging dominant knowledge and power structures: Black feminist thought critiques dominant knowledge and power structures that perpetuate oppression. It highlights the importance of diverse voices and calls for the recognition of marginalized knowledge.
4. Activism and social justice: Black feminist thought is not only a theoretical framework but also a call to action. It emphasizes the importance of activism and social justice work to create meaningful change. Black feminists often engage in grassroots organizing, advocacy, and community-building efforts to transform oppressive systems.
5. Intersectionality: Black feminist thought recognizes that individuals experience oppression and privilege in ways influenced by multiple factors such as race, gender, class, sexuality, and ability. It emphasizes the importance of addressing these intersecting systems of oppression.

As an element of protest, Black feminist pedagogy is a radical pedagogy designed to enable students to see the world through a perspective that would instill a revolutionary, conscious, liberating ideology (Joseph, 1995). It not only identifies institutionalized oppressions in the classroom, it also demands insight into power structures that challenge Black women's presence in academic spaces (Perlow et al., 2018). Thus, Black feminist pedagogy is premised upon the possibility of social and political change, fostering a more equitable educational environment for all.

Unlike traditional feminist pedagogy, initially founded on the basis of Western feminist thought, the theoretical roots of Black feminist pedagogy are based on the unique systematic oppressions Black women have encountered in their plight for social and political justice, and that these distinctive experiences are interconnected rather than independent. Intersectionality, a concept coined by Kimberle Crenshaw (1989, pp. 139–167), recognizes that individuals experience multiple intersecting systems of oppression and privilege based on identities such as race, gender, class, sexuality, and more. Because of the Black woman's unique position in society, the need to reexamine and even challenge the original assumptions about feminism becomes necessary to account for the experiences and lives of all women, not only middle- and upper-class White heterosexual women. Black feminist pedagogy offers the framework to challenge the hidden assumptions and thereby effect change that can improve the lives of those previously invisible, powerless, and disenfranchised.

The primary goal of Black feminist pedagogy is to critique traditional educational systems by providing new ways of thinking about standard curricula and by offering alternative interpretations to help students' consciousness (Henry, 2005). These critiques address three main areas: the dominant patriarchal education system, which serves a White elite; White academic feminist pedagogy, whose analyses of class and race are often irrelevant for the majority of Black women (hooks, 1981); and Black educational thought, which privileges masculinist discourse and ignores the educational needs of Black women and girls (Omolade, 1987).

Joseph (1995) and Collins (1986, 2000) assert that Black feminist pedagogy not only challenges traditional content, but the processes that structure learning. Prominent Black feminists, scholars, and activists (Collins, 2000; hooks, 1981; Omalade, 1987) agree that the practice of Black feminist pedagogy embodies four principles: the use of dialog in assessing knowledge claims; the centrality of personal expressiveness; the ethic of personal accountability; and concrete experience as a criterion of meaning. These principles not only it challenge the consideration of truth, but they also question the process of how one arrives at the truth (Collins, 2000). Ultimately, Black feminist pedagogy positions itself on principles that critique Western (that is, White and masculine) education. These two primary power structures, Whiteness and maleness, continue to dominate music education.

Black feminist pedagogy insists on a critical examination of power structures, emphasizing representation and working to dismantle oppressive systems in music education and performance spaces. For decades, music education has struggled to address the lack of diversity in the teacher workforce (DeLorenzo & Silverman, 2016), the withdrawal of non-White students from public-school music programs (Elpus & Abril, 2019), and the absence of multicentric teaching practices. Educators, researchers, and policy makers have responded by offering promising antidotes for these challenges, from recruitment efforts targeting non-White music teachers to the promotion of multiculturally inclusive curricula. Although these optimistic efforts may provide solutions, educators must seek sustainable change by addressing the root reasons for absent spaces for Black women and other systematically oppressed groups.

The liberation of Black women serves as a vital catalyst for broader societal freedom. It opens the door to dismantling systemic racism, sexism, and class oppression that affect all marginalized groups. Since Black women's lived experiences are situated at the intersection of race, class, gender, and sexuality this awareness empowers music educators to challenge other spaces in which inequalities converge. As music curricula are developed and classrooms and rehearsal spaces are shaped, it is essential to explore how these intersectionalities impact not only Black women but all systematically oppressed people. By centering these experiences in curriculum design and teaching strategies, music educators can create learning environments that address complex layers of identity. Understanding these intersections leads to transformative pedagogical approaches that account for how systems of inequality influence both the classroom content the interactions in classrooms and rehearsals. This awareness fosters a deeper, liberating educational experience that challenges oppressive structures in music education and beyond.

Consciousness and cultural empowerment emphasizes a teaching environment in which students' multifaceted identities are not only acknowledged but affirmed, their cultural knowledge is viewed as a valuable asset, and they are empowered to challenge oppressive structures. At the HBCUs where this type of empowerment is practiced, students can raise their consciousness about issues related to their lived experiences. Moreover, the faculty do more than just teach music; they help students reclaim their intellectual and artistic identities in environments that value their social and cultural heritage. HBCU music programs navigate both the visible and the invisible curricula, balancing the teaching of foundations while addressing the challenges that students from systematically oppressed communities face, feelings of alienation or cultural invalidation. This pedagogical approach to music education goes beyond technical proficiency or note accuracy. It reinforces students' sense of self-worth, encouraging them to see themselves not only as musicians but as empowered individuals capable of driving change.

Affirming Identity

In today's increasingly diverse educational landscape, the conversation around identity in higher education has never been more salient. For oppressed groups, particularly African Americans, identity affirmation is not simply a matter of self-perception, but how they are nurtured in academia. The affirmation of a student's identity has the power to foster self-worth, which directly enhances both academic engagement and musical success. In addition, students see themselves reflected both in the curriculum and the faculty. While validation of students' identities can help unlock their potential, the emphasis on Western Classical music often forces students to subordinate their identities in order to succeed in these systems. Consciousness and cultural empowerment resists stereotypes by asserting students' rightful place in both the Black and Western musical traditions, and by proving that their artistry is not one-dimensional. Students are given the tools to define their own artistic identity, which allows them to transcend multiple consciousnesses by integrating historical awareness, artistic innovation, and personal authenticity.

Value of Cultural Assets

Validating and celebrating cultural assets is another key tenet of consciousness and cultural empowerment, which recognizes that the value of cultural knowledge whether it stems from family, community, or experience. This framework challenges dominant narratives by insisting that such knowledge be integrated into education, providing students with the opportunity to leverage their cultural assets to excel both academically and socially. HBCUs create environments that incorporate African American cultural heritage and enable students to capitalize on their community's cultural wealth through tools that harness familial, linguistic, and communal experiences as valuable assets. Black feminist pedagogy emphasizes the intersectionality of race, gender, class, and other identities, ensuring that the cultural experiences of marginalized populations are centered in the curriculum. Moreover, this approach acknowledges the importance of a student's cultural background as a foundation and recognizes the value of cultural capital—the skills, knowledge, and experiences that provide social and academic advantages.

Transformative Empowerment

The third tenet of consciousness and cultural empowerment, that of transformative empowerment, asserts that education should not merely equip students to navigate oppressive structures but also prepare them to reconstruct those systems in ways that center equity, justice, and cultural pride. For Black students at HBCUs, the integration of cultural knowledge is more than self-recognition, it is a transformative act that deepens their connection to Black musical heritage and its broader socio-cultural significance. At HBCUs this connection is affirmed and celebrated. Students at such institutions cultivate critical consciousness and develop the agency to reshape dominant narratives. This process not only affirms their cultural heritage but also empowers them to challenge the hegemonic power structure and emerge as catalysts for social transformation.

In summary, HBCUs offer the consciousness and cultural empowerment blueprint for creating spaces in which music education provides both instruction and a pathway to liberation. Students not only learn music; they use music to unlock their full potential and challenge, if not dismantle, the barriers before them. Music educators must recognize that their role transcends technical training: they are part of the process for transformation. By embracing the consciousness and cultural empowerment approach, educators can cultivate a new generation of empowered, culturally grounded musicians and future educators set to reshape the future of music.

Applying the holistic approach of consciousness and cultural empowerment to music education can seem daunting. Music educators must meet musical standards, manage limited resources, prepare for demanding performance schedules, and ensure student engagement. Creating a truly empowering educational environment goes far beyond simply diversifying course content, hanging posters of non-White composers on classroom walls, or performing music by non-White composers. While these efforts are important, they represent a surface-level engagement. A deeper, transformative commitment is needed, one that addresses the cultural dynamics of the learning environment itself. At HBCUs, this deeper commitment has long been exemplified through an intentional approach to music education. Although consciousness and cultural empowerment may not always be explicitly articulated, HBCU music programs have consistently embodied its principles.

References

Alcoff, L. M. (2006). *Visible identities: Race, gender, and the self.* Oxford University Press.

Berger, J. B., & Milem, J. F. (2000). Exploring the impact of historically Black colleges in promoting the development of undergraduates' self-concept. *Journal of College Student Development, 41*(4), 381–394.

Bonner, F. B. (2001). Addressing gender issues in the historically Black college and university community: A challenge and call to action. *The Journal of Negro Education, 70*(3), 176–191. https://doi.org/10.2307/3211209

Bourdieu, P. (1973). Cultural reproduction and social reproduction. In R. Brown (Ed.), *Knowledge, education, and cultural change* (pp. 71–84). Tavistock Publications.

Bourdieu, P., & Passeron, J. C. (1990). *Reproduction in education, society and culture* (2nd ed., Vol. 4). Sage Publications. (Original English publication in 1977)

Brown, M. C., Donahoo, S., & Bertrand, R. D. (2001). The Black college and the quest for educational opportunity: The Black college: New perspectives and emerging possibilities. *Urban Education, 36*(5), 553–571.

Carter, P. L. (2003). "Black" cultural capital, status positioning, and schooling conflicts for low-income African American youth. *Social Problems, 50*(1), 136–155. https://doi.org/10.1525/sp.2003.50.1.136

Ciccariello-Maher, G. (2009). A critique of Du Boisian reason: Kanye West and the fruitfulness of double-consciousness. *Journal of Black Studies, 39*(3), 371–401. https://doi.org/10.1177/0021934706297569

Collins, P. H. (1986). Learning from the outsider within: The sociological significance of Black feminist thought. *Social Problems, 33*(6), S14–S32. https://doi.org/10.1525/sp.1986.33.6.03a00020

Collins, P. H. (2000). *Black feminist thought: Knowledge, consciousness, and the politics of empowerment.* Routledge.

Constantine, M. G., & Watt, S. K. (2002). Cultural congruity, womanist identity attitudes, and life satisfaction among African American women attending historically Black and predominantly White institutions. *Journal of College Student Development, 43*, 184–194.

Crenshaw, K. W. (1989). *Demarginalizing the intersectionality of race and sex: A Black feminist critique of antidiscrimination doctrine, feminist theory, and antiracist politics.* University of Chicago Legal Forum.

Davis, A. (1983). *Women, race, and class.* Vintage Books.

DeLorenzo, L. C., & Silverman, M. (2016). From the margins: The underrepresentation of Black and Latino students/teachers in music education. *Visions of Research in Music Education, 27*(1), 3.

Du Bois, W. E. B. (1903). *The souls of Black folk.* A. C. McClurg & Company. (reprinted by Dover 1994)

Elpus, K., & Abril, C. R. (2019). Who enrolls in high school music? A national profile of U.S. students, 2009–2013. *Journal of Research in Music Education, 67*(3), 323–338. https://doi.org/10.1177/0022429419862837

Gasman, M. (2009). African American female students at historically Black colleges: Historical and contemporary considerations. In V. B. Bush, C. R. Chambers, & M. B. Walpole (Eds.), *From diplomas to doctorates: The success of Black women in higher education and its implications for equal educational opportunities for all* (pp. 73–84). Routledge.

Gilroy, P. (2000). *Against race: Imagining political culture beyond the color line.* Harvard University Press.

Guiffrida, D. A. (2004). Friends from home: Asset and liability to African American students attending a predominantly White institution. *Journal of Student Affairs Research and Practice, 41*(4), 693–708. https://doi.org/10.2202/1949-6605.1394

Henry, A. (2005). Black feminist pedagogy: Critiques and contribution. In W. Watkins (Ed.), *Black protest thought and education.* Peter Lang Publishing.

Hirt, J. B., Amelink, C. T., McFeeters, B. B., & Strayhorn, T. L. (2008). A system of othermothering: Student affairs administrators' perceptions of relationships with students at historically Black colleges. *NASPA, 45*(2), 210–236.

hooks, b. (1981). *Ain't I a woman: Black women and feminism* (2nd ed.). Routledge.

Joseph, G. (1995). Black feminist pedagogy and schooling in capitalist White America. In B. Guy-Sheftall (Ed.), *Words of fire: An anthology of African-American feminist thought* (pp. 462–471). The New Press.

King, M. L. Jr. (1967, October 26). *What is your life's blueprint?* Speech presented at Barratt Junior High School.

Lareau, A., & Weininger, E. B. (2003). Cultural capital in educational research: A critical assessment. *Theory and Society, 32*, 567–606.

Lorde, A. (1984). Age, race, class, and sex: Women redefining difference. In *Sister outsider: Essays and speeches* (pp. 114–123). Crossing Press.

McCall, J. M. (2015). *Degree perseverance among African Americans transitioning from historically Black colleges and universities (HBCUs) to predominantly white institution (PWIs)*. Publication No. 1682266271 Doctoral dissertation. Arizona State University. ProQuest Dissertation & Theses.

Meer, N., & Du Bois, W. E. B. (2019). Double consciousness and the "spirit" of recognition. *The Sociological Review, 67*(1), 47–62.

Omolade, B. (1987). A Black feminist pedagogy. *Women's Studies Quarterly, 15*(3/4), 32–39.

Orr, A. J. (2003). Black-White differences in achievement: The importance of wealth. *Sociology of Education, 76*(4), 281–304. https://doi.org/10.2307/1519867

Palmer, R. T., & Gasman, M. (2008). It takes a village to raise a child': Social capital and academic success at historically Black colleges and universities. *Journal of College Student Development, 49*(1), 52–70.

Perlow, O., Wheeler, D., Bethea, S., & Scott, B. (2018). *Black women's liberatory pedagogies: Resistance, transformation, and healing within and beyond the academy*. Springer.

Preston, D. C., & Palmer, R. T. (2018). When relevance is no longer the question. *Journal of Black Studies, 49*(8), 782–800.

Ricard, R. B., & Brown, M. C. (2008). *Ebony towers in higher education: The evolution, mission, and presidency of historically Black colleges and universities*. Stylus Publishing.

Roscigno, V. J., & Ainsworth-Darnell, J. W. (1999). Race, cultural capital, and educational resources: Persistent inequalities and achievement returns. *Sociology of Education, 72*(3), 158–178.

Strayhorn, T. L. (2010). When race and gender collide: Social and cultural capitals influence on the academic achievement of African American and Latino males. *The Review of Higher Education, 33*(3), 307–332. https://doi.org/10.1353/rhe.0.0147

Turpin, C. A. (2007). Feminist praxis, online teaching, and the urban campus. *Feminist Teacher, 18*(1), 9–27.

Vogel, L. (2000). Domestic labor revisited. *Science & Society, 62*(2), 151–170.

Welang, N. (2018). Triple consciousness: The reimagination of Black female identities in contemporary American culture. *Open Cultural Studies, 2*(1), 296–306.

Yosso, T. J. (2005). Whose culture has capital? A critical race theory discussion of community cultural wealth. *Race, Ethnicity and Education, 8*(1), 69–91. https://doi.org/10.1080/1361332052000341006

PART TWO

EXEMPLARS OF TEACHING AND LEARNING MUSIC AT HBCUs

Over the course of a year, I embarked on an immersive journey across eight Historically Black Colleges and Universities (See Appendix C): Fisk University (Nashville, Tennessee), Florida Agricultural and Mechanical University (FAMU) (Tallahassee, Florida), Howard University (Washington, D. C.), Jackson State University (Jackson, Mississippi), Morehouse College (Atlanta, Georgia), Spelman College (Atlanta, Georgia), Tennessee State University (Nashville, Tennessee), and Tuskegee University (Tuskegee, Alabama). I immersed myself in the daily campus life by attending rehearsals, performances, and informal gatherings. My goal was to examine the academic environments and cultural landscapes of each institution and to understand how these contexts influence the teaching and learning within their music programs.

In Chapters 6, 7, and 8, I began each section with descriptions of my campus visits. I aim to offer readers—particularly those unfamiliar with HBCUs—a vivid portrayal of campus life. My personal narratives capture the sights, sounds, and atmospheres that define each institution, illustrating how music is situated in the historical and cultural context of its surrounding community, institutional mission, and students' experiences.

During these visits, I engaged in semi-structured interviews with a diverse group of individuals, including music majors and minors, students participating in various music ensembles, and faculty members within the music departments. To ensure confidentiality and protect the identities of participants, I have assigned pseudonyms to all individuals referenced in these chapters.

CHAPTER 6

AFFIRMING IDENTITY

ABSTRACT

Facilitating identity-affirming music education at Historically Black Colleges and Universities (HBCUs) reflects a core tenet of consciousness and cultural empowerment. Chapter 6 explores how HBCU music programs at Morehouse, Howard, and Tuskegee affirm identity through culturally grounded instruction. At Morehouse, students redefine Black male musicianship through cultural duality, excelling in both Western Classical and Black musical traditions. Howard provides cultural immersion through jazz and gospel and encourages students to locate themselves inside a broader musical and historical continuum. Tuskegee cultivates self-affirmation through heritage by fostering belonging even as its program grapples with diminished institutional support.

Implementing identity-affirming practices can present challenges. Educators must remain vigilant not to reproduce dominant hierarchies under the guise of "excellence." Integrating Black musical traditions alongside Western Classical curricula can create dual expectations, pressuring students to demonstrate proficiency in both to be viewed as legitimate musicians. Encouraging students to embrace cultural duality may foster empowerment, but can also create burdens of representation. Similarly, validating lived experience as a source of knowledge is essential, but risks being reduced to tokenism if not supported by deeper structural changes.

Immersing students in their own musical heritage affirms identity, yet may result in isolation if the broader institutional culture continues to privilege Eurocentric norms.

Implementing identity-affirming pedagogy requires intentional and sustained effort. Historically Black Colleges and Universities (HBCUs) model how music education can affirm, empower, and transform, but doing so demands institutional commitment and curricular structures that center students as cultural, historical, and artistic agents.

In his seminal autobiography, *The Narrative of the Life of Frederick* Douglas (1849), Douglas shared his belief of one's most authentic identity. He believed that the soul—one's core identity, humanity, and inner truth—was beyond the reach of those who seek to oppress it. This belief resonates deeply in HBCUs, in which students' identities are nurtured in ways that defy societal attempts to marginalize them. HBCU music programs serve as catalysts for self-definition, self-discovery, and self-affirmation by centering African American musical traditions in their curricula. Integrating these traditions not only enriches the academic experience but also empowers students to reimagine their potential for success (Gasman & Perna, 2011). Music educators at HBCUs, or any instructors teaching students of color, must navigate dominant cultural frameworks. It is crucial to understand the concept of double (or multiple) consciousness that shapes students' experiences. This awareness is particularly vital in educational systems in which Western Classical music traditions often marginalize other culturally significant musical forms.

The affirmation of a student's identity fosters positive self-worth, which directly enhances academic success; it is foundational to students' personal and intellectual growth. HBCUs have long served as identity-affirming spaces that support the academic, social, and psychological development of Black students (Allen, 1992; Wenglinsky, 1996). The most significant barrier to African American students' success at predominantly White institutions is the school's failure to address racial tension and cultural disconnect (Baber, 2012). By contrast, HBCUs create environments in which students can integrate their racial and cultural identities into their academic experiences, fostering a deep sense of belonging. Eurocentric curricula have dominated music education and often failed to reflect the lived experiences and cultural expressions of Black students (Borisoff & Chesebro, 2011).

When HBCUs affirm students' cultural strengths, students do not merely study music; they actively shape their artistic identities. These institutions expose students to culturally relevant content and facilitate critical discussions around systemic barriers, cultural diversity, and the enduring impact of racism. Such programs foster a strong sense of agency, enabling students to see themselves as part of a rich legacy of Black musical excellence.

Through this affirmation, students not only gain confidence in their craft but also deepen their understanding of their artistic roots.

Self-Defining Through Cultural Duality: Morehouse College

Morehouse College, the nation's only historically Black private liberal arts college for men, stands in the heart of Southwest Atlanta as a beacon of legacy. As part of the Atlanta University Center—along with Spelman College, Clark Atlanta University, Morris Brown College, and Morehouse School of Medicine—Morehouse has shaped Black men who have transformed the world.

Walking the campus, I think of Martin Luther King Jr., who entered Morehouse at 15, and the countless trailblazers who followed: philosopher and theologian Howard Thurman, Atlanta's first Black mayor Maynard Jackson, Olympic gold medalist Edwin Moses, filmmaker Spike Lee, actor Samuel L. Jackson, and Georgia's first Black senator Raphael Warnock. Their legacies echo through Morehouse's halls, inspiring the next generation.

On this cool fall afternoon, maroon and white banners bearing the school's motto, Et Facta Est Lux (And there was light) line the walkways. Morehouse students pass by, embodying the vibrant diversity of Black manhood. Afros, cornrows, dreadlocks, fades, and silk-pressed hair frame faces full of determination. Some stride purposefully to class, backpacks slung over their shoulders, while others linger on the steps of the bookstore, exchanging laughter and daps, the hand gesture, nonverbal form of communication. Their attire is as varied as their personalities: three-piece suits beside Adidas tracksuits, ripped jeans paired with designer sweatshirts, Jordans complementing gender-neutral ensembles.

Among them, I notice sweatshirts bearing images and messages of Black empowerment: Tupac Shakur, Malcolm X, Black Boy Joy, Black + Gay = PRIDE, and one that reads Black Man: Endangered Species. These young men defy stereotypes that seek to confine them to one-dimensional portrayals—hypersexualized, hyperaggressive, violent, or uneducated. Instead, they move through the world as scholars, creators, and leaders, unbound by society's imposed limitations.

As I make my way to the Martin Luther King Jr. International Chapel, memories of my time as a Spelman student performing in the Annual Spelman–Morehouse Christmas Carol Concerts flood my mind. In front of the chapel, a larger-than-life statue of King stands resolute, pointing toward the horizon, as if urging us all to press forward.

A short walk from the chapel brings me to the Ray Charles Performing Arts Center, or RayPAC, where the music department lives. From the nearby stadium,

I hear the rhythms of the Morehouse Marching Maroon Tigers preparing for a game. Inside RayPAC, the hallways hum with activity. Passing the music library, I hear the glee club warming up. A student brushes past, rapping Kendrick Lamar's "Not Like Us" through his headphones. From one practice room, gospel melodies by Jonathan McReynolds rise, while from another Verdi's "La donna è mobile" from *Rigoletto* soars. This convergence of genres—gospel, rap, Classical—mirrors the students themselves: multifaceted, multi-talented, and multi-dimensional.

These young men from diverse backgrounds have chosen Morehouse to study music, uniting to resist stereotypes and defy narrow narratives. They proudly embrace the complexity of their identities while affirming their roles as scholars, artists, and creators. In doing so, they navigate the tension between Western Classical traditions and the rich musical heritage of the African diaspora and demonstrate a cultural duality that redefines dominant narratives.

Cultural duality—the embodiment of two distinct cultural identities (Janssens & Steyaert, 1999)—shapes identity, particularly when individuals must navigate multiple cultural expectations. In music education, this duality requires students and educators to balance several musical traditions. While culturally responsive teaching (Gay, 2018) addresses this phenomenon, a broader framework is needed to fully understand its impact on Black musicians.

This interplay between cultural influences is especially evident in the faculty's decision-making process for college music programs. Nearly all students interviewed cited Morehouse's historical and cultural significance in shaping Black men as leaders (and not just its music program) as their primary reason for attending. Their choice reflects a deep cultural investment. At Morehouse, students must excel in both Western Classical and Black musical traditions, a dual commitment that challenges narratives about Black musicians.

The Morehouse music program actively confronts negative stereotypes and reshapes the perception of Black musicians in higher education. It disrupts misconceptions that portray Black men as lacking intellectual depth or musical sophistication. According to Hendricks (2021), counternarratives challenge majoritarian biases by centering the lived experiences of marginalized groups and redefining dominant perspectives. For Morehouse music students and faculty, these counternarratives serve as tools for reclaiming their voices, affirming their humanity, and resisting historical exclusion.

By embracing cultural duality, Morehouse musicians challenge assumptions that devalue Black male intellectualism and diminish their musical potential. The musicians prove that intellectual and artistic brilliance can co-exist. The program empowers students to see their artistry as an extension of both heritage and scholarship, redefining Black musicianship in higher education. Morehouse provides a space in which cultural duality operates not as a limitation but as a strength.

"I Can Be More Than Just a Rapper"

Cultural duality functions not only as a negotiation between self-perception and societal perception, but also as an act of resistance against narratives that have sought to diminish Black intellectual and artistic contributions. In music education, this duality is particularly evident as Black musicians balance Western Classical traditions with the rich musical heritage of the African diaspora. By redefining musical excellence, HBCUs challenge stereotypes that portray Black musicians as reliant solely on raw talent rather than intellectual rigor and formal study.

Many Black men face the struggle to define their identity given conflicting cultural expectations, particularly when dominant narratives attempt to confine their potential. One persistent notion about Black musicians is the idea that they possess only inherited, instinctual talent and lack the intellectual capacity to produce sophisticated music (Ewell, 2020). From its earliest days, the media has played a critical role in reinforcing such stereotypes (Entman & Rojecki, 2001; Taylor et al., 2019). The Morehouse music program intends to dismantle these misconceptions not by dismissing the idea that many Black musicians possess extraordinary innate ability, but by asserting that Black musical excellence is rooted in both natural talent, hard work, and intellectual engagement. This philosophy is embedded in the Morehouse Department of Music mission statement.

> We produce Morehouse Men who understand music theory as the global language of music. Men who understand the terminology and tools employed in those styles, while not losing sight of the historical, socio-political, and ethical issues in the cultures that created them. Whether in the Western tradition or the African diaspora, our alumni are prepared to effectively communicate and advocate for music as an essential part of life. In our program, they acquire performance skills, such as proper technique and methods of preparation.

The program seeks to produce musicians who not only understand music theory and performance techniques but also recognize the socio-political and historical contexts that shape the music they study and create.

This dual emphasis on skill and scholarship challenges the belief that Black musicians only succeed through innate ability rather than through disciplined study and intellectual mastery. A senior Morehouse music faculty member spoke highly of the students in the program, emphasizing that they bring a wide range of musical experiences.

> Some students arrive with years of formal music study [This participant used air quotes to describe formal music study.] —private lessons, AP theory courses in high school, top-ranking chairs in All-State bands, etc. Others come with raw, untrained talent, having learned music through oral tradition—by ear, on the spot, in church or community spaces. (Marcus Jackson, personal communication, September 17, 2024)

Many students admitted that, before coming to Morehouse, they had limited exposure to, Classical music. Their formal training had been shaped by participation in high school choirs or by playing instruments such as piano, drums, or bass guitar in church. One instructor described this phenomenon.

> Oh, we see students who can play. I mean, they can play play! They do things on their instruments, and I think, "Who taught you that?" And they just say, "I taught myself," or "I play at church." They're doing things I know people I went to grad school with couldn't do! But then I ask them to read a jazz chart or simply identify the chords they're playing, and they struggle. So I tell them, "Your raw talent isn't enough to cut it in this department. We expect more from you, and we're going to help you get to that 'more.'" (Allen Thompson, personal communication, September 17, 2024)

Another faculty member echoed this sentiment and explained that their goal is to build upon students' existing skills rather than diminish them.

> I tell my students, I don't want you to just rely on your talent. If you come in with strong gospel chops, I'm not going to put you down because you can't read music. No, I'm going to celebrate what you already know. My job is to build on that skill, not take it away. I want you to be a musician who can stand your own in any musical setting. (Miller Adkins, personal communication, September 18, 2024)

Culturally relevant teaching (Gay, 2018), a fundamental practice in Morehouse's music program, seamlessly integrates into daily instruction. Faculty members consistently make lessons relevant by connecting Classical music concepts to the musical experiences of their students, making it easier for them to relate to the music of Classical composers and expand their technical abilities.

In my multiple observations of music history and theory courses, instructors demonstrated how they made lessons relevant by connecting Classical music concepts to the cultural experiences of their students. For example, in a form and analysis course, one instructor explained altered dominant chords in a Chopin piano sonata by comparing them to the harmonic progressions in Stevie Wonder's "You Are the Sunshine of My

Life." This teaching method resonated deeply with students, as one of them noted:

> A lot of times, we don't know what we're playing—we just play what we hear. But when I come to my theory class, and Doc spells out the chords I recognize from the music I love, I realize, "Oh, this is what I've been playing!" It all starts making sense. And once it clicks, I can better relate to what Classical composers were doing. He teaches theory in a way that gives me the language to understand my own music. (Shawn Davis, personal communication, September 18, 2024)

By integrating diverse musical genres into their pedagogy, Morehouse faculty validate students' identities and promote inclusivity. This approach allows students to see themselves as part of the broader musical tradition, rather than as outsiders learning an art form disconnected from their lived experiences.

Cultural duality serves as a powerful counternarrative to the notion that Black men are confined to a narrow set of musical professions in commercialized genres such as hip-hop, R&B, or gospel. Morehouse challenges this limiting narrative by training students in both Western Classical music and Black musical traditions, thus equipping them for careers in orchestral conducting, symphonic composition, and performance. One third-year music student articulated this point.

> I think because we [Black men] are usually portrayed as the rappers, R&B singers, or hip-hop artists, people think that's all we do. I mean, I can be more than just a rapper. And there's nothing wrong with being a rapper! But think about it; that's all that's promoted, all that's celebrated. But we are also opera singers, composers, Classical performers. How often are they highlighted and celebrated? (Tony Edwards, personal communication, September 19, 2024)

Representation is key to broadening these perceptions, and faculty members who reflect the lived experiences of their students play an essential role in helping them navigate multiple musical worlds (Henderson, 2021). Morehouse's predominantly Black and male music faculty play a critical role in expanding these possibilities for students. Many faculty members are alumni and remain active in their fields; they provide students with representation and mentorship that reinforces the idea that Black men can excel in academic and professional music areas. Such representation sets a powerful standard, one intertwined with the expectation that Black men must work twice as hard to get half as far.

For Morehouse students, the expectation to be twice as good is not merely a saying, but a necessary strategy to maneuver in the professional and academic worlds. Morehouse's program deliberately over prepares its students, ensuring they enter either the music industry or graduate programs with exceptional skill and knowledge. One faculty member explained that

> The expectation is that you will learn the canon, the traditional repertoire. And of course, we require our students to sing art songs by Black composers and spirituals in addition to the required rep. But my bar is that you can perform your senior recital at any graduate school audition and get in with no reservations. We don't have any room for doubt. Not for us. That's the standard. (Tracy Harris, personal communication, September 17, 2024)

Morehouse faculty understand the racial biases that require Black students to over prepare to gain the same recognition as White counterparts. Their curriculum ensures that students not only meet but exceed industry expectations, excelling in multiple musical languages and pushing past limitations imposed by dominant narratives.

Morehouse music students are expected to excel in Western Classical traditions while also preserving their cultural musical heritage, ensuring they are exceptional in any setting. As do several HBCUs mentioned in this book, Morehouse trains students to excel in both Western Classical and Black musical traditions, opening doors to a wide range of careers. This commitment to excellence, however, does not come without generating criticism.

Grundy (2022) explores the intersection of race, gender, and class at Morehouse College, arguing that its culture is structured to appeal to the White (and patriarchal) gaze. This inquiry raises a critical question regarding the music program: if students are trained to master the Eurocentric musical canon, does this validate their success through assimilation? While some view it as a form of respectability politics, others see it as an intention to break down barriers and expand access to places where Black musicians have been historically excluded. One music faculty member directly countered the idea that Morehouse's program encourages assimilation.

> Morehouse students do not assimilate. We simply teach them to master both worlds as a strategy. First, they must preserve and perform our culture, our musical traditions, with quality and excellence. I need to hear them in the practice rooms studying Hall Johnson and Samuel Coleridge-Taylor just as much as their Schubert and Schumann. Our students have to fight to resist the erasure of our music. Second, we expand their opportunities. When they are able to do both—Black music and Western European Classical music—the doors open. They are no longer confined to society's expectations of what they should be playing. (Jackson Robinson, personal communication, September 18, 2024)

For Morehouse music students, cultural duality is both a burden and a form of empowerment. They carry the weight of historical exclusion while simultaneously shaping a future in which Black musicians are fully recognized for their intellectual and artistic excellence. They are taught to acknowledge the history of exclusion that Black musicians have faced and actively work to create spaces in which their artistry is valued. Excelling in both musical worlds is not just about survival; it is about ensuring that Black music and musicians are celebrated in all spaces. Morehouse's music program not only affirms the identities of its students but also asserts their rightful place as scholars, innovators, and cultural leaders in the broader musical landscape.

Self-Discovery Through Cultural Immersion: Howard University

I finally arrived at The Mecca: Howard University, the legendary institution that has shaped Black excellence for generations. Stepping onto The Yard, the heartbeat of the campus, I was immediately drawn to its southern border, anchored by the iconic Founders Library. More than just a building, Founders Library stands as a monument to knowledge, resilience, and the pursuit of justice. Thurgood Marshall and Charles Hamilton Houston once walked here and crafted the legal strategy that led to the *Brown v. Board of Education* victory.

I took a moment to digest my surroundings. Towering oak trees flanked The Yard, their trunks painted with the Greek letters of Black fraternities and sororities, a tribute to a legacy of leadership, scholarship, and service. As I stood, an explosion of sound erupted: a step show! Omega Psi Phi fraternity had taken center stage, their synchronized stomps and chants commanding attention. Other Greek organizations responded with their signature calls, while cheers and laughter rippled through the crowd, an impromptu celebration of Black culture and unity.

Turning toward the northernmost edge of The Yard, I made my way to Lulu Vere Childers Hall, home to the Chadwick A. Boseman College of Fine Arts named for the alumnus and actor, forever immortalized as Black Panther. Inside, I thought of internationally renowned opera singer Jessye Norman and Grammy-winning Roberta Flack, both of whom once studied here. I wondered how many other artists had walked these halls and found their voices in these very spaces.

On the third floor, the music classrooms and studios buzzed with activity. As I walked down the hallway, the unmistakable sound of gospel music drew me. Peeking into the student lounge, I saw a group of music students singing Walter Hawkins's "Thank You, Lord." Some were lounging on the couch, others sat cross-legged on the floor. Their voices blended in harmony as they swayed and waved their hands, fully immersed in the spirit of the music, much like a Sunday service in a Black church.

In the basement were more faculty studios, the band rehearsal room, and several practice rooms. I caught the sound of students working through an arrangement of "Take the A Train." Curious, I wandered past other rooms:

one was filled with the soaring notes of Italian arias and Negro spirituals, another housed a pianist perfecting Chopin's Ballade no. 1. Next door, a saxophonist ran modal scales against the steady tick of a metronome. By the time I returned, the "A Train" students had seamlessly transitioned into "Total Praise," layering harmonies with effortless precision. More than music, it was a shared spiritual moment, a testament to Black musical traditions. Finally, I found myself in the jazz band rehearsal room, surrounded by posters celebrating the legacy of the Howard University Jazz Ensemble. I reflected on the irony: jazz, once resisted by the department, was now a centerpiece of the program.

At Howard, students embark on a journey of self-discovery through immersion in Black musical traditions. They come to see themselves part of a broader historical and cultural continuum. Their artistry becomes part of something greater, a lineage of innovation, resilience, and excellence that has defined Black music. As they navigate these traditions, they not only learn, they discover who they are, where they come from, and how their voices contribute to the narrative of Black music.

This was, indeed, The Mecca.

Cultural immersion is described as the active engagement with a culture beyond one's own that fosters a deep understanding through direct interaction with people, customs, and traditions. Such experiences help teachers recognize the role culture plays in education (VanDeusen, 2019; Delano-Oriaran et al., 2018). In music education, such immersion is widely encouraged as a way for educators to develop cultural confidence (Abril, 2009; Ball & Ladson-Billings, 2020).

Much of this discourse focuses on engaging with cultures outside one's own. An important question arises: what happens when students immerse themselves in musical in environments that affirm their cultural identities rather than those environments that have historically prioritized Western European traditions? This question is particularly relevant at Howard University, where music education actively resists the marginalization of Black musical contributions.

Western Classical traditions have long dominated formal music education, often forcing students from marginalized backgrounds to assimilate into traditions that do not reflect their heritage. This cultural detachment can create a disconnect between students and their own musical identities. Howard challenges this dynamic by offering Black students an academic place where they can engage with their own musical traditions.

As the first HBCU to offer a Bachelor of Music degree in Jazz Studies in 1970, Howard defied the historical exclusion of Black music from academia. At a time when HBCU music curricula largely mirrored those of White schools, Howard carved out space for jazz and affirmed its academic legitimacy. This validation of Black American music allows students to fully engage with their traditions without external constraints.

By studying Black music in an affirming environment, students develop a deeper sense of ownership of their artistry and cultural legacy. They come to understand that their music is not to be defined, restricted, or devalued by external forces, but rather a tradition rich with history, creativity, and excellence. This immersion empowers students to define their musical identity on their own terms.

"I Finally Found *My* Story"

Cultural immersion at Howard University offers students a transformative experience that deepens their connection to Black musical heritage and its socio-historical significance. As an incubator for Black musical traditions, Howard ensures that students see themselves reflected in both the curriculum and faculty. Many find a sense of belonging in jazz, gospel, and popular music. As one instructor noted, "Students don't understand the legacy they are upholding. We have to teach them their place in this historical continuum." (Lance Smith, personal communication, April 3, 2024).

Unlike traditional music programs in which Black music is secondary to Western Classical traditions, Howard provides a place where students do not have to navigate between two musical worlds. Instead, they are given the tools to define their own artistic identity by integrating historical awareness, artistic innovation, and personal authenticity. For some, Howard becomes their first real immersion into Black musical traditions and reshapes how they see themselves as musicians. One student reflected that his perspective shifted after arriving at the university.

> I didn't listen to jazz like that before coming to Howard. My parents played it here and there, but it wasn't a thing in our house. Even in my performing arts school, jazz was just an elective. When I was looking at music schools, Howard caught my eye because it offered jazz, which was new for me. After coming here and seeing how jazz is celebrated by our teachers, it makes me feel good about myself and what I'm doing. Like, I made the right choice to study music here. (Shandra Conner, personal communication, April 5, 2024)

A second-year vocal performance major, originally planning to major in African American Studies, switched to Jazz Voice after realizing this music was her true calling. She described her experience as life-changing, helping her reconnect with music after losing confidence during the pandemic. Similarly, a third-year jazz vocal major, shared this:

> When I perform jazz, especially here at Howard, I feel like I am contributing to the legacy of those who made it possible for me to even study jazz here. I could have studied jazz anywhere else, but I don't think the environment would have been the same. Dr. Hollis always says, "Jazz isn't just music; it's our story." It's my story! It's like I'm finding little parts of what makes up who I am, creatively.

> I finally found *my* story! (Kendrick Greene, personal communication, April 3, 2024)

This student's testament aligns with Black feminist pedagogy, which emphasizes positionality and lived experiences. Students see themselves not as passive learners of Western music but as part of a lineage of Black musical excellence. Through cultural immersion, they reclaim their narratives, understanding that Black music is not only a tradition to be studied but a living legacy they could shape.

Like students at Morehouse, many Howard music students arrive with little formal background in Classical music and, in some cases, no exposure to jazz. One faculty member explained:

> Most of them come in with no experience in jazz. . . . They don't understand its relevance to popular culture now, or just the fact that it was the pop music back in the day. But they do know they do not want to sing Classical music. A lot of them tell me they have no connection to it. So they pick jazz because it offers courses that are closer to what they can relate to. (LaShay Chester, personal communication, April 4, 2024)

This resistance to Eurocentric definitions of musical excellence mirrors Black feminist pedagogy's principle of challenging dominant knowledge structures. At Howard, students are taught that their musical traditions are valuable, intellectually rigorous, and foundational to American music history. This counters the long-standing marginalization of Black music in academia and ensures that students develop confidence in their artistry without feeling pressure to assimilate.

Many students enter Howard without fully grasping the historical weight of jazz, therefore faculty intentionally connect students to its social and political movements. In one class, an instructor introduced vocal improvisational techniques. After students performed, he urged them to consider the historical context of the music.

> I hear what you guys did today, and it was great. I can tell you studied what these artists were doing vocally. But now, I need you to consider what was happening in America when these artists recorded these tunes. What was life like for Black men or Black women at that time? When you perform this music, you can't just sing the notes. You have to know your connection to it. That's when you know you're a part of jazz, and not just performing it. (Anissa Wallace, personal communication, April 4, 2024)

This approach reflects Black feminist pedagogy's focus on intersectionality and social justice. More than technique, jazz is storytelling, resistance, and a reflection of Black life. Music education at Howard does more than teach music history or theory; it encourages students to see themselves as cultural and historical contributors using music as a tool for both self-definition and activism.

I asked students how the discussion on historical context shaped their perspective on jazz. Cameron, a third-year jazz vocal major, recounted:

> I remember struggling to sing a piece I was working on. My teacher already knew what was going on with me. She got me to think about where I fit in with all the chaos.... At first, I didn't get it. Then she told me about Abbey Lincoln and how she used her voice, and it clicked. I realized that when I'm practicing my scales and improv, that's just one layer. It made me think about my role. (Cameron Morrison, personal communication, April 2, 2024)

Another faculty member explained:

> The challenge here is blending the academy with the street. And by street, I mean everything outside these walls. I tell my students, "I'm here to teach you and open your eyes to something that's part of your DNA. Together, we're going to discover how that shows up in your life. Because it's going to look different for you than it does for me." You have to make the music feel good to yourself before it feels good to anybody else. (Thomas Black, personal communication, April 2, 2024)

These statements capture how jazz education at Howard incorporates both formal training and the cultural, historical, and social essence of jazz as an organic Black art form. Students learn that music is more than a skill, but storytelling and cultural reclamation.

Howard University's music program extends beyond building technical skills. It affirms Black identity and empowers students to shape their artistic paths through immersion in Black musical traditions. By honoring the past while embracing new forms of expression, Howard provides students a space to define their own artistry. One faculty member described this approach:

> I'm not just teaching them music theory. I'm teaching them how to see themselves differently, how to dream beyond what they thought was possible. I tell them to look at me! I never thought that music could open doors and take me the places I've been. I've been able to travel all around the world. And when you experience different cultures, you get to know yourself better. (George Lacey, personal communication, April 2, 2024)

Howard's evolving curriculum ensures students are not only preserving Black music but also shaping its future. Faculty emphasize understanding Black musical traditions and adapting them for contemporary audiences. This balance allows students to appreciate jazz's historical significance and see themselves as part of its evolution.

Howard's faculty take a culturally relevant approach to teaching, meeting students where they are. One professor reinforced this idea: "It's okay to be like Beyoncé, but you can be that and more! That's what we want to see." (Leonard Brown, personal communication, April 2, 2024). This philosophy allows students to envision their full creative potential while remaining rooted in the traditions that paved the way for them.

Throughout my course observations, I noticed that instructors incorporate sermonettes that reinforce themes of identity, history, and purpose. Phrases such as "It's important to know who you are," "This is part of your history," and "We're depending on you to do big things" affirm students' roles as the next generation of Black musical innovators.

This pedagogy creates an environment in which Classical, jazz, and popular music coexist and positions Black music as an integral part of music education. The cross-genre interactions reinforce the idea that Black music is multifaceted, interconnected, and continuously evolving.

Howard's dedication to honoring Black music while embracing contemporary trends has sparked critical discussions about which Black musical traditions receive full academic recognition. Fifty years ago, Howard fought to legitimize jazz in its curriculum. Today, students are raising their voices about the need for gospel music to receive the same institutional validation.

Gospel music remains a vital but underrecognized academic discipline in university music programs. Although widely popular among Black colleges, gospel music still faces resistance in academic curricula due to bias, a lack of formalized training, and its association with religious practice (Walker & Young, 2003). One student expressed frustration over gospel's marginalization at Howard.

> Here, we have the Howard Gospel Choir, and they're pretty big. They get to perform everywhere! But I'm not sure our [music] department *fully* embraces them. Me and my friends feel like gospel should be part of the curriculum too, just like jazz is. (LeKeisha James, personal communication, April 5, 2024)

This ongoing struggle for the academic validation of Black music—even in historically Black institutions—raises important questions about whose musical traditions are considered worthy of formal study. While jazz has been institutionalized at Howard and even at predominantly White conservatories, gospel, despite its profound influence and technical sophistication, remains treated as an extracurricular activity rather than a legitimate academic discipline.

For many students, gospel is an essential part of their artistic identity and musical upbringing. They argue that its rich history, theoretical complexity, and technical contributions warrant its inclusion in the curriculum. This perspective challenges traditional academic hierarchies and questions why certain Black musical traditions are prioritized.

As students continue to voice their concerns, they highlight a broader conversation about the definitions of Black musical excellence in academia.

Expanding the curriculum to embrace gospel would not only affirm students' lived experiences but also reinforce Howard's legacy as a leader in Black music education. Recognizing gospel as a legitimate field of study would continue Howard's commitment to honor the full spectrum of Black musical traditions and to acknowledge them as essential contributions to music.

Self-Affirmation Through Cultural Heritage: Tuskegee University

In Tuskegee, a Alabama town with fewer than 9,000 residents, stands the nation's only university campus designated a National Historic Site, Tuskegee University. Every landmark, from its historic buildings to its traditions, affirms the power of education and cultural pride. Walking its grounds was more than a journey through history, it became an act of self-affirmation, a reminder that embracing one's heritage means claiming its strength and wisdom.

As I entered the area around Tuskegee University, the first landmark I passed was The Oaks, the Victorian-style home of the university's founder, Booker T. Washington. A testament to his legacy, the home stands as a physical reminder of his leadership. Continuing toward the main campus, I paused at the George Washington Carver Museum, where Carver's lab remained intact, a tribute to his groundbreaking agricultural work. Nearby, the Booker T. Washington Monument, Lifting the Veil, commanded my attention. The statue depicts Washington lifting a veil from a crouching man seated on an anvil, an open book in his lap. The inscription reads, "He lifted the veil of ignorance from his people and pointed the way to progress through education and industry."

I continued to Chambliss Hall, a red-brick building once an elementary school for Black children. Now home to the Department of Fine and Performing Arts, it houses the Marching Crimson Pipers, whose sounds often fill the air and blend past and present through music. I made my way to the Tuskegee University Chapel, where the Golden Voices Concert Choir rehearsed. In the narthex, my eyes were drawn to the breathtaking Singing Window, a towering stained-glass tribute to Negro spirituals. Although a reproduction of the original lost to fire, its impact remains profound. I stood in quiet reflection, taking in the luminous colors and sacred imagery. The panels depicted 11 spirituals, including "Go Down, Moses" and "Swing Low, Sweet Chariot." Biblical figures are rendered as people of African descent. At the center, beneath the window for "Rise Up, Shepherd, and Follow," Jesus appeared as a Black infant swaddled in vibrant blue, a striking affirmation of royalty.

Next to the Chapel lies the Tuskegee Institute Cemetery, the final resting place of Booker T. Washington, George Washington Carver, William L. Dawson, and other distinguished faculty. Sitting on a bench by Washington's gravesite, I reflected on his lifelong dedication to education and innovation. Shortly after founding Tuskegee, he had encouraged students to sing Negro spirituals in worship, insisting they remain a shared experience and an enduring tradition. Wandering through the cemetery, I stopped at the grave of William Dawson, the dean of African American Choral Music. A master composer and arranger of spirituals, Dawson reshaped choral music, ensuring that the voices of enslaved ancestors would never be forgotten.

The legacies of Washington, Carver, Dawson, and countless others endure not only in monuments and gravesites, but in the lived experiences of every student who walks these grounds. At Tuskegee, history is studied but also lived, a foundation upon which students affirm their own identity.

Self-affirmation theory explores how individuals respond to experiences or information that challenge their concepts of themselves (Steele, 1988). Because cultural heritage—values, traditions, and identity—forms a fundamental part of one's sense of self, self-affirmation is deeply intertwined with cultural expression. At Tuskegee University, music serves as a powerful means of self-affirmation, allowing students to connect with their heritage, uphold cultural values, and take pride in their history. Through music, students reinforce their sense of meaning, the belief that their contributions matter, and efficacy, the confidence in their abilities (Batory-Ginda, 2022).

Tuskegee has long been recognized as a leader in producing African American professionals in Science, Technology, Engineering, and Mathematics (STEM) fields. The school is the nation's top producer of Black aerospace science engineers and a leading institution for African American graduates in chemical, electrical, and mechanical engineering. The university's strong emphasis on STEM over STEAM (which includes the arts), however, presents challenges for the music program that limit its growth and visibility. Despite this, music remains an essential, although often overlooked, force in shaping students' identities. More than an academic subject or extracurricular activity, music is a vital conduit for personal expression, cultural appreciation, and self-affirmation.

Music at Tuskegee plays a crucial role in affirming students' both individual and collective identities. It provides a place where students see themselves reflected in the historical continuum of Black artistic contributions, which reinforces their sense of purpose and agency. In addition to being a creative outlet, music acts as a cultural bridge that connects generations and preserves and revitalizes Black musical traditions. Whether through performance, composition, or cultural preservation, Tuskegee students challenge dominant narratives and assert their rightful place in the rich legacy of Black music.

Hess (2020) argues that music education needs to be more than skill development; it should also operate as a tool for self-recognition and validation. At Tuskegee, self-affirming musical experiences such as participating in ensembles offer students a deeper sense of belonging and identity. Even in an institution in which the arts struggle for recognition alongside STEM disciplines, music remains a source of empowerment. It allows students to define themselves on their own terms and sustain the traditions that affirm their cultural legacy.

"I Take Pride in Making Music Here!"

Tuskegee's musical legacy is inseparable from its broader cultural and historical significance; it fosters a sense of pride and belonging among its students. Music here serves as both an artistic discipline and an active affirmation of identity, linking students to a lineage of excellence. Through engagement with Tuskegee's rich musical traditions, students internalize a deep connection to their history that cultivates both personal pride and a sense of agency. This process of self-affirmation not only strengthens individual identity, but also empowers students to confidently assert their place in the world (Steele, 1988).

Making music at Tuskegee is not merely about performance but honoring a tradition that accompanies the history of the institution. One faculty member underscored the importance of embedding historical awareness into music instruction.

> Tuskegee has probably one of the richest and oldest histories in music when it comes to HBCUs, and really all colleges and universities. I tell my students all the time, "Look, you guys should take pride in making music here." Of course, I have to give them the historical significance of it all, but that's okay. I don't mind taking time out of my instruction time to give them that. I also tell my colleagues to do the same. You know, it's important for us to know the history of where we are, so we can then transfer that history to our students. That way, they feel good about what they're doing and *where* they're doing it at! (Curtis Jamison, personal communication, March 11, 2024)

This emphasis on history is an act of self-affirmation. When students recognize their connection to a broader narrative, they begin to understand the weight of their contributions. Music becomes an active process of reclaiming identity, asserting cultural value, and challenging narratives that have historically minimized the contributions of Black musicians.

Tuskegee's commitment to cultural preservation extends beyond its faculty who ensure that students engage directly with contemporary figures shaping Black music. One such opportunity occurred when composer Ayatey

Shabazz visited the Tuskegee Wind Ensemble to discuss his composition *Red Tails*, a tribute to the legendary Tuskegee Airmen. Shabazz's visit provided students technical insights into the piece and a deeper understanding of the events it honored. A student recalled the significance of that experience.

> We were learning this piece called *Red Tails* and as we were learning the music, we were learning the story. Then he came in and spoke to us about it. There were things about the Tuskegee Airmen that I never knew. But it meant more to have the composer come to us. It eventually hit me that, man, here I am at Tuskegee getting to perform a piece about the Tuskegee Airmen at the concert for the Music Institute. That was like a double honor. For me, it was bigger than just learning that piece. (Melinda Johnson, personal communication, March 12, 2024)

Such direct engagement, arranged by the instructor, between composer and student reminds students that the music they perform is an extension of their history and identity.

Tuskegee's musical tradition not only preserves history; it instills self-confidence and agency in students. Performing the works of composers such as William Dawson both diversifies content and affirms their role in a broader cultural continuum. Iris, a member for the Golden Voices Concert Choir, recalled how her perception of spirituals shifted after learning about Dawson's legacy.

> I remember being a freshman, and Dr. Williams gave us "Ain'-a That Good News" to learn for spring tour where we would go to Texas, Arkansas, Illinois, Tennessee, and Missouri. I had heard the piece before and knew it was a spiritual, but that was about it. Dr. Williams gave us the whole story behind the song and told us about William Dawson and how Mr. Dawson was right here at Tuskegee writing a lot of these spirituals for the Golden Voices. Now, every time we sing a Dawson piece, I feel like a part of that history! (Iris Hogan, personal communication, March 12, 2024)

For students such as Iris, music becomes more than sound, but a vehicle for discovery and empowerment. By recognizing their role in continuing this legacy, students realize that their contributions matter, which reinforces their self-worth and place in history.

Tuskegee's music program fosters a deep sense of ownership and responsibility among its students. Many students discussed the importance of their contribution to the growth of the program. For them, to make music at Tuskegee is a commitment to revitalize a significant musical, historical, and cultural tradition. One student reflected on this sense of duty of Tuskegee's band, the Marching Crimson Pipers.

> I take pride being a part of the Crimson Pipers. It's about making sure that what I'm able to experience, the next person gets to experience that as well. . . .

> After coming here [to Tuskegee] and seeing how much work we actually put in, it kind of gave me the perspective of feeling the responsibility to be a part of the band and making it better for the next person. (Jaquon Davis, personal communication, March 12, 2024)

This pride is rooted in the collective effort to build something lasting. Another band student likened their contributions to nurturing a living entity.

> When it's something that you're passionate about, you want to see it grow. Even after you're gone. If you have that love for the band program, you make the commitment to make it great. I feel like you should take pride in playing in the band or singing in the choir because you're putting your brick in the building. (Deonte Smith, personal communication, March 12, 2024)

For these students, their work in Tuskegee's ensembles means more than rehearsals and performances; it is an act of preservation, growth, and self-affirmation. Through their dedication, they not only witness the evolution of the program but also solidify their place in its legacy, which then reinforces their own sense of self-worth and agency.

Music at Tuskegee fosters a sense of ownership and agency, allowing students to shape their identities through artistic expression. Beyond preserving Black musical traditions, it instills confidence in students' ability to excel across all genres. In one Golden Voices Concert Choir rehearsal, students were as energized singing Randall Thompson's *Last Words of David* as they were performing one of Dawson's arranged spirituals. Their enthusiasm reflected an understanding that excellence in music transcends genre, honoring heritage while embracing a broad array of musical experiences.

After the rehearsal, a student explained the excitement behind performing Thompson's pieces.

> We like it because it's just good music. Dr. Williams always picks good music for us. And he teaches it to us in a way that we're able to do all types of music. I think he wants us to understand that it's about knowing our heritage, regardless of what we sing. (Jamarcus Thomas, personal communication, March 13, 2024)

This perspective highlights the dual impact of Tuskegee's music program: students learn music and they also cultivate an awareness of their place in a continuum of artistic excellence. Their pride in performance reinforces a belief in their ability to contribute meaningfully to the world, which strengthens their sense of self-worth.

At Tuskegee, taking pride in making music makes one feel good at what one does and helps shape identity. Whether through performances of Dawson's spirituals, engaging with composers such as Shabazz, or the everyday affirmations of faculty members who remind them of their place in this storied institution students are constantly encouraged to see themselves as bearers of a legacy far greater than themselves. This deep connection between music, identity and self-affirmation is not unique to this institution: it reflects a broader legacy shared by HBCUs that have long been pioneers in music education. Yet, despite their historic influence, these programs now face growing challenges to maintain their prominence.

Tuskegee represents many other HBCUs that were once trailblazers in music education, institutions with strong historical legacies and rich traditions of making music. At one time, music programs at institutions such as Tuskegee set the standard, templates for excellence in higher education. As national priorities have shifted toward STEM, however, music programs at HBCUs have struggled for resources and institutional support. This situation reflects a trend in higher education, in which many music departments, once thriving centers of innovation, are now relegated to service roles, that is providing music for campus and community events rather than receiving recognition as essential academic disciplines.

This shift raises important questions about the function of music in today's academic life. A fundamental tenet of Booker T. Washington's educational philosophy was that the curriculum should address both the individual needs of students and the demands of society. It should be functional, practical, and utilitarian. Is music no longer seen as functional or practical, especially for systematically marginalized groups? Could this perception be the reason why music has increasingly become a service rather than a primary field of study at Tuskegee, as at many HBCUs? For students of color, the issue of whether music is a viable and utilitarian occupation cannot be ignored.

Recognizing this need, Tuskegee is considering implementing a music education program to address the lack of a formal degree pathway in music. Williams notes,

> The interest to study music has always been there. Each year, several students apply at Tuskegee and say, "I want to major in music education," assuming we have a music education program because music is such a big part of this place. ... Music will always have a place here. It's part of our legacy, even when we didn't have the music degree for over 60-plus years, it still remained vibrant, but our society is at a different time in history, and we have to consider that. It will take support from the university to help us invigorate music [education]. (Anthony Williams, personal communication, March 11, 2024)

Implementing a music education program would both restore a vital academic discipline and address the issue of diversity in music education. Research has shown that the lack of diversity among school music teachers (Hancock, 2008; Henderson, 2021) is directly linked to the underrepresentation of marginalized students in music education programs. By reestablishing a music education program at Tuskegee, the university could once again play a key role in fostering diversity in the field, ensuring greater representation of Black music teachers in schools.

In summary, music programs that emphasize consciousness and cultural empowerment equip students to critically examine the multiple facets of their identities—race, culture, class, gender, and sexuality, etc.—while providing a supportive environment in which to navigate these complexities. This heightened consciousness allows them to reconcile their personal and cultural identities with dominant narratives, thus fostering resilience, empowerment, and confidence.

The music program at Morehouse College, the only HBCU for men, challenges the narrative that limits Black men's professional opportunities in the music industry and in academia. Through this dual mastery, students expand their career trajectories, proving that Black men can excel in musical spaces previously dominated by Whites. At Howard University, music students are encouraged to imagine their own artistic paths. The curriculum consisting of core coursework in music history and theory, coupled with culturally grounded instruction immersed in Black music genres, ensures that students engage with Black musical heritage in a meaningful way.

Although Tuskegee University is revitalizing their music program's historical legacy, students nevertheless make meaningful connections to the institution's musical heritage and find affirmation and pride through their involvement in the choir and marching band. Regardless of how Morehouse, Howard, or Tuskegee achieves identity affirmation, their collective aim is to empower students to claim a sense of self-worth and to underscore the vital role of music in affirming identity through cultural heritage.

Research has shown that HCBUs such as Morehouse, Howard, and Tuskegee foster a deep sense of belonging and identity among students, making these institutions vital spaces for academic and personal growth (Johnson & McGowan, 2017; Squire & Mobley, 2015; Van Camp et al., 2010). Their campuses are unapologetically Black, where African American history and culture is woven into the tapestry of the college experience. While the educational environments often focus on the students' racial identity, many HBCUs fail to affirm students' sexual or gender identities (e.g., Carter, 2013; Mobley & Hall, 2020; Patton, 2011). Collins's concept of "outsiders within" (1986) offers insight into this dichotomy at HBCUs at which LGBQT+ students are often racial insiders, but gender or sexually outsiders. The presence of LGBQT+ students forces HBCUs to expand their definitions to include the full range of all identities within the Black community.

By centering Black musical traditions and engaging students in critical discussions about race and identity, Morehouse, Howard, and Tuskegee demonstrate the impact of affirming environments and identity-based coursework (Fiorentino, 2020). These institutions offer students the opportunity to explore their musical heritage and aspirations in spaces free from judgment or exclusion. Yet, the full realization of a consciousness and cultural environmental pedagogy demands more than racial affirmation alone. It calls for an expansion of inclusive practices that affirm the identities of all students, including those of gender, sexuality, and class.

References

Abril, C. R. (2009). Responding to culture in the instrumental music programme: A teacher's journey. *Music Education Research, 11*(1), 77–91.

Allen, W. R. (1992). The color of success: African-American college student outcomes at predominantly White and historically Black public colleges and universities. *Harvard Educational Review, 62*(1), 26–45. https://doi.org/10.17763/haer.62.1.wv5627665007v701

Baber, L. D. (2012). A qualitative inquiry on the multidimensional racial development among first-year African American college students attending a predominately White institution. *The Journal of Negro Education, 81*(1), 67–81. https://doi.org/10.7709/jnegroeducation.81.1.0067

Ball, A. F., & Ladson-Billings, G. (2020). Educating teachers for the 21st century: Culture, reflection, and learning. In N. I. Nasir, N. Lee, C. R. Pea, & M. McKinney de Royston (Eds.), *Handbook of the cultural foundations of learning* (1st ed., Vol. 1, pp. 387–403). Routledge. https://doi.org/10.4324/9780203774977-27

Batory-Ginda, A. M. (2022). Strengthening identity by affirming one's most important values. *Journal of Constructivist Psychology, 35*(3), 1079–1094. https://doi.org/10.1080/10720537.2021.1929598

Borisoff, D., & Chesebro, J. W. (2011). *Communicating power and gender*. Waveland Press.

Carter, B. A. (2013). "Nothing better or worse than being Black, gay, and in the band": A qualitative examination of gay undergraduates participating in historically Black college or university marching bands. *Journal of Research in Music Education, 61*(1), 26–43.

Collins, P. H. (1986). Learning from the outsiders within: The sociological significance of Black feminist thought. *Social Problems, 33*(6), 14–32.

Delano-Oriaran, O. O., Penick-Parks, M. W., & Fondrie, S. (Eds.). (2018). *Culturally engaging service-learning with diverse communities*. IGI Global.

Douglas, F. (1849). *Narrative of the life of Frederick Douglas, an American slave*. Anti-Slavery Office.

Entman, R. M., & Rojecki, A. (2001). *The Black image in the White mind: Media and race in America*. University of Chicago Press.

Ewell, P. A. (2020). Music theory and the White racial frame. *Music Theory Online, 26*(2). https://doi.org/10.30535/mto.26.2.4

Fiorentino, M. C. (2020). *What preservice music teachers learn about diversity during student teaching*. Publication No. 2594546904 Doctoral dissertation. University of Illinois at Urbana-Champaign. ProQuest Dissertation and Theses.

Gasman, M., & Perna, L. W. (2011). Promoting attainment of African American women in the STEM fields: Lessons from historically Black colleges and universities. In G. Jean-Marie & B. Lloyd-Jones (Eds.), *Women of color in higher education: Changing directions and new perspectives* (pp. 73–88). Emerald Group Publishing.

Gay, G. (2018). *Culturally responsive teaching: Theory, research, and practice*. Teachers College Press.

Grundy, S. (2022). *Respectable: Politics and paradox in making the Morehouse man*. University of California Press.

Hancock, C. B. (2008). Music teachers at risk for attrition and migration an analysis of the 1999–2000 schools and staffing survey. *Journal of Research in Music Education*, 56(2), 130–144. https://doi.org/10.1177/0022429408321635

Henderson, C. (2021). Preparing future music teachers for dealing with minority students: A profession at risk. *Visions of Research in Music Education*, 16(17). https://digitalcommons.lib.uconn.edu/vrme/vol16/iss4/17

Hendricks, K. S. (2021). Counternarratives: Troubling majoritarian certainty. *Action, Criticism and Theory for Music Education*, 20(4), 58–78.

Hess, J. (2020). Finding the "both/and": Balancing informal and formal music learning. *International Journal of Music Education*, 38(3), 441–455.

Janssens, M., & Steyaert, C. (1999). The world in two and a third way out? The concept of duality in organization theory and practice. *Scandinavian Journal of Management*, 15(2), 121–140.

Johnson, J. M., & McGowan, B. L. (2017). Untold stories: The gendered experiences of high achieving African American male alumni of Historically Black Colleges and Universities. *Journal of African American Males in Education*, 8(1), 23–44.

Mobley, S. D., & Hall, L. (2020). (Re) defining queer and trans* student retention and "success" at historically black colleges and universities. *Journal of College Student Retention: Research, Theory & Practice*, 21(4), 497–519.

Patton, L. D. (2011). Perspectives on identity, disclosure, and the campus environment among African American gay and bisexual men at one historically Black college. *Journal of College Student Development*, 52(1), 77–100. https://doi.org/10.1353/csd.2011.0001

Steele, C. M. (1988). The psychology of self-affirmation: Sustaining the integrity of the self. *Advances in Experimental Social Psychology*, 21, 261–302. https://doi.org/10.1016/S0065-2601(08)60229-4

Squire, D. D. & Mobley, S. D. (2015). Negotiating race and sexual orientation in the college choice process of Black gay males. *The Urban Review*, 47(1), 466–491. https://doi-org.ezproxy.bu.edu/10.1007/s11256-014-0316-3

Taylor, E., Guy-Walls, P., Wilkerson, P., & Addae, R. (2019). The historical perspectives of stereotypes on African-American males. *Journal of Human Rights and Social Work*, 4(3), 213–225. https://doi.org/10.1007/s41134-019-00096-y

Van Camp, D., Barden, J., & Sloan, L. R. (2010). Predictors of Black students' race-related reasons for choosing an HBCU and intentions to engage in racial identity—relevant behaviors. *Journal of Black Psychology*, 36(2), 226–250. https://doi-org.ezproxy.bu.edu/10.1177/0095798409344082

VanDeusen, A. J. (2019). A cultural immersion field experience: Examining preservice music teachers' beliefs about cultural differences in the music classroom. *Journal of Music Teacher Education*, 28(3), 43–57.

Walker, L. B., & Young, S. (2003). Perceptions about gospel choir in the college and university music curriculum: A preliminary investigation. *Contributions to Music Education, 30*(1), 85–93.

Wenglinsky, H. H. (1996). The educational justification of historically Black colleges and universities: A policy response to the U.S. Supreme Court. *Educational Evaluation and Policy Analysis, 18*(1), 91–103. https://doi.org/10.3102/01623737018001091

CHAPTER 7

VALUING CULTURAL ASSETS

ABSTRACT

Historically Black Colleges and Universities (HBCUs) exemplify the core principle of consciousness and cultural empowerment by valuing students' cultural assets as essential foundations for meaningful learning and artistic development. Rather than viewing students through a deficit lens, HBCU music programs recognize community, familial, and artistic knowledge as essential tools for academic and creative excellence. Chapter 7 examines how Fisk University, Tennessee State University (TSU), and Florida A&M University (FAMU) center Black musical traditions not as supplements to the curriculum, but as its very core.

At Fisk, faculty engage in historiographic and storytelling pedagogies that position students as inheritors of a living musical archive, affirming the spirituals and oral histories as critical forms of knowledge. At TSU, educators embrace an ethnographic, student-driven approach aligned with the music-teacher-as-producer model. This approach encourages creative autonomy and industry relevance, allowing students to draw from their musical roots to shape commercially viable, award-winning work. At FAMU, culturally sustaining pedagogy integrates students' lived musical experiences, from gospel and jazz to marching band, into a curriculum that resists assimilation and reclaims cultural space, even amid external political pressures.

While these institutions succeed in amplifying Black cultural expression, the work demands constant responsiveness to institutional constraints, funding disparities, and the pressures of dominant norms. Through intentional pedagogy and structural commitment, Historically Black Colleges and Universities (HBCUs) model how valuing cultural assets can empower students to thrive artistically, academically, and culturally, while simultaneously and shaping the future of music education in higher education.

HBCUs are both spaces for academic achievement and transformative hubs in which students unlock their musical potential while validating their cultural assets. These institutions have long been seen as preservers, producers, and promoters of African American musical and cultural heritage since their founding. By leveraging the unique knowledge, skills, and abilities that students bring with them, HBCU music programs operate on an asset-based model, one that deliberately shifts educators away from deficit-based assumptions, in which students are seen as lacking in some area, toward an approach that recognizes and builds on their inherent strengths and cultural wealth (San Pedro, 2018).

While curricula include Eurocentric music traditions, HBCUs actively cultivate environments that celebrate various musical languages as a source of strength (Yosso, 2005). This asset-based approach encourages music educators to foster inclusive classrooms in which diversity is not only accepted but also inspires innovative musical expression. In doing so, they combat implicit biases that can otherwise pressure students to conform to Western Classical standards for validation. Instead of a one-size-fits-all curriculum, HBCU educators value the lived experiences of African American students and transform their personal narratives and cultural practices into the learning process. As a result, students thrive not in spite of their lived experiences, but because of them.

Often described as "safe, positive, accepting, supportive, and culturally relevant" (Tatini-Smith et al., 2013, p. 77), HBCUs provide a counterpoint to predominantly White institutions in which traditional barriers limit the recognition of non-White contributions. At Fisk University, Tennessee State University, and Florida Agricultural and Mechanical University students find that their artistry is an extension of both their heritage and their academic endeavors, which fosters agency. By embracing students' unique knowledge and abilities as essential assets, HBCU music programs empower students to view their cultural strengths as tools for creative expression. This recognition not only combats deficit-based thinking often found in higher education music programs, but also transforms the educational and artistic landscape.

Preservers of Cultural Assets: Fisk University

Nestled in the heart of Nashville's historic African American community, where indications of a once-thriving culture now mingle with signs of gentrification, is Fisk University, the oldest higher education institution in Nashville. I searched for the famed Jubilee Singers painting, an artwork I had admired in countless books and television specials about Negro spirituals. I felt I was on my way to a grand gallery at the Louvre, hunting for the Mona Lisa. Queen Victoria, who commissioned this portrait and presented it to Fisk University in 1887, had ensured that this iconic image would be forever entwined with the school's story. I asked a student where could I find the painting. He pointed me to Jubilee Hall, the campus's largest and most stately Victorian Gothic building, a National Historic Landmark that stands as a proud emblem of Fisk's enduring spirit.

Jubilee Hall, the oldest building on campus, is named in honor of the Fisk Jubilee Singers who had toured the country to raise funds for its construction. Inside the Appleton Room, a vibrant space for lectures, workshops, and collaborative discussions, was the striking floor-to-ceiling painting of the eleven original Jubilee Singers. Studying the portrait, I was struck by the quiet power in the faces of these young women and men: some wore faint, hopeful smiles, while others maintained stoic, resolute glares, their eyes narrating stories of courage, sacrifice, and unwavering determination. I could not help but imagine the harrowing journeys they must have undertaken traveling the nation and the globe, all in pursuit of right to be educated, at a time when Black lives were devalued and freedom severely curtailed. In that moment, tears welled not out of sorrow but from profound gratitude for the sacrifices made by those seven women and four men whose musical legacy still inspires the world.

Tucked between the Fisk Memorial Chapel and the John Hope and Aurelia Elizabeth Franklin Library, the unassuming Harris Music Building, named after Richard Harris, Fisk's first Black trustee, houses a small music theory and history classroom, a compact piano lab, faculty office studios, and a few practice rooms. I had expected a larger facility to reflect Fisk's historical connection to Black music. Instead, I marveled at the irony that the funds raised through sharing Black music had helped establish Fisk but the building itself remains modest. Brick and mortar do not guard Fisk's musical heritage, however; it is the people, the Fiskites themselves. The dedicated faculty, passionate students, and the entire Fisk community serve as living archives of a storied tradition, preserving cultural assets cherished at Fisk and around the world.

HBCUs show that effective music teaching requires not a surface-level appreciation of culture, but a deep understanding of the history that shaped it. This historiographic approach to pedagogy ensures that students see themselves reflected in the curriculum; this reflection fosters a deep connection to their musical heritage and enhances their artistic and academic growth. Music educators must go beyond mere acknowledgment of the influences that students bring. To truly value cultural assets requires moving past basic familiarity or a passive appreciation of a culture to actively researching, integrating, and validating these assets (Smith, 2023). In essence, educators need to actively engage with and understand the historical context and significance behind these assets.

Preserving one's heritage is an act of empowerment and continuity. Fisk's legacy, epitomized by the renowned Fisk Jubilee Singers, draws students, whether pursuing Classical, jazz, or contemporary genres, like a magnet to connect with this Black musical tradition. Students interviewed for this book noted the importance of Fisk is more than that of a university. For them, it represents a homecoming that reaffirms a historical legacy and validates their musicianship and sense of belonging.

At Fisk University, teaching and learning music take place in a culturally rich curriculum grounded in historical awareness. This framework emphasizes music's role in shaping identity and cultural consciousness. It encourages students to explore how African Americans have used music for survival, empowerment, and cultural preservation. Students gain insight into how musical traditions that shape collective identity and resilience have been sustained and transformed.

"You're a Living Archive"

A historiographic approach to pedagogy involves teaching from a critical historical perspective in a way that connects the past to the present and allows students to see themselves as part of an ongoing cultural legacy. Fisk University exemplifies this approach by integrating conservatory-style training with African American traditional music, ensuring students are both rooted in Classical technique and engaged with the historical foundations of their heritage. While the conservatory model is traditionally associated with Western European Classical training, Fisk reinterprets it through an African American musical lens.

At Fisk University's music department, culturally responsive teaching makes students feel valued, while historiographic pedagogy ensures they understand their role in a larger historical tradition. These methods combined create a music education model that is both culturally affirming and historically grounded, one that empowers students to carry forward Black musical traditions. One professor reflected,

> Every now and then, I have to remind my students that "Hey, you're a living archive." I understand that my teaching is not seen as traditional. Shucks, some may even say that I'm old fashioned. But my goal is to make sure our students value their culture and the music that's in their blood. And they can't value it unless they know the history behind it. They're gonna get what they need for a music degree—you know, theory, music history, private lessons,

and all that—but you can get that anywhere. And they didn't come to Fisk to get what they can get anywhere, they came here to get something more, and it's my job to give them that something more. (Jonathan Willis, personal communication, March 24, 2024)

Fisk instructors do not simply teach Black music as a genre, but rather frame it in its cultural context. By embedding music in its historical framework, instructors reinforce the idea that Black music is not only an aesthetic form but a cultural artifact shaped by social realities.

Historiographic pedagogy (Tröhler, 2006) examines how history is written, whose voices are included, and how interpretations evolve over time, while storytelling pedagogy serves as the method through which history is conveyed, remembered, and made meaningful. Storytelling values the students' cultural assets by incorporating their lived experiences, histories, and identities (Gunawardena & Brown, 2021). Rather than adhering to a one-size-fits-all model, storytelling transforms education into a culturally responsive experience that honors students' backgrounds, skills, and talents.

Instructors at Fisk often use a storytelling approach rather than a lecture-based method to humanize historical events and make learning engaging. Students respond positively to this approach, demonstrating how oral traditions function as an intentional teaching strategy:

> [Student 1:] Dr. Dillard rarely has any [lecture] notes. I mean, most days, he just comes in, sits down, and starts talking. [Student 2:] Yeah, and whatever we're talking about that day, he's always gonna bring it back to Fisk some kind of way. Like, we can be talking about R&B music or even hip-hop, but by the end of class he's gonna find a way to connect it to something that has to do with the Jubilee singers. [laughs] It's wild! [Student 1:] To be honest, I probably remember the most from this class than my other classes. (Marshawn Johnson & Jason Nelson, personal communications, March 25, 2024)

This approach challenges Western academic norms of a neutral telling of history, affirming that oral history and lived experience are valid sources of knowledge. Storytelling in education is most effective when it bridges historical knowledge and modern relevance, helping students understand their world by linking new information to the already familiar (Landrum et al., 2019).

Storytelling has long been a tradition in African and African American culture, used to transmit the history not found in textbooks and Western academic settings. One student recalled a powerful storytelling-based lesson:

> I remember that time we had class in front of Jubilee Hall. Dr. Dillard wanted us to actually be in that place while he told us about spirituals and the Fisk Jubilee Singers. He told us stories about how this school wouldn't even exist if it wasn't for them singing music from our roots. He told us about the time

> he was a student here and when he was in the choir and how his teacher did the same thing with him, you know, brought them in front of Jubilee Hall to teach them the legacy. (Dravius, Dawkins personal communication, March 25, 2024)

By engaging physical spaces as historical sources, the instructor demonstrated that history is found not only in books, but is embedded in landscapes, architecture, and institutions that shape students' present-day realities. Teaching in this way makes history tangible, allows students to experience rather than study the past, and reinforces that awareness of history is fundamental to valuing cultural assets.

Current members of the Fisk Jubilee Singers play an important role in the preservation of cultural assets. The 2021 Grammy Award-winning ensemble for Best Root Gospel Album carries forward a historical legacy, affirms Black musical traditions, and serve as cultural ambassadors. One instructor described how the Jubilee Singers' performances are historical documents.

> You know, that's actually an interesting story behind winning that Grammy. They [Jubilee Singers] took the recordings from the historic Ryman Auditorium concerts. So the first half of the concert, they sung spirituals, then later on in the second half, Professor Kwami, the Fisk Jubilee Singers Director, would feature other Nashville artists of various genres from gospel to country. So, the Jubilee Singers did and used many of those as recording for that project was just something archival or you know something to sell as a fundraiser. And we ended up getting a Grammy for it! (Richard Donahue, personal communication, March 25, 2024)

This statement highlights the Jubilee Singers' contribution to cultural preservation by their creation of recordings that become historical archives. Their work demonstrates that valuing cultural assets does not mean isolating them. It means elevating them and demonstrating their influence on broader musical traditions.

At Fisk, cultural assets are preserved through linguistic capital with both storytelling and music serving to transmit knowledge and sustain traditions. Familial capital further reinforces this preservation and fosters a sense of belonging through shared, intergenerational histories. Fisk students and faculty emphasize the institution's legacy, recognizing themselves as part of a broader historical tradition of Black music. Preserving these cultural assets, however, comes with challenges.

Fisk University's commitment to preserving spirituals operates in tension with its location. Nashville, famously known as Music City, is a global hub for music: its industry is heavily dominated by country, rock, and contemporary commercial music, which leaves historically Black music traditions, particularly Negro spirituals, in a precarious position.

This struggle is not new. Some of the original Fisk Jubilee Singers in the 19th century even resisted performing spirituals; many students saw them as painful reminders of slavery. Some Jubilee Singers initially refused to sing slave songs because they felt that these songs represented a traumatic past rather than a source of cultural pride. Similarly, today's Fisk students grapple with how to honor these songs in an industry that does not always value them.

According to several Fisk music faculty, the preservation of spirituals involves more than historical recognition. "It is about ensuring that these songs remain a living, breathing part of not just Black music, but American music." (Katherine Milton, personal communication, March 25, 2024) With the growing dominance of contemporary popular music, spirituals seem to be increasingly treated as museum pieces rather than dynamic art forms. Despite the fact that the Fisk Jubilee Singers received a Grammy award, spirituals are not commercially lucrative. Nonetheless, HBCUs such as Fisk actively ensure that spirituals remain a living tradition and not a relic of the past.

Producer of Cultural Assets: Tennessee State University

Tennessee State University (TSU), the only state-funded HBCU in Tennessee, sits at the western edge of Jefferson Street, a street once pulsing with the rhythms of Black music. While Nashville is celebrated for Music Row, the city's famed entertainment district, Jefferson Street holds a different, lesser-known legacy. Here rock and roll and R&B icons Jimi Hendrix, Aretha Franklin, and Ray Charles found inspiration and performed in packed venues that electrified the city's Black community. TSU's music program, deeply connected to this historic corridor, continues to echo those legendary sounds.

As usual, I wanted to take in the sights of the campus before heading to the music building. A passing student, proudly sporting a TSU hoodie, recommended that I visit the Averitte Amphitheater, the heartbeat of student life. Sitting on one of its concentric concrete rings, I observed the campus rhythm unfold before me. This space would normally be packed for pregame rallies, Greek step shows, or student-led concerts. On this cool spring afternoon, however, clusters of students lounged in conversation. A group laughed as they scrolled through pictures on their phones. Nearby, a faculty member, speaking with an animated voice, held the attention of a few students, passionately recounting the history of Jefferson Street's musical heyday. Others sat cross-legged on makeshift picnic blankets, lost in their own worlds, headphones draped over their ears.

I headed south to the Marie Brooks Strange Music Building and Performing Arts Center, named for the TSU faculty member who, in 1931, founded the renowned Tennessee A&I State College Concert Singers. A symbol of Black Classical excellence, the building carries a rich legacy. I was greeted by two students, Darius and Jada, wearing blue windbreakers embroidered with the name Aristocrat of Bands. Their warm smiles and Southern charm came through their "Yes, ma'am" and "No, ma'am" responses as they guided me through the space.

As we walked, they shared their aspirations. Darius, who honed his skills playing keyboards in church, dreams of becoming a producer, while Jada, already landing gigs on Music Row, aims to be a songwriter. We passed bulletin boards for music organizations Phi Mu Alpha Sinfonia and Sigma Alpha Iota where students animatedly debated a recent recital. Near the band room, I saw a poster that read "Congratulations to the Aristocrat of Bands, 2023 Grammy-Award Winners for Best Roots Gospel Album—*The Urban Hymnal.*" Catching my reaction, Jada beamed, "Yes, we got a Grammy!" Darius quickly corrected her, "Actually, we got two."

They led me to a corridor of practice rooms and music classrooms. Horn players riffed on Earth, Wind & Fire, a saxophonist reimagined "Crazy" in a neo-soul groove, and vocalists belted Chaka Khan and Jill Scott covers. Down the hall, a gospel duo harmonized the Sister Act II rendition of "His Eye is on the Sparrow." This music making was an expression of their identities. Jefferson Street's musical legacy, infused with the students' own experiences, was being nurtured at TSU. Through gospel, pop, hip-hop, and soul, they were unapologetically shaping the sound of their generation. I asked Darius and Jada, "Is this part of the Grammy-Magic? They smiled and answered in unison, "Yes, ma'am!"

Critics have long argued that many colleges and university music programs remain outdated, adhering primarily to Western Classical traditions while failing to integrate the diverse musical genres that students actively engage with outside of school (Jorgensen, 2003; Koza, 2010; Powell et al., 2020). In response, Randles (2016) introduced the concept of the music teacher as producer, a reimagined role in which educators act not only as instructors but also as facilitators, collaborators, and cultural curators. In this model, the music teacher becomes a multi-faceted guide, "part musician, part technician, part guidance counselor, and part magician," equipped to bridge the gap between formal music education and students' own musical landscapes. While this approach presents an exciting vision, it raises a question: how can music educators practically negotiate this gap in their teaching?

Sirek (2018) proposed that adopting an ethnographic approach to teaching music provides a pathway for teachers to embody the teacher-producer model. Ethnography, both a process and a product aimed at understanding cultural practices (Wolcott, 2008), offers educators a framework for valuing students' cultural assets and centering their lived experiences. By engaging in ethnographic methods such as participant observation, interviews, and cultural analysis, teachers gain deep insight into students' musical identities, creative processes, and the broader social contexts that shape their artistry.

The TSU music program stands at a unique crossroads where tradition meets innovation and Classical music techniques intersect with student-centered, culturally relevant pedagogy. This duality is an intentional effort to prepare students for the realities of today's musical landscape while honoring their musical experiences. Further shaping TSU's identity is its geographical and cultural backdrop of Nashville, Music City, USA This setting provides an immersive environment in which both faculty and students engage in collaborative music making. By embracing an ethnographic approach that honors the past while pushing creative boundaries, TSU faculty position themselves as producers of cultural assets who influence both music education and music.

"If You're Not Producing, You're Not Teaching"

The ethnographic approach to teaching and the music-teacher-as-producer model interconnect; beyond traditional music education, both prioritize cultural assets, student experiences, and creativity. These frameworks challenge Western-centric, teacher-led models by shifting the focus toward student agency, cultural relevance, and real-world application. These approaches assert that students' lived musical cultures themselves form the curriculum.

At their core, both models require a new mindset. Ethnographic teaching demands that educators immerse themselves in students' cultural and musical realities to create an inclusive, meaningful learning environment. The music teacher as producer applies these insights, much as does a music producer guiding an artist in the studio, to shape the student's creativity into professional-level artistry.

At TSU, this approach thrives in its HBCU environment, which acts as a home away from home for students, reinforcing both their academic development and cultural identity. The music program integrates traditional Black music and performance practices with contemporary forms, ensuring that students' experiences drive the curriculum. TSU faculty recognize the importance of meeting students where they are and adjusting pedagogy to reflect the evolutions of Black music and of the music industry.

> I hear some of my colleagues say they're moving further away from having our students play a bunch of music from the 1700s and 1800s. So much good music has happened since then. My mindset is moving further away from it, too. The [music] industry moves so much quicker than we do in education. (Thomas Grey, personal communication, June 6, 2024)

Another professor acknowledges how student-driven innovation has changed their approach.

> I've been teaching college music for the past 15 years, and I feel like I'm behind. I need to catch up with my students! I watch what they're doing with their music, especially on social media. They have their own Instagram followers, their own YouTube channels promoting their music! I can't even say that for myself! (Timothy Anderson, personal communication, June 5, 2024).

The model of music teacher as producer requires educators to be not only instructors but innovators, collaborators, and facilitators of creative work.

> If you're not producing, you're not teaching. And I don't just mean producing in the sense of studio production. If you're not innovative, if you're not creating, if you're not pushing your students to be innovative, what's the use of you teaching music here? (Mark Brunson, personal communication, June 6, 2024)

Many students enter TSU's music program for the HBCU experience, rather than with a clear understanding of what it means to be a college music major. Some arrive with formal music training while others come from high school marching bands, gospel choirs, or are self-taught. Students from Black musical traditions often possess exceptional aural skills, improvisational ability, and performance instincts, particularly in gospel, jazz, and R&B. Some lack formal training in music theory, sight-reading, or applied instrumental techniques.

One faculty member illustrates how these differences require rethinking traditional academic expectations.

> We get kids who come in and can play a pretty good gospel piano, or maybe even good jazz piano. But they can't read a note. They may not even be able to tell you what the chord is, and their fingering might be a little rough. But it's good stuff! They can transpose and modulate, pick up a soloist in any key and play. That's good stuff. I went to graduate school with people who can't do that! We want to keep that! (Lawrence Brown, personal communication, March 26, 2024)

This approach aligns with Yosso's (2005) concept of familial capital, which recognizes the value of cultural knowledge passed down through Black communal spaces such as the church or family traditions. Rather than viewing these informal learning methods as deficiencies, TSU instructors see them as enriching students' overall musicianship.

To support this diversity, TSU offers three undergraduate music degrees that accommodate three career paths: Bachelor of Science in commercial music, Bachelor of Science in music education, and Bachelor of Science in music—liberal arts. The university also offers a Master of Education in curriculum and instruction for students who wish to advance their studies in music education. Faculty recognize that students enter the program at various levels of ability, which requires a curriculum that supports both foundational and advanced learning. One faculty member notes that "The important thing is to meet them where they are and curate their journey, to challenge them at a level that fits them, not pushes them toward what a Curtis Institute or Eastman-trained musician's next level would be" (Nathan Williams, personal communication, March 26, 2024).

This revamped curriculum at TSU has been successful largely due to its diverse faculty, who come from elite conservatories, universities, and industry backgrounds (e.g., Juilliard, Indiana University, Eastman, and Nashville's commercial music scene). The department has recruited specialists in jazz, pop, country, opera, and commercial songwriting to better serve its students.

> A plus for us is that we have a diverse faculty that reflects the needs and aspirations of our students. It's important that our students see professional musicians from different music backgrounds, even different ethnic backgrounds. Now we have people from all over—Russia, Serbia, Turkey, the Middle East, all over the United States. We have Grammy-winning songwriters, people who specialize in country music, opera, jazz, and commercial songwriting. Many of our faculty even invite students to perform with them on professional gigs. (Craig Oliver, personal communication, March 14, 2024)

By expanding faculty expertise, TSU broadens its musical scope and ensures students receive exposure to multiple genres, career pathways, and industry connections.

Understanding students' cultural backgrounds also means acknowledging the personal challenges they bring into the classroom. Many students not only come from diverse musical backgrounds but also face socio-economic hardships that impact their education. Music faculty member Larry Jenkins emphasizes the importance of teaching "with" rather than "beyond" students' challenges.

> I don't know if I'd even say "beyond," it's just it's like a "with." Sometimes with this challenge, we have no choice right now. You know, I still need you to learn XYZ. Look, this instrument; I'm sorry that it's running sharp, but you need to pull that slide out a little bit more and we gotta keep it pushing. (Larry Jenkins, personal communication, March 26, 2024)

Jenkins highlights that material barriers such as financial struggles, lack of quality instruments, and life circumstances should not prevent learning. Instead, faculty work with these realities to create meaningful learning experiences. This approach reflects ethnographic teaching in action: teachers do not ignore students' lived realities but find creative ways to help them succeed despite challenges. "We work with what we have.

If a student is struggling, we don't just let that be a stopping point—we adjust. That's part of the HBCU experience. We teach the whole student, not just their technical ability" (Larry Jenkins, personal communication, March 26, 2024). This philosophy reinforces the music-teacher-as-producer model, in which faculty not only teach: they problem solve, support, and lift up students in ways that value both their talent and their personal struggles.

Ethnographic teaching and the music-teacher-as-producer approach extend beyond the classroom into real-world music creation, as demonstrated by TSU's 2023 Grammy-winning album, *The Urban Hymnal*. TSU faculty member Luke Johnson played a pivotal role in reinventing the traditional HBCU band sound by treating the performance group Aristocrat of Bands as a recording ensemble.

> We pretty much turned the band room into a studio. We brought the band in and had an area mic. And you know, we recorded, we would break down to sections, bring in certain students who are really good players to layer at the top and solo. (Luke Johnson, personal communication, June 6, 2024)

Rather than reproducing existing marching band traditions, Johnson and his team used professional production techniques to elevate HBCU music to commercial-level quality and broader cultural visibility.

> We decided that we were going to reinvent Black music, combine the many genres of Black music through the lens of the HBCU marching band. The win was not just a moment for TSU, but it's recognizing Black musical excellence at HBCUs. It proves that our sound, our style, deserve to be seen and celebrated on the biggest stages, especially among those who, so call, make the rules about what excellence in music look or sound like. (Luke Johnson, personal communication, June 6, 2024)

The success of *The Urban Hymnal* serves as a cultural validation through mainstream industry recognition. It also serves as a blueprint for how HBCU bands can move beyond halftime shows into professional recording, film scoring, and music industry collaborations.

Ethnographic teaching values students' cultural assets, while the music-teacher-as-producer model amplifies them. Rather than impose rigid standards, TSU faculty foster creativity, innovation, and professional readiness. Whether through curriculum reform, faculty diversification, or producing Grammy-winning albums, the TSU music community actively shapes Black music education and its influence in the industry. Through these pedagogical approaches, educators seamlessly integrate Black music with cutting-edge production methods.

TSU's Grammy win proves that HBCU music programs are cultural powerhouses, yet a dearth of funding restricts their ability to innovate. Cooper (2023) examines the ongoing disparities in funding for HBCUs, particularly in contrast to their predominantly White institutional counterparts.

Despite being a leader in HBCU music education, TSU faces financial constraints that hinder its expansion, innovation, and ability to provide students with industry-level opportunities. Faculty members acknowledge the disparities in how state funds are distributed; TSU receives significantly less support compared with public White institutions such as the University of Tennessee.

> A lot of our struggles come from the fact that we just don't have the resources that other institutions in the state have. When you look at the University of Tennessee, their funding structure is completely different. We have to fight for what should already be allocated to us. (Ronald Willis, personal communication, March 26, 2024)

The historical underfunding has directly affected TSU's ability to sustain its music program and elevate Black cultural assets. Cooper notes that many Southern states have funneled resources into White institutions while neglecting Black land-grant institutions, a practice that has left many HBCUs with outdated facilities, fewer academic programs, and limited financial resources for students and faculty.

TSU's struggle mirrors that of other HBCUs discussed by Cooper (2023), a fight for funding that should have been equitably allocated but was instead diverted to White schools. Faculty members stress that talent is not the issue. Resources are.

> We have students coming in with real talent, but they don't always have the same resources as students at UT or Vanderbilt. Some of them come in with broken instruments or no instrument at all. We could be producing the next music educator of the year, but without adequate funding owed to us, we will never know. (Mark Brunson, personal communication, June 6, 2024)

Despite these financial challenges, TSU faculty remain steadfast in their commitment to lift up students both academically and artistically. TSU continues to provide a high-quality education in the face of resource limitations. The music program stands as a powerful embodiment of both the struggles and triumphs that define the HBCU experience and demonstrates that Black musical excellence not only endures but flourishes. Yet, the continued success of programs such as TSU's cannot rest on resilience alone. Achieving true artistic and educational equity requires sustained funding and policy support that acknowledges past injustices and invests in Black educational institutions.

Promoters of Cultural Assets: Florida Agricultural & Mechanical University

Florida Agricultural and Mechanical University (FAMU) has long stood as a cultural and educational beacon, not only in Tallahassee but across

Florida. Just as profound as my experience at FAMU was the journey that led me there. Charles Dickens's famous opening lines from *A Tale of Two Cities*—a meditation on light and darkness, hope and despair—felt particularly resonant as I traveled along US Highway 319, marked by its unsettling designation: Plantation Parkway.

The landscape along this route tells a layered and complex story. Plantations such as Pebble Hill, Forshalle, and Cherokee stand as relics of a past defined by both economic prosperity and unimaginable oppression. These grand homes and meticulously maintained grounds embody Dickens's duality. The wealth they represented was built on the suffering of enslaved people. As I passed, I wondered how many of their descendants found refuge and empowerment at institutions such as FAMU and other HBCUs throughout Georgia and Florida.

Arriving at FAMU, affectionately known as The Hill, was like stepping into a space of defiant hope. The university's location atop the highest of Tallahassee's seven hills is both geographical and symbolic. It is a summit of possibility, a place where generations of African Americans have ascended in pursuit of knowledge and self-determination. It stands in stark contrast to the historical injustices in the land surrounding it.

As I drove through campus, I took in the sights of students between classes, the lush greenery, and the unmistakable energy of The Hill. Then, a familiar sound from my childhood stopped me in my tracks: the Marching 100 in rehearsal. I pulled over, drawn by the unmistakable pulse of the tubas swaying in rhythm to Tevin Campbell's "Can We Talk." The closer I got to The Patch, the ground where the Marching 100 perfects its craft, the music transported me to another time and place. This was not any R&B arrangement. This was the FAMU Sound, made iconic by Lindsey B. Sargent. Since the 1970s, Sargent's arrangements have defined the band's signature blend of brass intensity, wind fluidity, and extended jazz harmonies that transformed familiar melodies into something uniquely FAMU.

I made my way to the Foster-Tanner Arts Building, the heart of FAMU's music program. William P. Foster, who led the Marching 100 for over 50 years, revolutionized college marching bands, elevating showmanship, precision, and musical excellence. The building also honors Henry O. Tanner, one of the first internationally recognized African American painters who broke racial barriers in the late 19th and early 20th centuries. On the outside of the Foster-Tanner Arts Building, a newly mounted plaque caught my eye: "Home of the Julian 'Cannonball' Adderley and Nathaniel 'Nat' Adderley Music Institute." The inscription honored these FAMU alumni, whose contributions to jazz resonate worldwide.

Standing before it, I was reminded of Dickens's duality, FAMU exists as a counterpoint to the history that surrounds it. The plantations I passed once commodified Black labor, extracting wealth while denying education and suppressing Black culture. Yet here on The Hill, FAMU does the opposite: it cultivates, celebrates, and promotes the cultural assets of its community. It stands as the spring of hope in a land shaped by a winter of despair, a testament to resilience, brilliance, and the unshakable power of Black scholarship and artistry.

HBCUs exemplify how music programs actively promote students' cultural assets while fostering academic achievement. This approach, known as culturally sustaining pedagogy (Paris, 2012; Paris & Alim, 2017), builds upon culturally relevant pedagogy not only by recognizing cultural diversity but by ensuring that students' cultural identities are celebrated. For music educators to truly value cultural assets, they must move beyond mere acknowledgment of diversity and actively promote students' home cultures.

The promotion of cultural assets in colleges and universities is essential to sustaining cultural heritage and fostering community pride. While preservation focuses on safeguarding traditions, promotion expands their visibility and encourages appreciation. At HBCUs, cultural assets are often promoted through their marching band, symphonic band, jazz ensembles, choir, and orchestra. These ensembles not only provide students with rigorous musical training but also promote the centrality of Black musical traditions in performance. FAMU's Marching 100 serves as a global ambassador for this vision, but is only one part of a broader ecosystem.

Students are drawn to FAMU's music program not only for its prestigious ensembles but for what the program represents, a space where Black music is actively nurtured, sustained, and celebrated. While The Marching 100 is globally recognized for its precision, innovation, and electrifying performances, its deeper significance lies in its role affirming Black cultural expression on the international stage. Beyond the marching band, FAMU's ensembles serve as cultural ambassadors, ensuring that Black music is preserved in academia and prominently showcased.

"We're Not Just Teaching Music; We're Sustaining a Legacy"

FAMU's commitment to both academic and cultural excellence has long defined its mission to serve African American students. The music program's embodiment of culturally sustaining pedagogy ensures that Black musical traditions are deeply integrated into the educational experience. This ethos is embedded in every facet of the music program, a microcosm of the university's larger commitment to Black cultural wealth.

Many faculty members, themselves FAMU alumni or HBCU graduates, recognize the importance of teaching music through a culturally relevant lens. Their pedagogy reflects the experiences and backgrounds of their students, reinforcing the Department of Music's mission: "To provide the highest quality of music education at the undergraduate level for aspiring teachers, scholars, performers, and composers, while also engaging non-majors and the broader community in music as a vital part of human culture and experience."

This mission extends beyond traditional music instruction, fostering a familial, community-centered atmosphere, a defining characteristic of HBCUs. Familial capital rooted in family traditions, communal support, and cultural knowledge shapes FAMU's learning environment (Smith, 2023; Yosso, 2005). Unlike institutions that include multicultural music only for diversity's sake, FAMU ensures that Black students do not just learn about other musical traditions but also see their own cultural wealth affirmed in the curriculum.

Culturally sustaining pedagogy demands that racial identity development be actively incorporated into education, ensuring that Black students recognize their cultural legacy in what they study. One faculty member explains:

> Our curriculum is pretty much the same as any traditional music degree. But what's different here is that we center our music. And that's a must! Maybe it's easier to do that with the band or the choir . . . but the faculty who teach music history, music appreciation, or even music theory, they too are expected to teach to the backgrounds of our students. These students should see themselves in what we teach. If our students don't, then we have failed at our jobs. Like our mission says, we provide "high-quality music instruction" for our students. But we're not just teaching music; we're sustaining a legacy. (Matthew Neilsen, personal communication, November 12, 2024)

This sentiment encapsulates FAMU's unwavering dedication to preserving Black musical traditions as a central pillar of its academic mission. By ensuring that students' cultural assets are both acknowledged and deeply integrated into their education, FAMU exemplifies culturally sustaining pedagogy. Music education at FAMU does not strive to assimilate Eurocentric norms but to sustain the Black musical heritage for future generations.

Promoting cultural assets includes and sustains students' cultures in academia. Rather than using Black music as a bridge to Eurocentric education, instruction rooted in culturally sustaining pedagogy ensures that Black musical traditions remain central to students' educational experiences.

The Adderley Institute at FAMU exemplifies this pedagogy, designed to advance Black musical traditions while giving students meaningful opportunities to engage with their cultural heritage. Faculty emphasize that the Institute is a force dedicated to elevating the creative and intellectual contributions of Black musicians.

Faculty stress the importance of branding and institutional recognition in solidifying FAMU's place among prestigious institutions. The naming of the

Julian Cannonball and Nat Adderley Music Institute ensures that FAMU's legacy is sustained and respected, particularly in jazz and popular music. One faculty member states, "We have to claim our culture, and it's metaphorical for everything else we're talking about" (Darrell Farris, personal communication, November 11, 2024). This naming represents a deliberate effort to cement FAMU's musical and cultural legacy, ensuring that students recognize the accomplishments of the Black artists who paved the way.

The Institute is committed to both scholarly research and artistic excellence and focuses on Black popular music. As noted in its founding mission:

> The Institute's research and academic arm focuses on popular music in its historical, cultural, and aesthetic domains and its linkages to other artistic forms of representation. While it promotes scholarly inquiry in all world music, its core research centers on Black popular music of the Americas.

Rather than treating jazz and Black popular music as secondary to Western Classical traditions, the Institute positions them as core to music education. Students' cultural knowledge must be preserved, not erased or reduced to a transitional step toward dominant traditions. The Adderley Institute fulfills this mission by ensuring that Black music remains central to FAMU's curriculum.

This commitment to centering Black musical forms extends beyond the classroom into performance spaces, most notably through FAMU's world-renowned Marching 100. At FAMU, the Marching 100 is more than a band; it is a cultural institution with a global impact. To students, it represents a connection to their heritage and a platform to showcase Black musical excellence on the world stage. Many students join the band both because of their love for music and to become part of a lasting legacy.

> [Student #1:] I'm not a music major, but when I came to FAMU, I knew I wanted to be part of the band. I wanted to be part of that musical legacy. When I told my family I made it, they were so excited! They come to all the home games to support me.

> [Student #2:] "I'm a mechanical engineering major, but the band is my family. We literally call each other brothers and sisters. We spend most of our time together, but it's all good. I love traveling and seeing the world with my family. I wouldn't have this kind of experience if I wasn't in the band." (Shenae Thompson & Gregory Lankford, personal communications, November 11, 2024)

Beyond its cultural significance, the Marching 100 serves as a financial and promotional asset to FAMU, drawing national attention and thereby elevating the university's reputation. Faculty member Thomas provides insight to this significance:

> The band has been a godsend for us because it's very popular. We raise a lot of money because people value what we do. When we played at the University of Florida, they lost hundreds of thousands of dollars in concessions during halftime because people wouldn't leave their seats—they wanted to see the Marching 100! (James Thomas, personal communication, November 12, 2024)

Black musical traditions not only command admiration but wield financial and institutional power, leaping over the gap between artistic excellence and mainstream visibility.

While the Marching 100 is its most recognized ensemble, FAMU's entire music department shapes cultural identity not only globally but in the broader Tallahassee community. Ensembles frequently perform for local audiences, including churches, retirement homes, and public schools, which reinforces FAMU's dedication to cultural outreach.

A faculty member describes how band members serve as role models for younger students, inspiring future generations of musicians.

> We teach our students that people are watching you and that you represent something bigger than you. When they go to elementary schools, middle schools around this city—both Black and White—the students tell their teachers, "We want a drumline like that." They're always calling for the FAMU drumline to come in, play with them, and lead them around the campus. (Jennifer Robinson, personal communication, November 12, 2024)

FAMU's deep cultural connections contrast with the experiences of Black students at predominantly White institutions. Faculty members note that FAMU's culture of musical and cultural celebration attracts students who seek a sense of belonging.

> When you promote your culture, people outside the campus recognize it. You become a light, as well as a sanctuary. A lot of Black students who are in school at FSU [Florida State University] come over all the time to FAMU music activities for the culture. What they get here, they can't get at FSU. (James Thomas, communication, November 11, 2024)

This dynamic reinforces FAMU's role as a cultural refuge in which Black students experience representation, protection, and celebration. Through local school engagement, programming, and high-profile performances, FAMU ensures that Black cultural pride remains strong, allowing future generations to see themselves reflected in music.

Beyond promoting and sustaining Black musical traditions, institutions such as FAMU must also confront broader challenges related to representation in music education. While HBCUs have long championed diversity, equity, and inclusion, systemic barriers still exist to ensuring that students have access to opportunities and recognition in the music industry and academia. This raises a critical question: how can such institutions such continue to advance diversity efforts while maintaining their mission to sustain Black cultural excellence?

A core aspect of culturally sustaining pedagogy is ensuring that students' cultural identities are not erased. This preservation is particularly critical in music education, in which Black contributions have been excluded from mainstream curricula. Educators must resist erasure and Whitewashing by ensuring that Black musical traditions remain central to instruction rather than treated as secondary to Western Classical music.

Music educators now face political pressures that threaten their ability to teach the history of marginalized people. At Florida's only public historically Black university, some students now fear that political constraints could interfere with how their history is taught. One student said,

> That's the main reason why I chose to come to FAMU. I wanted to be at a place where my music was promoted. I got accepted to Florida State, but I knew as a Black man, I wouldn't have the same experience learning my music. There's nothing like learning your music in a place where all facets of your music are genuinely promoted and respected. But now the governor is trying to take that away. (LeShawn Lewis, personal communication, November 11, 2024)

Senate Bill 266 signed into law on May 15, 2023 by Governor Ron DeSantis blocks public colleges from using taxpayer money on diversity programs and forbids instruction on racism and oppression. This law poses a direct challenge to FAMU's mission of preserving Black cultural wealth. Music is deeply tied to cultural identity, history, and lived experience. The legislation limits the ability of music educators to engage students in critical discussions about Black music's racial and historical context. When educators are restricted from teaching about the systemic barriers that shaped Black musical traditions, they are not only limiting knowledge but actively erasing students' identities.

> [Faculty 1:] Our music is American music. Jazz, hip-hop, country, you name it. You can't have American music without Black music.
>
> [Faculty 2:] How can I talk about jazz without talking about the blues; and how can I talk about the blues, without talking about spirituals and fields songs; and how can I talk about spirituals and fields songs without talking about slavery. So you can pass all the laws you want, when we teach music, and American music at that, oh, we're automatically gonna be part of the story! (James Thomas & Matthew Neilsen, personal communications, November 12, 2024)

FAMU's music program actively resists this erasure by ensuring that Black students learn and create in a framework that values their cultural heritage. Sustaining diversity, equity, and inclusion principles at HBCUs, however, requires continuous advocacy, institutional support, and an intentional restructuring of curricula to ensure Black musical traditions remain central.

In summary, music programs that incorporate consciousness and cultural empowerment, by valuing the cultural assets in the classroom, go beyond appreciating diversity. They serve as a means of empowerment, identity formation, and resistance actively challenging the erasure of marginalized histories and creating a space for students to assert their cultural identities. Fisk University, Tennessee State University, and Florida Agricultural and Mechanical University exemplify the multifaceted role HBCUs play in preserving and promoting Black musical traditions to ensure that these assets are securely archived and also shaping contemporary and future musical landscapes.

Fisk University's efforts to preserve spirituals underscore the school's maintenance of historical continuity, in which music is not only remembered but revitalized for modern audiences. As a producer of cultural assets, Tennessee State University embodies the dynamism of musical creation and trains students to contribute to Black musical expression. FAMU, in its role as a promoter of cultural assets, ensures that these traditions reach national and global stages.

As Elliott (2012) asserts, music education serves as a vehicle to foster musicianship, listenership, and cultural expression. Educators must recognize their responsibility to shape musical cultures and guide students to view their artistry as both an individual and collective force for change. Music educators must engage with a broad range of cultural values, positioning themselves as facilitators who amplify students' cultural voices rather than subsuming them under dominant narratives (Gellerstein, 2021). Particularly at HBCUs, however, this practice must be paired with preparing students to thrive in broader musical and professional arenas that may not reflect their cultural backgrounds.

While HBCUs provide support for Black students, especially in music programs, they must also prepare students for realities beyond the HBCU community. After experiencing culturally affirming environments, many students face culture shock after graduation. In graduate schools, for example, their culture is not as valued. McCall (2015) recommends that music students not be limited to the musical and cultural experiences at HBCUs. They need to broaden opportunities by attending conferences and performances and engage with a global network of music professionals and students.

The examples of Fisk, TSU, and FAMU nonetheless show that when music education is rooted in consciousness and cultural empowerment, not only does it celebrate the artistic contributions of its students, but also actively invests in their futures. By centering cultural assets in the curriculum, these schools allow music students to reimagine their future in music on their own terms. From performing on the world's largest stages to winning multiple Grammy awards, the possibilities are limitless.

References

Cooper, J. N. (2023). Battle of the lands: The creation of land grant institutions and HBCUs: Fostering a still separate and still unequal higher education system. *Washington and Lee Journal of Civil Rights and Social Justice, 30*(2), 247–287.

Elliott, D. J. (2012). Music education philosophy. In G. E. McPherson & G. F. Welch (Eds.), *The Oxford handbook of music education* (Vol. 1, pp. 63–88). Oxford University Press.

Gellerstein, B. A. (2021). *Daring to see: White supremacy and gatekeeping in music education.* Publication No. 2525691107 Doctoral dissertation. University of Massachusetts. ProQuest Dissertation & Theses.

Gunawardena, M., & Brown, B. (2021). Fostering values through authentic storytelling. *The Australian Journal of Teacher Education, 46*(6), 36–53. https://doi.org/10.14221/ajte.2021v46n6.3

Jorgensen, E. R. (2003). Western Classical music and general education. *Philosophy of Music Education Review, 11*(2), 130–140.

Koza, J. (2010). Listening for whiteness: Hearing racial politics in undergraduate school music. In T. A. Regelski & T. J. Gates (Eds.), *Music education in changing times: Guiding visions for practice* (pp. 85–95). Springer.

Landrum, R. E., Brakke, K., & McCarthy, M. A. (2019). The pedagogical power of storytelling. *Scholarship of Teaching and Learning in Psychology, 5*(3), 247.

McCall, J. M. (2015). *Degree perseverance among African Americans transitioning from historically Black colleges and universities (HBCUs) to predominantly white institution (PWIs).* Publication No. 1682266271 Doctoral dissertation. Arizona State University. ProQuest Dissertation & Theses.

Paris, D. (2012). Culturally sustaining pedagogy: A needed change in stance, terminology, and practice. *Educational Researcher, 41*(3), 93–97.

Paris, D. & Alim, H. S. (Eds.) (2017). *Culturally sustaining pedagogies: Teaching and learning for justice in a changing world.* Teachers College Press.

Powell, B., Hewitt, D., Smith, G. D., Olesko, B., & Davis, V. (2020). Curricular change in collegiate programs: Toward a more inclusive music education. *Visions of Research in Music Education, 35*(1), 16.

Randles, C. (2016). *Why music lessons need to keep up with the times.* The Huffington Post. https://www.huffpost.com/entry/why-music-lessons-need-to_b_10314552

San Pedro, T. (2018). Abby as ally: An argument for culturally disruptive pedagogy. *American Educational Research Journal, 55*(6), 1193–1232.

Sirek, D. (2018). Our culture is who we are! "Rescuing" Grenadian identity through musicking and music education. *International Journal of Music Education, 36*(1), 47–57.

Smith, Q. L. (2023). *Black cultural wealth: Exploring the application and measurement of a new construct.* Publication No. 2817253750 Doctoral dissertation. The University of North Carolina at Chapel Hill]. ProQuest Dissertation & Theses.

Tatini-Smith, L., Lewis, N. D., Maynie, J., McCou, K., Swanson, R., & Williams, R. (2013). I'm Black and I'm Proud: The centrality of race and racial regard at an HBCU: A pilot study. *Researcher: An Interdisciplinary Journal, 26*(2), 77–86.

Tröhler, D. (2006). History and historiography of education: Some remarks on the utility of historical knowledge in the age of efficiency. *Encounters in Theory and History of Education, 7,* 1–17. https://doi.org/10.24908/eoe-ese-rse.v7i0.606

Wolcott, H. F. (2008). *Ethnography: A way of seeing.* AltaMira Press.

Yosso, T. J. (2005). Whose culture has capital? A critical race theory discussion of community cultural wealth. *Race, Ethnicity and Education, 8*(1), 69–91. https://doi.org/10.1080/1361332052000341006

CHAPTER 8

TRANSFORMATIVE EMPOWERMENT

ABSTRACT

Historically Black Colleges and Universities (HBCUs) exemplify the tenant of consciousness and cultural empowerment by positioning transformative learning as central to music education. Rather than treating music instruction as isolated from students' social realities, HBCU music programs integrate identity, activism, and community engagement into the fabric of their curricula. Chapter 8 explores how Jackson State University and Spelman College cultivate liberatory learning environments that prepare students not only as musicians, but as culturally grounded leaders and social change agents.

Chapter 8 examines how Jackson State University (JSU) and Spelman College model transformative empowerment through music education rooted in critical consciousness and social responsibility. At JSU, students engage with Black history, cultural resistance, and community through a curriculum shaped by Freirean conscientization. Teachers function as mentors, not only teaching content but preparing music education students' social awareness and commitment to justice. At Spelman, Black feminist pedagogy grounds instruction in intersectionality, creating liberatory learning environments where Black women's voices, histories, and musical identities are centered. Faculty use storytelling, role modeling, and culturally responsive practices to help students claim their space as artists and changemakers.

These approaches exemplify that music education can foster both artistic development and political agency. As the chapter cautions, however, transformation is not guaranteed by good intentions alone. It requires reflexive practice, structural support, and the courage to challenge exclusionary traditions. When grounded in both critical pedagogy and cultural affirmation, music education becomes a vehicle for liberation and equips students not just to perform, but to transform.

Historically Black Colleges and Universities (HBCUs) have long served as powerful platforms for an education that extends beyond the classroom and integrates activism, community engagement, and leadership development. Since the 1800s, service and social responsibility have been foundational to HBCUs, rooted in the belief that educating freed Blacks would empower the entire race (Daniels et al., 2017). Despite their under representation in the literature on civic engagement, HBCUs have a rich history of working with local communities, training individuals to challenge civil rights injustices, and promoting social justice (Gasman & McMickens, 2010; Gasman et al., 2015). This commitment continues today, shaping the economic, civic, and social fabric of their communities.

Developing socially conscious change agents remains a goal for HBCUs in the 21st century. Beyond preparing students for careers, these institutions cultivate leaders equipped to address national and global challenges (Gasman & Tudico, 2008; Lomax, 2006). Civic engagement is core to the academic experience; service and social justice are deeply embedded in the curriculum (Lomax, 2006). Students actively work to address social issues, which ensures a continuous pipeline of leaders prepared to advocate for change.

Inside this socially conscious framework, music education assumes a transformative role. Grounded in the principles of Black feminist pedagogy, this approach fosters critical engagement by empowering students to challenge societal norms, lift up marginalized voices, and use artistic expression in the service of activism. Music education becomes a vehicle for identity affirmation, critical thinking, and community-centered learning. It equips students to confront injustices in academia and beyond.

Hess (2019) asserts that music education should embrace activism and encourage students to develop socio-political awareness to challenge oppressive systems. Traditional music education often lacks critical pedagogy; HBCUs, however, provide a counter narrative by fostering community and resistance to injustices. Students are trained both as musicians and as cultural leaders who challenge dominant narratives. They use their music education as a tool for social change.

At HBCUs such as JSU and Spelman College, this vision is realized when students see themselves as advocates. These institutions create liberatory spaces in which students recognize their power as leaders and change agents. They ensure that students' education involves not only acquiring knowledge but that it produces liberation through music.

Transformation through Purpose-Driven Teaching: JSU

Located in the heart of Mississippi, JSU, the state's largest HBCU, stands as both an academic and a cultural pillar. As I entered the gates, I made my way down the campus's main artery, Gibbs-Green Memorial Plaza, affectionately known as The Plaza. Near the entrance was a table for voter registration and volunteer signup for the 2024 elections. On the other side of The Plaza students were distributing flyers for that night's event. Students moved through The Plaza in clusters, some deep in conversation, others laughing, dancing, rushing to class, or relaxing on the benches along the bricked walkway.

I wondered about the name Gibbs-Green. Perhaps it honored an esteemed alumnus? My eyes caught a sign that read Jackson State Tragedy. Intrigued, I stopped. One of Mississippi's Freedom Trail Markers, the sign detailed an event that shaped JSU's legacy of activism.

I learned that on May 14, 1970, Mississippi police opened fire on unarmed student protestors demonstrating against the Vietnam War and racial injustices. Phillip Lafayette Gibbs, 21, a political science major, and James Earl Green, 17, a high school senior, were killed. Now filled with students laughing and debating, The Plaza was once a site of resistance and mourning.

A tour group of potential students approached, led by a student guide who proudly shared the tragic story. "Once you come to JSU, you'll learn more about this [pointing at the sign] and how JSU has always been important to the Civil Rights Movement." His words resonated. More than a university; JSU was a training ground for change makers.

Taking it all in, I continued my walk toward the FD Hall Music Center, named after Frederick Douglas Hall, the university's first official music department chair. A group of students brushed past me, clad in JSU and Sonic Boom gear. Their energy was contagious. "Hey, need help finding something?" one asked. They were members of JSU's internationally acclaimed marching band, the Sonic Boom of the South. They were going to perform, and I was not about to miss the performance.

Back at The Plaza, faculty, students, and staff—even campus security—were their moving and dancing to the Sonic Boom playing "Get Ready" by The Temptations. The J-Settes, JSU's legendary dance line, captivated my attention. They embodied the energy and spirit of JSU, not only a show, but an experience.

The irony struck me. I stood on the same ground that once bore the weight of tragedy and protest, yet now pulsed with celebration and resilience. In this moment, past and present converged: activism, transformation, and the unbreakable musical spirit of JSU.

One of the defining strengths of HBCUs is their ability to create learning environments that foster growth, empowerment, and success. Research consistently demonstrates that HBCUs cultivate scholars, leaders, and change-makers through providing supportive educational spaces (Albritton, 2012; Freeman & Gasman, 2014; Palmer & Young, 2023). This transformative impact is made possible by an environment in which students' intellectual abilities are affirmed, their presence is integral to campus culture, and their educational experiences are enriched by a strong sense of belonging (Stewart et al., 2008). This community fosters confidence, self-empowerment and a deep engagement with learning that allows students to develop critical thinking, social awareness, and cultural reflection.

At JSU, this philosophy is deeply embedded in the music program; students are challenged to think critically, engage in social awareness, and use music as a tool for transformation. Although the iconic marching band The Sonic Boom of the South is widely recognized as the public face of JSU's music program, the university's true legacy lies in its producing Black music educators at a higher rate than any other institution in Mississippi (NASM, 2024). Over half of JSU's music graduates each year are music education majors, and even those who graduate without a concentration in education often find their way into teaching or mentoring. This pipeline of Black music educators reinforces JSU's commitment to preparing students to become change agents in classrooms, communities, and beyond.

The foundation of JSU's music program is deeply rooted in Freire's (1974) concept of transformative learning known by the term *conscientization*. This process develops the ability to question, debate, and take action on the social, political, cultural, and economic forces in one's life. Schmidt (2005) builds on Freire's conscientization by examining its application in music education. He contends that music education should move beyond a focus on performance and aesthetics to actively pursue social transformation, to challenge educators to engage with their communities, and to root their practice in relevance, dialog, and social responsibility.

Similar to several academic disciplines at JSU, the music program extends the university's connection to social transformation. By developing students' critical consciousness and preparing them for transformative impact—both musical and social—education at JSU bridges theory with action. In doing so, it equips students not only to transform music classrooms but also to lift up their communities.

"You Won't Leave Here like You Came"

At the heart of JSU's music program is a pedagogy grounded in critical consciousness, a foundational expectation at HBCUs, at which education is intrinsically tied to cultural affirmation and social change. As Lewis and Lee (2009) emphasize, students come to HBCUs expecting more than academic content; they seek instruction that reflects and affirms their lived experiences as Blacks navigating a racially stratified society. JSU meets this demand through a customized core curriculum structured to

> develop their critical consciousness by learning to ask essential questions, to use habits of the mind that support critical and analytical thinking to answer them, to think deeply and effectively communicate, and to collaborate with others to address societal problems.

This approach transcends the confines of traditional coursework. Faculty describe the JSU experience as one that transforms students intellectually, emotionally, and socially. This transformative journey is especially profound in JSU's music program, in which faculty extend the reach of music education far beyond performance or theory. As one professor explains,

> You're going to be challenged and you're going to be changed. We expect transformation from the day you walk through those gates from your freshman year to the day you walk across that stage [at graduation]. That's why we say, you won't leave here like you came. My job is to, first, change how you think about yourself. If I can do that, teaching you this [picks up a music score] is easier. (Catherine Kendall, personal communication, October 21, 2024)

At JSU, students are immersed in a campus environment in which Black excellence is visible, celebrated, and normalized. "To be at an institution in the South, especially in Mississippi, but yet you have positive images of Blackness around you is transformative in itself," a faculty member explains (James Bryant, personal communication, October 22, 2024). These images of success and leadership help students take ownership of their own potential. Another professor emphasizes that

> We're taught to own our Blackness. And if we don't protect it, and if we don't teach it the way it should be taught, then others are not going to respect you, respect us, and respect the history from which we came. (Brenda Woodall, personal communication, October 21, 2024)

This message reinforces the notion that cultural pride is both transformative and a form of resistance and advocacy.

Music faculty at JSU understand their role as not only teaching music but reshaping how students see themselves and the world. Through deliberate engagement with cultural and socio-political issues, instructors foster a learning environment in which students are encouraged to analyze society and their place in it. This pedagogical strategy is not always formally documented in syllabi or departmental handbooks. Instead, it exists in a powerful hidden curriculum, one that imparts values, affirms identity, and cultivates a sense of purpose.

The hidden curriculum at JSU refers to the ways in which Black culture, history, and heritage are woven into students' educational experience. Described by Wilkerson et al. (2021), this includes culturally relevant pedagogy, fictive kinship, that is, family-like relationships not connected by blood (Nelson, 2013), and traditions that affirm students' identities and provide a sense of belonging. These elements, along with formal instruction, shape how students understand their place in society. Two students remarked,

> [Student 1:] At JSU, we meet people who look like us, who are doing the things we want to do. For me, it's life-changing when I see successful people who look like me, who came from similar backgrounds as I did. If they could do it, so can I.
>
> [Student 2:] What I appreciate most is that I have professors who really care for us. They check on us outside of class, have lunch with us, making sure we're OK, not just with our music, but me as a person. And because we have that kind of relationship, we can talk about anything. They talk to me like my mama or uncle you know, telling me [disguises voice], "You better get yourself together 'cause can't call yourself a music major here and can't get your act together. Do I need to drive down to Hattiesburg and visit yo' Mama?" [Students laugh] (Shanae Thompson and Darius Harrison, personal communications, October 22, 2024)

The anecdote of a professor threatening to call a student's mother is humorous but poignant. It reflects the intimate, accountability-driven community that drives students' growth.

In JSU's music classrooms, students are reminded to consider the broader implications of their craft. Observing several music classes and rehearsals, I saw that the faculty's theme was one of musicianship grounded in social awareness. As one faculty member told students, "Let's take all the things that you're learning right now, and let's see how these principles translate into real life. Because life is bigger than just playing or singing." (Allen Rogers, personal communication, October 22, 2024) In this way, music serves as a medium through which students critically engage with the world, making connections between their artistry and broader social issues.

"From Mindset to Movement"

HBCUs such as JSU have long recognized the importance of raising critical consciousness among students, helping them understand their social position while empowering them to become change agents (Lewis & Lee, 2009). Freire's conscientization (1974) underscores this process: individuals evolve from a passive awareness of oppression to an active role in transforming it. This journey is embedded in the ethos of JSU's music program, in which students are not only taught to think critically but to act with purpose. Diemer et al. (2021) explain that the power of critical consciousness lies in its ability to move people toward meaningful action against oppression.

At JSU, this notion comes alive in music education classrooms, in which faculty prepare students to question dominant narratives, reject stereotypes, and apply their education to real-world contexts. Students are challenged to teach themselves about current events. One stated, "To be informed is to be everything. And that is what we're taught here. Social justice can't start unless we're knowledgeable of our purpose" (Nicole Griffin, personal communication, October 22, 2024). In one of the music education courses I observed, the teacher pushed students to resist deficit thinking, urging them not to "satisfy the negative expectations" placed on them or on their own students. This emphasis on intellectual and cultural empowerment positions JSU as both a center of activism and a launch pad for leadership.

The music program's commitment to action is reflected in its outcomes. With a claimed 97% placement rate into teaching roles or graduate programs, according to the director of the music education program, JSU ensures its graduates are making tangible impacts in education. The university's influence is deeper than numbers, however. Music education at JSU is intentionally designed to develop excellent educators and socially conscious leaders. JSU embeds critical reflection throughout its curriculum. Students are placed in public school classrooms, required to write about what they observe. Students internalize this charge.

> When we come back from our classroom observations, we discuss what we saw, not just rehearsals and things like that, but what did we see as far as equitable resources and treatment of young Black and Brown students in music classes. Then we discuss what we need to do to make things better once we are in those teaching positions. (Christopher Lockett, personal communication, October 22, 2024)

This approach ensures students are grounded in classroom realities before graduation. They not only recognize inequities, but they are also taught to confront them.

One student recalled entering a school in which administration failed to advocate for students, prompting the music education student to attend and speak up at board meetings, becoming the change they wanted to see. Such activism is deliberately nurtured. Faculty urge students to pursue terminal degrees, reinforcing their capacity to become decision-makers in the world of education. When I observed a conversation between a faculty member and music education students, the faculty member stated,

> This degree is just the beginning. After you graduate, come back and get your masters, and after that, find a good doctoral program. We need you with terminal degrees so you can be in places where your knowledge is respected. We need you to be at the table where decisions are made. We need you to be a decision-maker. (Harriet Mitchell, personal communication, October 21, 2024)

This proactive approach ensures that students do not only participate in the system but actively shape it.

JSU challenges students to interrogate Western-centered music education models and develop culturally relevant frameworks that preserve Black musical traditions. Through its pedagogical approach, JSU instills a sense of cultural responsibility, leadership, and the drive to lift up others. As Adams et al. (2016) write, social justice education aims to provide the tools to analyze oppression and take action to reform oppressive systems. JSU does precisely this. It transforms students from learners into leaders, from musicians into movement builders. Faculty encourage students to "think outside the box" because "some of these standards don't reflect who we are." In every facet of the music education program students are called to imagine, lead, and liberate. By fostering a culture of critical inquiry, cultural pride, and civic engagement, JSU ensures its graduates are prepared not only to succeed but to transform the world around them. In doing so, JSU affirms that music education is not only about the course content but about who is teaching, why the subject matter is taught, and how that teaching can shape a more equitable future.

JSU's cultural environment undoubtedly nurtures social consciousness and critical awareness. One must ask how this approach prepares students to transform predominantly White or institutionally rigid spaces after graduation. Are students being equipped to both affirm their identity and strategically challenge those systems that may not affirm them? A fine line exists between empowerment and insularity. Students must be trained to navigate systems of power while also resisting them. If the message is rooted in internal affirmation without providing strategies for external engagement, the risk is creating a sense of empowerment that may not be sustained under systemic resistance.

The push toward terminal degrees and leadership roles is also complicated. Encouraging advanced degrees is vital to increase Black representation in decision-making spaces. It also raises issues of gatekeeping in academia:

are students being guided into graduate programs with clear understanding of the labor expectations, debt burdens, and often exploitative dynamics found in institutions of higher education? In advocating for more Black doctoral-level educators, the field must also be held accountable for transforming those structures that have historically excluded them.

Lastly, there is the risk of romanticizing the JSU experience without examining its limitations. While students and faculty testimonies highlight life-changing mentorship and community, critical pedagogy must resist the temptation to frame institutions, especially HBCUs, as inherently liberatory. Even those institutions rooted in social justice are still constrained by larger systems. A critical response to JSU's music program would benefit from further reflection on challenges, in funding, institutional support, curriculum reform, or broader educational policy. How do these factors impact the university's ability to deliver a transformative educational experience. To summarize, transformation is not guaranteed by intention alone. It requires rigorous reflection, structural support, and a willingness to interrogate our most cherished narratives of empowerment.

Empowerment through Liberatory Learning Spaces: Spelman College

Regarded as the oldest institution of higher education for women of color in the United States, Spelman College stands at a powerful intersection of race and gender in education. For me, Spelman has always been a sacred space, one rooted in empowerment. It empowered me over 25 years ago and, remarkably, continues to empower me now as a faculty member. Many of the buildings remain just as I remember them, silent witnesses to my journey.

As I walk the campus, not a day goes by that I do not find myself transported to my time as a student. The memories usually rush in, especially when I walk The Oval. Its perfectly manicured lawn, laced with vibrant perennials, returns me to my new student orientation week. I remember the night before our induction into sisterhood, a tradition that still continues. Before sunrise, we were abruptly awakened and led to The Oval. Hand in hand, linked with our sisters in a circle that stretched around the green, we sang the Spelman hymn: "Spelman, thy name we praise, standard and honor raise . . . "

The crown jewel of The Oval is the Sisters Chapel. Six towering white columns frame its entrance, upholding the weight of generations of women's prayers and determination. Large semi-stained glass windows once opened wide during the sweltering Atlanta summers (when the chapel had no central air conditioning). There I first experienced the feeling of empowerment.

I sat beside my newfound sisters as Johnetta B. Cole, Spelman's first woman president, gave us our charge. Tall, poised, and wrapped in Spelman-blue Afro-centric regalia, she made her way to the podium. Her voice, deep and full of presence, rang out as she addressed us as "My Spelman Sisters." Her words were deliberate, each syllable enunciated with care. I felt goosebumps rise on my arms. Something was happening.

Was this excitement? Was it anxiety? Was it the weight of being the only one among my siblings who had chosen a college over 500 miles from home, that is, leaving Arkansas for Spelman instead of attending the University of Arkansas of Pine Bluff (UAPB)? Perhaps it was the beginning of something deeper. Whatever it was, it stayed with me. It grew over time and evolved, a spiritual awakening in the form of an indescribable sense of belonging. I knew that I belonged here. I am supposed to be here. For a young Black woman raised in Arkansas, that knowledge alone was transformative.

Perhaps it was fate—or divine intention?—that led me back to my alma mater. I walk these same grounds today not only as a graduate, but as an educator, a mentor, and a witness to what this institution continues to offer, a space to empower the next generation of leaders. I come to this campus, this sacred space, no longer a student, but as an example for my students, reminding them of what I have always known for myself. This place was built for me.

Spelman College, one of two Historically Black Colleges and Universities exclusively dedicated to the education of women (the other is Bennett College in Greensboro, North Carolina), represents a specialized space in which women are empowered to become leaders of positive social change. Black women are uniquely situated because they stand at the focal point at which three prevalent systems of oppression intersect: race, gender, and class (Collins, 2000). The concept of intersectionality (Crenshaw, 1989, pp. 139–167) recognizes that people experience multiple intersecting systems of oppression and privilege based on the social identities of race, gender, class, sexuality, and others. It acknowledges that the experiences cannot be understood by examining only one identity but rather through an intersectional lens that accounts for the interacting forms of oppression and privilege that shape people's lives.

Two primary power structures, Whiteness and maleness, have dominated music education. Black women play a pivotal role in understanding intersectionality due to their experiences of oppression and their position at the nexus of multiple marginalized identities (Collins, 2000). Because Black women's lived experience stands at the focal point of systems of oppression, that is of race, class, gender, and sexuality, awareness of this intersectionality enables music practitioners to look for other spaces in which inequality arises.

These spaces have fostered conditions in which Black women were accepted, validated, and able to thrive without being subject to stereotypes or the constant need for self-justification. For a Black woman, having her own space means having a place in which she feels safe, empowered, and free to be her authentic self. This space that allows her to express her thoughts, feelings, and experiences without judgment or fear of discrimination (Grissom-Broughton, in preparation).

Spelman College embodies this mission by providing both a culturally and gender responsive education. An array of courses helps students develop rhetorical skills, an awareness of social processes, and a vision of themselves as social change agents (Jordan, 2011). This environment empowers young African-American women who are subjected to racial and gender oppression.

"A Choice to Change the World"

Spelman prides itself in offering students a unique learning environment to become agents of social change. The school is intentional in its efforts to ensure its students are equipped to become critical thinkers and to raise their consciousness on issues related to women and women of color. Key aspects that contribute to Spelman's distinctiveness are (1) an emphasis on the holistic development of Black women, (2) a commitment to sisterhood and community, (3) acknowledgment of the intersectionality of its students' identities, (4) representation of Black women in leadership, (5) a focus on social justice and activism, and (6) preservation of its rich history and legacy.

From their arrival on campus, Spelman students are immersed in the college's mission: to empower the whole person, cultivate an appreciation for global cultures, and inspire a commitment to positive social change (Spelman College, 2024) Even before entering the gates, visitors are greeted by bold banners along the driveway and campus walkways that display powerful messages and the faces of Spelman students and faculty. Among the most prominent is the college's signature phrase: A Choice to Change the World. This motto signals to all who enter that choosing Spelman is choosing to become a change agent.

Spelman's mission is not only communicated through banners and slogans but through music. In addition to learning the Spelman hymn, students are taught the College song, aptly titled after the motto. Written by Spelman music alumna Sarah Stephens Benibo this stirring piece has become Spelman's musical mantra, performed at major college events and at occasions that promote social justice. Its lyrics capture the spirit of Spelman's charge:

> It's my choice, and I choose to change the world.
> It's my voice and I speak with pride and courage.
> I'll be the change I wanna see, I'll scream out loud and say,

> It's my choice, and I choose to change the world.
>
> The change begins today, with every choice that I make.
>
> Spelman, look around and see where the changes need to be.
>
> End poverty, fighting overseas; Another dies from a disease.
>
> End hypocrisy, starving on the streets, and no one does a single thing (https://www.youtube.com/watch?v=Ww-UeXL87r0)
> (Spelman College, 2024)

This ethos of empowerment is further instilled through the First-Year Experience Seminar, a two-semester, required general education course that introduces students to Spelman's core values: academic excellence, leadership, and service. Through reflective essays, community service projects, seminar discussions, and the development of a writing portfolio, students begin to examine ethical leadership and social change in both personal and collective contexts.

Such an institutional culture shapes how music is taught at Spelman. Students are seen not simply as musicians, singers, or educators but as Black women and future leaders who use music as a tool for justice, expression, and healing. Music becomes a vehicle for social transformation.

Across the curriculum, faculty employ culturally responsive pedagogies that reflect the lived experiences of Black women. Classrooms are nurtured as safe spaces in which students are encouraged to express their ideas without fear of judgment. These environments foster student agency through discussion, research, and creative projects.

Even in traditionally Eurocentric courses such as History of Western Music, Spelman faculty reframe the narrative to include Black women's presence. According to the course syllabus, students facilitate class discussions by reflecting on how each unit connects to their identity as Black women. One student says,

> At the beginning of class, Dr. Green reminds us every week to center ourselves in the topic. At first, I thought music history was just about a bunch of old dead white men! But Dr. G always finds a way to include a woman composer. Even if they're not Black women, she gets us to see ourselves in the story. Like, when we studied medieval music, she showed us paintings with Black people playing instruments. That made me feel like, "Oh wow. I was there too." Even if they didn't include me in the book! (Tiana Mitchell, personal communication, February 20, 2024)

Another students adds:

> Right! And that we [Black women] were making all kind of music [starts counting fingers] in Mali, Ghana, Nigeria . . . Oh, we were still doing our thing! If these books just now including Hildegard, it's gonna be another

100 years before they find some music by a Black woman written in the Medieval period. Maybe I should find it!! [Students erupt in laughter.] (Malia Watkins, personal communication, February 20, 2024)

Through such liberatory practices, Spelman fosters learning spaces in which students, especially those who may not have previously felt empowered to share their voices, can be heard. These pedagogical approaches validate students' experiences and help them see themselves as artists, scholars, and agents of change.

"My Presence Is My Social Justice"

Spelman College offers a liberatory educational environment that centers the lived experiences, identities, and empowerment of young African American women, particularly in the face of the racial and gendered oppression. The music program exemplifies this liberatory vision. It has evolved in tandem with the Spelman's mission, shaped by social, political, and cultural movements that have influenced the lives of Black women. The curriculum prioritizes issues central to Black women's musical experiences and affirms their cultural and creative contributions.

While Collins (2000) was not referring to Spelman specifically, her assertion that the presence of Black women in academic spaces is a radical act can certainly be applied to the context of Spelman College. For Black women to occupy academic, artistic, and professional music spaces from which they have historically been excluded is a political statement. Their presence challenges cultural erasure, disrupts academic gatekeeping, and redefines who belongs and whose knowledge holds value. To be a Black woman, fully visible and unapologetically authentic, is an act of resistance. As one aptly states, "In a world that often renders Black women invisible, Spelman's music program makes them the center of the narrative" (Sage Davis, personal communication, February 23, 2024).

This pedagogical approach draws on resistant capital (Yosso, 2005), which refers to the knowledge and strategies marginalized people develop to challenge inequality. At Spelman, students and educators engage in practices that resist normative standards in music education, standards that often invalidate Black women's musical contributions or demand assimilation into Eurocentric ideals. The idea that "My presence is my social justice" encapsulates the daily resistance by Spelman students and faculty. One educator reflected,

> You don't always have to be on the picket lines to be political. Learn your craft, practice, study. Be better than the best. When you sit in certain rooms,

you're making a political statement. When you get accepted to certain graduate programs, you're making a statement. For me, as a Black woman, my presence is my social justice. (Janice Spencer, personal communication, February 22, 2024)

This intentional, informed, and empowered presence is transformative. It resists invisibility, challenges oppression, and makes space for future generations. Hess (2019) reminds us that music education should not be limited to technical skill or aesthetic appreciation; it must also be about empowerment, activism, and social justice, particularly at a time when young people are navigating the forces of racism, sexism, classism, and other systems of oppression.

One of the most powerful examples of this philosophy is the Music Seminar, a weekly gathering of music students that includes student recitals, guest performances, lectures, and workshops. What distinguishes this space is its focus on celebrating Black women in music. Many of the guest speakers and workshop leaders are accomplished Black women working in various sectors of the music industry. One student reflects,

I especially like Music Seminar because of all the women we get to meet. Like, there are Black women in fields where I didn't think we exist. To meet women like Rhianna Giddens and to be able to talk with them one-on-one and talk about their life, and just how they're able to overcome so much as a woman of color, lets me know that I can make a huge impact on the world too. Even if I just start in my community or just here on campus. (Allana Smith, personal communication, February 28, 2024)

The intimate, affirming environment of Music Seminar encourages students to engage with questions of identity, creativity, and resistance. It raises their consciousness about how race, gender, and other forces intersect with their musical journeys. Showcasing Black women as leading experts and artists in the music industry sends a powerful message that their contributions are both vital and celebrated.

Seeing Black women's impactful roles can inspire other underrepresented people, showing them that they, too, can make a significant impact in music. By amplifying the experiences of underrepresented groups, colleges can challenge traditional norms that have perpetuated inequality in music education. This act encourages an inclusive representation in the music industry, enriching the learning experience for all students. Moreover, this approach helps dismantle the barriers that have prevented certain groups from pursuing careers in music and leads to greater representation in the profession.

Spelman College serves as a powerful model of what is possible when learning environments are designed to affirm and empower Black women and other marginalized groups. While single-sex institutions are often assumed to be inherently empowering for women, McCall (2019) reminds us that they, like coeducational settings, are shaped by broader cultural forces. McCall's work highlights the importance of examining how factors such as race, gender, class, religion, and ethnicity intersect. What sets it apart is Spelman's ability to cultivate a liberatory environment in which women of color can fully integrate their cultural heritage into their academic journey.

Rather than debate whether music education for Black women in higher education should occur in single-sex or coeducational settings, the more urgent question may be: what can we learn from environments like Spelman, spaces crafted for those whose identities lie at the intersection of multiple systems of oppression? These institutions offer a compelling vision of what music education can be when liberated from the constraints of exclusionary traditions. Research affirms that women's colleges provide critical components such as personal support, visible role models, inclusive curricula, and institutional missions grounded in excellence and equity (Collins, 2001).

Spelman exemplifies this educational vision. Its music program is neither focused on female dominance or feminist theory nor limited to teaching about women. Rooted in a pedagogy of liberation, it creates a space in which all students, regardless of gender, are invited to engage critically, creatively, and collectively in their own education. When education affirms identity, honors culture, and resists oppressive structures, it becomes a transformative force. As higher education institutions work to dismantle systemic inequities, they would do well to draw inspiration from Spelman's example in which music education is empowerment, affirmation, and a radical act of justice.

In summary, consciousness and cultural empowerment in music education represents a transformative approach that presents a culturally inclusive curricula, emphasizes music's historical role in resisting oppression, and prioritizes affirming identity while fostering personal and collective empowerment. Both JSU and Spelman College exemplify this transformative vision through their distinct, yet aligned, commitments to music education that cultivates leadership, critical consciousness, and social agency.

JSU's coeducational model, rooted in the traditions of HBCU bands and instrumental music, builds empowerment through ensemble performance, community identity, and the collective power of sound. Spelman, on the other hand, engages a Black feminist pedagogical framework designed exclusively for Black women, offering a liberatory space in which students' voices, culture, and experiences are centered. Despite their differences in focus, both institutions share a common goal: to promote music education as a catalyst to develop students who can challenge societal norms and become agents of change.

DeAngelis's (2022) research underscores the impact of institutions such as JSU and Spelman have in diversifying music education. The research notes that HBCUs and Hispanic-serving institutions account for nearly one-third of all Black and one-fourth of all Latino music education graduates. Further research is needed to understand the unique experiences of pre-service teachers of color in HBCU music education programs, and to examine the broader role these institutions play in reshaping the music teaching profession.

Black feminist pedagogy (not always labeled as such) is transformational in nature and has long been practiced in HBCUs through their mission to shape students committed to social justice. As hooks (1994) and Love (2019) caution, the presence of impressive and empowering mission statements do not guarantee liberatory teaching practices. Indeed, HBCUs can at times reproduce authoritarian models of education that stifle students' voices and reinforce hegemonic norms. As hooks (2003) reminds us, "White supremacy thinking can be taught by teachers of any race," (p. 79) and the dominance of conservative values in some HBCUs may perpetuate mainstream ideals centered on obedience and conformity rather than critical thought and transformation. Empowering students requires educators to engage in transformation themselves, often in ways that resist dominant cultural and institutional norms.

Ultimately, the examples of JSU and Spelman highlight the power of music education to serve as a liberatory force, one that affirms identity, cultivates resistance, and equips students to employ their artistry to engage in social change. These institutions offer compelling models to reimagine how music can be taught, not merely as a discipline of sound and technique, but as a practice of freedom.

References

Adams, M., Goodman, D., Joshi, K. Y., & Bell, L. A. (2016). *Teaching for diversity and social justice.* Routledge.

Albritton, T. J. (2012). Educating our own: The historical legacy of HBCUs and their relevance for educating a new generation of leaders. *The Urban Review, 44*(3), 311–331. https://doi.org/10.1007/s11256-012-0202-9

Collins, P. H. (2000). *Black feminist thought: Knowledge, consciousness, and the politics of empowerment.* Routledge.

Collins, A. C. (2001). *Socialization at two Black women's colleges: Bennett College and Spelman College.* Publication No. 249993735 Doctoral dissertation. University of Pittsburg. ProQuest Dissertation & Theses.

Crenshaw, K. W. (1989). *Demarginalizing the intersectionality of race and sex: A Black feminist critique of antidiscrimination doctrine, feminist theory and antiracist politics.* University of Chicago Legal Forum.

Daniels, K., Hicks, K., & Plummer, M. (2017). Historically Black colleges and universities: A history of community engagement. In C. Dolgon, T. Mitchell, & T. Eatman (Eds.), *The Cambridge handbook of service learning and* community engagement (pp. 64–70). Cambridge University Press. http://doi.org/10.1017/9781316650011.007

DeAngelis, D. R. (2022). Recent college graduates with bachelor's degrees in music education: A demographic profile. *Journal of Music Teacher Education, 32*(1), 25–37.

Diemer, M. A., Pinedo, A., Bañales, J., Mathews, C. J., Frisby, M. B., Harris, E. M., & McAlister, S. (2021). Recentering action in critical consciousness. *Child Development Perspectives, 15*(1), 12–17.

Freeman, S., & Gasman, M. (2014). The characteristics of historically Black college and university presidents and their role in grooming the next generation of leaders. *Teachers College Record, 116*(7), 1–34.

Freire, P. (1974). Education for critical consciousness. *Continuum.*

Gasman, M., & McMickens, T. L. (2010). Liberal or professional education? The missions of public Black colleges and universities and their impact on the future of African Americans. *Souls, 12*(3), 286–305.

Gasman, M., Spencer, D., & Orphan, C. (2015). "Building bridges, not fences": A history of civic engagement at private Black colleges and universities, 1944–1965. *History of Education Quarterly, 55*(3), 346–379.

Gasman, M. & Tudico, C. L. (Eds.) (2008), *Historically Black colleges and universities: Triumphs, troubles, and taboos.* Palgrave Macmillan.

Hess, J. (2019). *Music education for social change: Constructing an activist music education.* Routledge.

hooks, b. (1994). *Teaching to transgress: Education as the practice of freedom.* Routledge.

hooks, B. (2003). *Teaching community: A pedagogy of hope.* Routledge.

Jordan, Z. (2011). "Found" literacy partnerships: Service and activism at Spelman college. *Reflections, 10*(2), 38–62.

Lewis, M. K., & Lee, A. K. (2009). Critical consciousness in introductory psychology: A historically black university context. *Pedagogy and the Human Sciences, 1*(1), 50–60.

Lomax, M. L. (2006). Historically Black colleges and universities: Bringing a tradition of engagement into the twenty-first century. *Journal of Higher Education Outreach and Engagement, 11*(3), 5–14.

Love, B. (2019). *We want to do more than survive: Abolitionist teaching and the pursuit of educational freedom.* Beacon Press.

McCall, S. D. (2019). *Girls, single-sex schools, and postfeminist fantasies.* Routledge.

National Association of Music. (2024). *The higher education arts data services (HEADS.* https://nasm.arts-accredit.org/services/heads/)

Nelson, M. K. (2013). Fictive kin, families we choose, and voluntary kin: What does the discourse tell us?. *Journal of Family Theory & Review, 5*(4), 259–281. https://doi.org/10.1111/jftr.12019

Palmer, R. T., & Young, E. (2023). The uniqueness of an HBCU environment: How a supportive campus climate promotes student success. In T. L. Strayhorn & M. C. Terrell (Eds.), *The evolving challenges of Black college students* (pp. 138–160). Routledge.

Schmidt, P. (2005). Music education as transformative practice: Creating new frameworks for learning music through a Freirian perspective. *Visions of Research in Music Education, 6*(1), 22. http://www.rider.edu/~vrme

Spelman College. (2024). Spelman's history and traditions handbook. *Spelman College Office of Alumnae Engagement.* https://www.spelman.edu/_1_Docs-and-Files/alumnae/FINAL-Spelman-HistTraditions-Brochure-95-20240806-Rev3.pdf

Stewart, G., Wright, D., Perry, T., & Rankin, C. (2008). Historically Black colleges and universities: Caretakers of precious treasure. *Journal of College Admission,* (201), 24–29. Fall.

Wilkerson, A., Stanislaus, E. P., & Hodge, L. (2021). Teaching first-year seminar: The hidden curriculum of culture, history, and heritage at historically Black Colleges and universities. *Race and Pedagogy Journal, 5*(2).

Yosso, T. J. (2005). Whose culture has capital? A critical race theory discussion of community cultural wealth. *Race, Ethnicity and Education, 8*(1), 69–91. https://doi.org/10.1080/1361332052000341006

Additional Reading

Grissom-Broughton, P. (In preparation). A space of our own. Perspectives of music education at a Black women's college. In N. McBride & C. Sears (Eds.), *The Oxford handbook of gender and queer studies in music education.* Oxford University Press.

Omolade, B. (1987). A Black feminist pedagogy. *Women's Studies Quarterly, 15*(3/4), 32–39.

CHAPTER 9

IMPLICATIONS, RECOMMENDATIONS FOR POLICY AND PRACTICE

ABSTRACT

Drawing on themes of consciousness and cultural empowerment explored through chapters 6, 7, and 8, this final chapter outlines tri-faceted model of education centered on resistance, cultural memory, and collective uplift. Chapter 9 positions Historically Black Colleges and Universities as models of a music education that affirms identity, resists marginalization, and centers Black musical traditions in and beyond the curriculum.

Three key pedagogical orientations emerge: a resistance pedagogy that challenges Eurocentric musical hierarchies and affirms Black musical excellence; a pedagogy of cultural memory that positions music as both historical record and living archive; and a pedagogy of collective responsibility that emphasizes service, intergenerational mentorship, and communal restoration through music. These intersecting approaches not only empower students to navigate dominant systems, but also equip them to reshape them through critical consciousness and artistic agency.

This chapter argues that the field of music education must move toward a decolonized, deconstructed, and democratized framework, one that centers Historically Black Colleges and Universities (HBCUs) not on the margins, but at the heart of the discourse. Listening to the voices of HBCU educators and students during this moment of social and educational reckoning offers a way forward, in which music education becomes a practice of freedom, and where cultural affirmation, justice, and transformation are its primary goals.

HBCUs continue to serve as epicenters of cultural preservation, artistic innovation, and educational justice. Far beyond their historical role in granting access to higher education for Black students, HBCUs have emerged as dynamic spaces in which identity is affirmed, Black musical traditions are elevated, and students are prepared to lead with pride. In music education these institutions offer a powerful counter narrative to frameworks that often marginalize the contributions of Black musicians, educators, and scholars.

Each HBCU carries its own unique cultural, historical, and pedagogical imprint. In this book, I have engaged with eight distinct institutions not as representatives of them all, but as microcosms of the varied ecosystem that is Black higher education. Through the lens of consciousness and cultural empowerment, I have explored how music programs across these campuses affirm identity, value cultural assets, and foster transformative empowerment.

Consciousness and cultural empowerment reflects what HBCUs have been accomplishing for generations: teaching that centers Blackness, lifts up cultural heritage, resists dominant deficit narratives, and empowers students to become agents of change. Study of each of these eight institutions reveals a unique story of how music becomes a pathway to self-knowledge, liberation, and leadership. In the order they appear in this book, these eight institutions are:

Morehouse College reflects self-definition through cultural duality, in which Black men are invited to resist external narratives and articulate their own definitions of identity through musical expression, brotherhood, and critical engagement. Morehouse cultivates artists rewriting what it means to be Black, male, and musically excellent in America.

Howard University exemplifies self-discovery through cultural immersion. As the first HBCU to offer a degree in jazz studies, Howard has long been a trailblazer in legitimizing Black musical forms. Its curriculum fosters deep engagement with Black musical traditions, in which students uncover their cultural power and develop a sense of self through artistic exploration.

Tuskegee University offers self-affirmation through cultural heritage. Once home to Booker T. Washington and a foundational site for Black music education in the South, Tuskegee invites students to see themselves

Implications, Recommendations for Policy and Practice   173

reflected in the music they perform and study, and to forge connections to cultural pride even on a campus known for its science, industry, and vocational excellence.

Fisk University stands as one of the great preservers of cultural assets. With a legacy rooted in the Jubilee Singers, Fisk continues to safeguard the historical soundscape of Black spirituals. Through its preservation of American music history, the university maintains its role as a steward of cultural memory earning Grammy recognition in the process.

Tennessee State University stands out as a producer of cultural assets, innovatively blending elements of Black musical traditions with the precision of HBCU band culture. Its Grammy-winning performance signals not only student excellence but affirms the HBCU's rightful place on the global stage of artistic innovation and recognition.

Florida A&M University (FAMU) emerges as a promoter of cultural assets. Through iconic performance traditions like the Marching 100 and the cultural work of the Julian Cannonball and Nathaniel Adderley Music Institute, FAMU ensures that Black music is not only performed and celebrated, but also critically studied, preserved, and passed forward.

Jackson State University (JSU) demonstrates transformation through purpose-driven teaching. Beyond its iconic Sonic Boom of the South, JSU has produced generations of music educators, men and women who return to classrooms, churches, and communities equipped to inspire and empower the next wave of musicians through culturally relevant and socially responsive pedagogy.

Spelman College offers empowerment through liberatory learning spaces. At Spelman, we see how music education affirms the lived experiences of Black women. Through this pedagogical approach, students are nurtured not only as musicians but as cultural thinkers and change agents equipped to use their voices for transformation.

Together, these eight institutions reveal a rich and diverse tapestry of Black musical pedagogy and expression. They show what is possible when music education is infused with cultural consciousness and historical awareness. They resist erasure and create space. They sound the alarm for a more just future. They demonstrate how, in the face of oppression, HBCUs have long created alternative spaces, places in which music is lived and students explore the fullness of their identities.

Three Common Themes

In Chapter 5, I posed a series of five critical questions to guide the exploration of the unique educational practices in HBCUs. These five questions are: What content is most relevant to teach in these spaces? Who should

Table 9.1.

Three Themes, Descriptions, and Approaches

Theme	Description	Pedagogical Approach
Multi-navigation of respectability, resistance, and activism	Black musical forms are centered, challenging eurocentric definitions of excellence	Resistance pedagogy
Music as historical memory and cultural archive	Music preserves and transmits Black history in the absence of official recognition	Culturally responsive and culturally sustaining approaches
Collective mission of community responsibility and musical uplift	Music is taught as a form of service and communal uplift, particularly for the Black community	Inter-generational mentorship and fictive kinship

be teaching (and learning) this content? How do cultural and historical factors influence pedagogical practices? What is the academic and musical transformation that takes place in these institutions? How is it exemplified in the lives of students and the broader community? The answers to these questions emerge through three key cross-case considerations that serve as this discussion's themes (See Table 9.1). Each theme is supported by a description of how it is manifested in practice, along with the corresponding pedagogical approach used to support student learning.

The Theme of Multi-Navigation of Respectability, Resistance, and Activism

Excluded from research on elite conservatories and White-dominated institutions, HBCUs have built rigorous and innovative music programs of their own. From Howard's pioneering efforts in Classical and jazz studies to Spelman's affirming work on Black women composers, these programs reflect a longstanding tradition of Black educational self-determination.

At many of these institutions the curriculum itself becomes an act of resistance (Regelski, 2014; Talbot & Williams, 2019). The inclusion of Black musical forms, the elevation of historically marginalized composers, and the centering of Africa and the diaspora in music history are forms of curricular justice. What is taught and how it is taught carries political and cultural weight in spaces long excluded from shaping the dominant musical canon. This pedagogical approach is expansion, not assimilation. HBCUs resist the idea that legitimacy be defined by Whiteness.

And yet there remains a paradox at the heart of many HBCU music programs: the emphasis on European Classical music, a tradition often viewed as the epitome of Western dominance among musical genres. Why would institutions dedicated to affirming Black identity center this repertoire? The answer lies in a both-and rather than an either-or approach. HBCUs understand the dominant culture. They teach Bach and Brahms to ensure students are fluent in the languages of power and access. This strategic navigation (Yosso, 2005) positions students to enter graduate programs, orchestras, and institutions that still gatekeep legitimacy. At HBCUs, that canon is taught in a context steeped in Black cultural pride, critique, and resistance; these transform its meaning.

This approach exemplifies multi-navigation: honoring technical discipline and artistic excellence while simultaneously disrupting the hierarchy that positions European music as superior. Students are encouraged both to master dominant forms and to reimagine them, placing gospel, jazz, hip-hop, and African diasporic traditions on an equal footing. Faculty teach European music alongside conversations about erasure, power, and cultural ownership. Not submission, it is subversion through fluency.

Such pedagogy is deeply political. HBCUs are spaces in which respectability, resistance, and activism are not contradictions but coexisting strategies of survival and transformation. The resilience here is not passive endurance but what Du Bois (1903) called a "dogged strength," an intellectual resistance that repurposes the tools of exclusion to serve the goals of liberation. Indeed, as Bonner et al. (2024) note, one forthright manifestation of Black resilience has been the ability to use counterculture and counternarratives to combat racism. HBCU music programs do precisely this: they counter the Eurocentric definition of musical excellence by embedding Black culture at the core of academic study.

This philosophy carries over into pedagogy. In many HBCUs classrooms students are not only recipients of knowledge, but active participants in shaping culturally inclusive music education. They are empowered to critique the canon, ask why certain composers are elevated over others, and propose alternatives rooted in their own lived experiences. The teaching approach itself becomes a form of activism by centering dialog, cultural affirmation, and critical consciousness.

Yet this navigation is not without tension. As McCall (2015) found, Black students who studied music at HBCUs and later pursued graduate degrees at primarily White institutions often found that their racial identity and their HBCU education were viewed as inferior. This response reveals the devaluation of Black institutions and culture in music academia, further underscoring the need for HBCUs to prepare students to navigate multiple worlds.

Through this multi-dimensional pedagogy students, having developed both technical fluency and critical awareness, are equipped to move fluidly among musical traditions. They gain not just the ability to perform, but the power to ask the question: Whose music matters? Who gets to decide? How do we honor our own?

At HBCUs, the curriculum embraces a both-and mindset:

> Both the technical discipline of Bach and the soul-stirring power of gospel.
>
> Both the respect for tradition and the courage to reimagine it.
>
> Both the mastery of dominant forms and the affirmation of Black cultural genius.

This both-and approach is a radical form of resistance and resilience. It refuses to choose between visibility and authenticity and declares that Black music is, in all its forms, central to the musical world.

The Theme of Music as Historical Memory and Cultural Archive

Far beyond their academic mandates, HBCUs function as living archives of Black life, embodying the collective struggle, triumph, and creativity of African Americans in a nation that has marginalized their voices. These institutions house historic structures that testify to the enduring fight for educational access and racial justice. In this way, HBCUs do not only preserve Black history, they assert its centrality in the American narrative. As Cotton et al. (2017) notes, these campuses are "living embodiments" of resilience, offering a counter-memory to the selective portrayals found in some cultural histories.

From the spirituals sung by Fisk University's Jubilee Singers to the legacy of William Dawson's spiritual arrangements at Tuskegee, HBCUs have served as the guardians of Black musical heritage. Through these practices, all eight institutions highlighted in this book demonstrated a mission to elevate Black music not only as tradition, but as an act of cultural preservation. Forms such as spirituals, gospel, jazz, and HBCU band culture are central to a pedagogy that insists Black cultural expression is essential not only to Black History, but to America's history.

In doing so, HBCUs actively resist erasure and affirm the value of cultural memory and production of the contributions of Black music. As Roebuck and Murty (1993) and Tatini-Smith et al. (2013) emphasize, HBCUs offer culturally relevant and racially affirming environments that foster a healthy Black identity and support students in their journey of self-discovery. Rather than adopt a deficit-based view, these institutions champion Black cultural capital and help students see themselves not as exceptions, but as extensions of a lineage of excellence. This effort is connected to what Favors (2019) describes as the "second curriculum," the ideological, artistic, and spiritual education that runs parallel to academic learning. Through this second curriculum HBCUs cultivate acts as sites of cultural archives where Black music is preserved, studied, and reimagined.

This work of cultural preservation is deeply political. HBCUs are uniquely positioned to combat historical amnesia (that is the tendency to reduce slavery, racism, and dispossession to past mistakes) and confront such dispossession as ongoing structures of oppression (Plummer et al., 2024; Thomas-Durrell, 2022). In a society in which identity erasure is normalized, HBCUs reclaim what has been silenced. Through intentional engagement with Black musical traditions, these schools offer students tools to locate themselves in a broader diasporic context. The schools help students see themselves as part of a historical and artistic lineage, a lineage that both resists Whiteness-centered narratives of musical knowledge.

This practice is particularly powerful in a music education system that embeds Whiteness and contributes to the erasure of racial and cultural diversity (Bradley et al., 2007), while Black cultural expression is often excluded, commodified, or trivialized. Hess (2019) argues that this erasure in music education can traumatize students, reproducing the coloniality in music education by denying the validity of musical forms rooted in African diasporic traditions. HBCUs counter this situation by restoring value to those forms through formal instruction, performance, and campus-wide cultural rituals in which choirs and marching bands are centerpieces of institutional identity.

W. E. B. Du Bois's concept of the veil offers a potent metaphor. The veil symbolizes the psychological and cultural alienation African Americans experience, being physically present in American society, but obscured in its dominant narratives and recognitions. HBCUs lift the veil. They both educate and illuminate, allowing students to see themselves reflected in the curriculum, the pedagogy, the institution's mission, and even in the physical landscape. This reflection offers the continuity of ensuring the longevity of one's culture. This notion is perhaps best captured in Beyoncé's "Black is King," when she states: "To live without reflection for so long might make you wonder if you even truly exist" (Knowles-Carter, 2020). HBCUs offer a mirror that reflects the depth, beauty, and power of the students' musical heritage.

Ultimately, HBCUs preserve more than sound. They serve as guardians of cultural memory, ancestral knowledge, and the rich musical legacy of the African American experience. Musical traditions in HBCUs provide a foundation through which students root their identities, reclaim their narratives, and connect to their heritage. When these traditions are sustained, future generations are empowered to explore their cultural history, understand their place in a broader historical and artistic continuum, and cultivate a strong sense of identity and pride. Such ongoing transmission fosters continuity and belonging, anchoring students in a lineage of artistic excellence and cultural resilience. In preserving these musical traditions, HBCUs do not only honor the past but ensure that the sounds of African Americans—their struggles, joy, resistance, and triumphs—continue to resonate across generations.

The Theme of Collective Mission of Community Responsibility and Musical Uplift

HBCUs' music programs are rooted in a legacy of collective excellence and communal responsibility. These institutions extend their mission beyond technical musical training to emphasize community uplift, cultural preservation, and intergenerational mentorship. In this framework, music is a vehicle for identity, service, and transformation.

A defining characteristic of these programs is their commitment to student well-being and collectivism. Rather than promoting individualism, HBCUs foster a pedagogy centered on care, cultural affirmation, and shared purpose. Success is measured not only by personal achievement but by one's contribution to the institution, the community, and the broader Black collective (Hawkins, 2021). This philosophy is lived out through curricula that embed civic engagement and social responsibility. As Lomax (2006) notes, service is a core academic value, not an extracurricular activity. Students are encouraged to engage directly with social issues through artistry and leadership.

Musical practice and social purpose are deeply intertwined in this context. Students are taught to view their craft not solely as personal expression or career preparation but as a tool for cultural affirmation and social justice. Ricard and Brown (2008) emphasize that HBCUs aim to cultivate leaders who understand the complexities of the African American experience and contribute meaningfully to broader societal progress. Music education, therefore, becomes a method of both personal empowerment and public service.

Integral to these programs is the tradition of musical lineage and mentorship. Knowledge is passed through enduring teacher-student relationships that often span several generations and multiple HBCU institutions. Such a musical genealogy can easily be traced. I experienced this firsthand during my studies at Spelman College with Joyce Finch Johnson, who had studied under John W. Work III at Fisk University. Jazz scholar Gary Thomas studied at Howard University with Fred Irby III, a Grambling State graduate mentored by Frederick Tillis of Wiley College. James Ferdinand, former director of the Aeolians at Oakwood University, studied conducting at Morgan State with Nathan Carter, a Hampton University alumnus.

Morehouse College presents a particularly vivid example: David Morrow, director of the Glee Club, noted that in over a century, the group has only had three directors, each a student of his predecessor. Composer Carlos Simon, a graduate of Morehouse, studied under composer and Morehouse alumna Uzee Brown, who was mentored by Wendell Whalum Sr., a lineage that speaks to the continuity of Black musical excellence.

This intergenerational transmission is reinforced by the ethic of fictive kinship, in which students, faculty, and alumni form familial bonds grounded in a shared cultural purpose (Nelson, 2013; Stewart et al., 2008). Faculty serve as othermothers, mentors, and elders who provide both academic rigor and emotional support (Guiffrida, 2004). Many students choose HBCUs because of this familial legacy, cultural pride, or historical significance. This legacy-based mentorship nurtures belonging and reminds students of their lineage of artistic and intellectual excellence. Through oral tradition and sustained guidance, HBCU music programs prepare not just musicians, but cultural stewards.

These values are embodied in the music itself. At HBCUs, music is treated as a form of cultural inheritance. Students are taught that their musical gifts carry a responsibility to honor the traditions from which they come and to serve others through their craft. This commitment extends beyond the campus. Many HBCU music programs provide free concerts, workshops, and cultural events that enrich surrounding communities and broaden access to the arts. These public offerings are both outreach initiatives and extensions of the institutional mission to democratize culture and preserve the HBCU's musical legacy.

In summary, HBCU music programs do more than affirm identity, value cultural assets, or embrace transformative empowerment. They collectively reimagine music education through a culturally grounded, community-centered lens. By centering Black musical forms and challenging Eurocentric definitions of excellence, these programs act as living repositories of historical memory, preserving and transmitting Black history in ways that often bypass official recognition. They uphold a collective mission of community responsibility in which music is taught both as a craft and as a form of service, healing, and communal restoration.

These themes reflect a broader educational vision: to cultivate not only excellent musicians but culturally rooted artist-scholars, sustainers of Black musical traditions who understand their work as both art and activism. Students are nurtured in environments that empower them to become socially conscious leaders capable of navigating multiple consciousnesses. While traditional institutions often need to create such affirming spaces, at HBCUs these environments are foundational, inherited, and lived.

A Template for Challenging Ideologies in Music Education

HBCUs have been integral to American higher education for over a century, yet they remain largely absent from research on music education. Only recently have scholars begun to critically examine the musical experiences in these institutions. Two of them, Jackson and Nunn (2003), assert that HBCUs were founded in response to two prevailing realities in the US: the legal enforcement of racial segregation and the societal norms that denied Black people access to equitable education, including in music. I argue that these same two realities—legal exclusion and racial bias—continue to marginalize HBCUs in music education. The historical forces that necessitated the founding of HBCUs remain the very ones that exclude them from scholarly discourse.

Understanding the origins of HBCUs is essential to understanding their omission in academic narratives about music education. Just as Black communities were systematically excluded from broader educational opportunities, HBCUs have been overlooked in favor of institutions that uphold the Western European musical canon as the benchmark of excellence. This narrow focus continues to marginalize the musical contributions of HBCUs, privileging traditionally White colleges and universities and Eurocentric traditions over culturally diverse expressions.

Despite the vibrant musical legacies that thrive on HBCU campuses, the lack of empirical research on the lived experiences of their students, faculty, and alumni is striking. These institutions offer critical insights into how music functions as cultural affirmation, resilience, and resistance, insights long ignored or undervalued in dominant educational books and major studies. The study of HBCU music programs not only uncovers their historical contributions but also provides powerful models for addressing urgent issues in music education today, including diversity, equity, inclusion, and political engagement. To move the field forward is to examine how historical oppression and ongoing biases have resulted in the academic neglect of HBCUs. Such an examination challenges the dominant ideologies that have long obtained in music education.

In Part One of this book I recommend using the historical and socio-cultural contexts, along with the themes explored in Part Two, as a framework for reimagining music education through three critical lenses: decolonization, deconstruction, and democratization. These interconnected approaches offer a necessary antidote to the exclusionary practices that have defined music education and provide a foundation for a more just, inclusive, and culturally responsive scholarship.

Decolonization

To colonize is to take control of a people or an area, often as an extension of state power. In education, colonization imposes cultural values and knowledge systems that marginalize other values and systems. Colonization goes beyond overt oppression to enforce a worldview that shapes how knowledge is defined, taught, and valued. Modern universities continue to reflect these colonial legacies in their curricula and in their determination of whose knowledge is considered legitimate. Stein (2022) explains that colonization in academia involves appropriating space and subjugating others in order to maintain dominance.

Ashcroft et al. (2013) define decolonization as "the process of revealing and dismantling colonialist power in all its forms," including the institutional and cultural systems that uphold it (p. 79). Rosabal-Coto (2019) calls for the removal of systems that maintain both material and symbolic forms of colonization. Decolonization does not simply concern representation but promotes a radical transformation of power structures, worldviews, and institutional practices that have long marginalized non-dominant voices.

Music education is a prime example of a colonized system. Hess (2015) argues that when Western Classical music is positioned as the default, the curriculum itself becomes a colonizing force. Various types of the music of the African diaspora, as well as that of Indigenous communities and popular genres, are often excluded or presented without a cultural context. This trivialization reinforces curricular hierarchies that act as forms of epistemic control and maintain the supremacy of Eurocentric traditions.

The foundations of many elite academic institutions were laid during colonial eras in order to educate but also to propagate White supremacy through the codification of knowledge. African Americans were deliberately excluded from these institutions for centuries, which barred them from formal music education and academic recognition. Meanwhile, vibrant Black musical traditions thrived outside academia in churches, communities, and performance circuits. Yet this music was either ignored or distorted in universities. When finally acknowledged, these traditions were offered through a lens of cultural superiority rather than in genuine appreciation of their artistic and educational value.

In response to this entrenched inequity, Hess (2015) offers a comparative musics model that reframes music education as relational rather than hierarchical. All forms of music, including Western Classical music, are understood as cultural practices shaped by specific social, historical, and political contexts. Such a model encourages students to draw on their lived experiences and their identities as legitimate sources of musical inquiry. It positions music as a medium to develop skills and as a tool to critically engage with systems of power, race, and colonialism.

HBCUs have long embodied this decolonized vision. Their very existence resists colonial structures both symbolically and materially. Established in response to the exclusion of Black students from White institutions, HBCUs were designed as spaces of resistance, affirmation, and excellence. They have challenged dominant hierarchies by centering culturally responsive teaching to counteract the legacy of colonization and validate Black intellectual and artistic traditions (Buzzetto-Hollywood, 2023).

In music education, HBCUs have modeled the principles that scholars such as Hess advocate. Not a recent trend at HBCUs, culturally responsive teaching is foundational. Instruction is student-centered and affirming. Curricula reflect the students' culture. Faculty prioritize meaningful relationships built on care and respect. Black music is central, not supplementary, both in music programs and in the broader institution.

For generations, HBCUs have incorporated a decolonized framework as a deeply rooted philosophical commitment. These institutions provide affirming educational environments in which Black students are seen, heard, and valued, and music serves as a means of liberation rather than of assimilation. By modeling what inclusive and culturally responsive music education can look like, HBCUs actively redefine the colonial system. For institutions serious about equity, HBCUs offer both an inspiration and a blueprint, one the broader academic community must embrace if it hopes to move past performative inclusion toward a real transformation.

Deconstruction

Deconstruction, a philosophical theory developed by Jacques Derrida in the 1960s, challenges the assumption that meaning is fixed, stable, or absolute (Kates, 2005). Instead, it reveals that meaning is fluid, layered, and open to reinterpretation. A text, a curriculum, or a piece of music can hold multiple meanings. What is considered central can easily become marginal and vice versa. Derrida's goal was not to destroy meaning, but to uncover and question the assumptions that shape our thinking. Deconstruction is neither destruction nor relativism. Rather, it is a critical inquiry that questions binary thinking and highlights how power shapes knowledge. Deconstruction encourages us to scrutinize frameworks we take for granted.

In music education, deconstruction examines how hierarchies of value are built. A common binary in traditional curricula places Western Classical music as legitimate and non-Western or Black musical traditions as secondary. The US college-level music programs have long privileged European art music, relegating genres such as gospel, jazz, hip-hop, and spirituals to the margins, if they appear at all. Deconstruction exposes this hierarchy as a cultural construct rooted in historical power dynamics, not as a reflection of inherent musical value.

Implications, Recommendations for Policy and Practice 183

Schmidt (2012) applies Derrida's notion of deconstruction to music education through what he terms "dialog as deconstruction." Instead of viewing dialog as a process leading to consensus, Schmidt frames it as a space of conflict and multiplicity, conditions that foster critical thinking and creative exploration. Central to this approach is the idea of mis-listening, a deliberate disruption of conventional listening norms that encourages students to engage with sound in unfamiliar ways. Mis-listening, which is not misunderstanding, is an opportunity to reimagine meaning beyond dominant interpretations.

This reframing of dialog and listening parallels the experiences of non-Black faculty teaching at HBCUs. Making up approximately half of HBCU faculty, these faculty often report a heightened sense of self-awareness as they navigate unfamiliar cultural environments. These educators not only gain deeper insight into African American culture, but also confront and unlearn many of their previously held, misinformed assumptions (Closson & Henry, 2008). Such encounters illustrate deconstruction in practice, in which dominant norms are challenged and meaning constantly reshaped through engagement with the Other.

Dawson-Smith's (2006) research illustrates deconstruction in action. The author notes that White faculty members in predominantly Black institutions often struggle with cultural dissonance, their inability to apply the institutions' cultural practices. In deconstructive terms, this tension reveals a displacement of normative power: the fact that their default cultural assumptions no longer hold sway. What once dominated is now decentered, what was once marginalized is now foundational. Deconstruction is made tangible in institutional dynamics.

In such settings, White faculty must process a pedagogical unlearning, a deconstructive act that mirrors Derrida's assertion that meaning is always provisional. This unlearning recognizes the Other and allows difference to remain rather than be resolved. True dialog requires an ethical openness to what cannot be fully understood.

HBCUs embody this approach. In their music programs, the traditional authority of Western Classical music is recontextualized, and Black musical traditions reshape curricular hierarchies. These institutions normalize diverse content that reflects their students and communities, both through classroom teaching and performance repertoire. Ensembles routinely perform spirituals, gospel, jazz, and works by African American composers along with the traditional canon. In doing so, HBCUs enact what Derrida called "a play of differences," which creates space for multiple voices and interpretations without requiring a single dominant narrative.

This vision aligns with a growing movement in music education. Scholars such as Schmidt (2012, 2020), Bradley et al. (2007), and McCall (2017) emphasize critically examining curricula, pedagogical norms, and notions of success. Who is included? Who is left out? What definitions of excellence are upheld and why? Through this lens, deconstruction becomes a pedagogy of possibility. It invites educators to challenge fixed meanings, unlearn assumed truths, and center all students' lived experiences and cultural identities.

Democratization

Democratization, in the context of education, not only extends access but reshapes the structures, values, and practices that determine who gets to learn, who is heard, and what is considered legitimate knowledge. Much like decolonization, democratization is a process. It demands that we interrogate traditional hierarchies and build learning spaces responsive to the lived experiences of all students, especially those historically excluded from educational opportunity (Cipollone et al., 2022).

Democratization in music education challenges the privileging of Western Classical music as the standard of excellence. It asks: Whose music matters? Whose knowledge is centered? Whose stories are told? For far too long, the field has upheld narrow definitions of value. Gospel, hip-hop, go-go, jazz, spirituals, and other Black musical forms have been marginalized, regarded as supplemental rather than central. Democratizing music education means dismantling those constructs and re-centering other musical practices as equally worthy.

Jung (2021) distinguishes two dimensions of this work: democratization *of* and democratization *through* music education. The former refers to reimagining the field itself, that is transforming pedagogies and curricula to reflect values such as mutual respect, shared authority, and equity. Democratization through music education speaks to the broader goal, that of preparing students to live as citizens in a democratic society. It uses music to cultivate habits of cooperation, critical thought, and cultural understanding.

This approach aligns with what Love (2019) calls abolitionist teaching, a pedagogy rooted in resistance, justice, and liberation. Love argues that educators must be willing to fight for a radically different system. Just as abolitionists risked everything to end slavery, democratizing educators must confront and dismantle the structures that reproduce inequity.

Since no single formula is available, democratizing music education requires courage. Some educators might challenge inequitable audition practices that favor students with early access to private lessons. Others might curate performance repertoires that reflect students' cultural identities or create projects that address issues of social justice. Some advocate for LGBTQIA + inclusion; others work outside school walls, investing in community-based initiatives that expand access. All of these are acts of creative activism (Talbot & Williams, 2019), efforts to redistribute power and redefine music education.

The need for this work is urgent. Research by Goodwine (2019) shows that African American students are often overexposed to performance-based ensembles in K–12 schools but underprepared in other foundational areas such as theory and history. This disparity is a failure of the system. Overrepresentation of students in certain performance-based ensembles exposes a mismatch between students' strengths and how success is defined in college music programs. Walker (2007) and Kelly (2019) argue that success in music should not be measured solely by technical skill, but by an educator's ability to recognize and nurture the social, cultural, and historical knowledge students already possess. Democratization means validating these assets, not pathologizing them.

HBCUs embody this vision. From their founding missions to educate the formerly enslaved to their present-day practices of curricular inclusion, HBCUs have modeled what democratized music education can look like. These institutions often adopt alternative admissions criteria that value musicality in its many forms, not only by Western Classical music standards. They offer students life-changing access to rigorous programs without requiring them to shed their cultural identities. Ensembles routinely perform gospel, jazz, spirituals, and works by African American composers along with the Classical canon.

Democratization is a state of mind. It means seeing students not as empty vessels, but as co-creators of knowledge. It requires teachers to release control and embrace uncertainty. It is often a struggle toward a destination of dignity and freedom. This struggle must take place in every rehearsal, lesson plan, and faculty meeting. In the face of inequity silence indicates assent. To democratize music education is to reject silence and choose action. In the final analysis democratization, like deconstruction or decolonization, is a pedagogy of possibility. It offers the chance to remake music education into something more just, humane, and true to the people it serves. Reaching such a goal will not happen automatically; it requires intention.

Concluding Thoughts and Recommendations for Policy and Action

Despite their extraordinary contributions to American society, the relevance of HBCUs is still questioned in some circles. This doubt is rooted less in evidence than in a lack of familiarity. For many Americans, particularly those who are White, Asian, Hispanic, or live outside the South or East Coast, knowledge of HBCUs is limited to occasional media depictions of marching bands or sports rivalries (Koch & Swinton, 2022). Even in music education, HBCUs are frequently overlooked, their histories marginalized in both research and practice.

Yet HBCUs continue to play a vital role in American higher education. As Martin Luther King Jr., a Morehouse College alumnus, once noted, while HBCUs were born of segregation, they themselves were never segregated. Their founding was not rooted in exclusion, but in possibility. Today, although they represent less than 3% of all postsecondary institutions and enroll only 8% of African American students, HBCUs produce 20% of all Black college graduates, a staggering figure that affirms their impact (United Negro College Fund, 2023).

This success is not limited to academic metrics. Research has shown that HBCUs provide students cultural affirmation, community support, and a self-confidence that can be difficult to foster in predominantly White institutions (Allen, 1992; Gasman, 2025; Ponder, 2023; Stewart et al., 2008). A Gallup study confirmed that Black graduates of HBCUs report significantly more positive college experiences than their peers at non-HBCUs. These institutions cultivate more than musicians; they shape self-aware students and visionaries equipped to transform the world around them.

Still, HBCU's contributions to music education remain underrepresented in scholarship. Despite rich musical histories, their music programs are rarely examined through scholarly lenses. We need research that critically engages with HBCU music programs from historical, pedagogical, and philosophical perspectives. Including these voices enriches our understanding of what music education can be. Centering these perspectives invites us to reimagine the field as more inclusive, more just, and more reflective of the spectrum of American musical experiences.

Structural Barriers and Policy Challenges

While HBCUs have demonstrated resilience, they continue to face at least three structural and societal challenges that hinder the growth of their music programs.

- Funding disparities: HBCUs often receive less support from federal and state governments and private donors, which leads to limitations in facilities, equipment, scholarships, and faculty resources (Goldman Sachs, 2023).
- Resource limitations: Inadequate rehearsal spaces, outdated technology, and limited course offerings (especially in areas such as music business, production, or ethnomusicology) put HBCU students at a disadvantage compared with their primarily White counterparts.
- Biased perceptions: Persistent stereotypes about the capabilities of HBCU students rooted in racism, classism, and elitism can affect accreditation, hiring, and the perceived legitimacy of their programs (Gasman, 2025).

These challenges are compounded by the growing political backlash against diversity, equity, and inclusion (DEI) initiatives. Executive orders and state legislation targeting DEI threaten to reduce vital funding streams and silence the voices HBCUs have historically empowered. Although White institutions are often able to withstand such attacks, HBCUs, with fewer resources, typically bear the brunt of policy shifts.

Moving Forward: Critical Dialog and Action

Music education must take seriously its responsibility to confront systemic inequities and embrace transformative practices. Drawing from Coeyman (1996), Singleton (2021), and others, educators and policymakers must be willing to engage in courageous conversations. Key questions include those that arise in at least four categories.

- Institutional awareness: Are we fostering spaces in which students can critically examine the racialized histories of American music and music education, or are we maintaining silence around these truths? What are the risks are you willing to take to disrupt inequitable systems in your institution? Are you challenging norms or merely navigating them?
- Leadership and advocacy: How can HBCUs lead national conversations about music education reform? How can their strengths and innovations shape certification standards and policy?
- Admissions and equity: Are our practices equitable, or are they gatekeeping in disguise? What alternatives to elitist audition and evaluation practices can better affirm diverse musical pathways? What myths about HBCU music students still linger, and how are we disrupting them?
- Student well-being and cultural grounding: Are we asking students to assimilate, or are we making room for their full cultural selves? Are we preparing future Black music educators to replicate systems or to lead with liberation by challenging oppressive systems?

These questions should not remain rhetorical. They must serve as a call to action across institutions, accreditation bodies, scholarly journals, and funding agencies. We must prioritize research collaborations between HBCUs and other institutions, inclusive publication practices, and investment in culturally relevant pedagogies. Policymakers need to advocate for equitable funding, and music educators should rethink what excellence looks like beyond Eurocentric traditions.

The Future of Music Education Runs Through HBCUs

The work of HBCUs in shaping Black musical identity is foundational. By their very nature these institutions affirm identity, validate cultural assets, and empower students to transform both themselves and the systems around them. Not only alternatives to primarily White institutions; they are exemplars of community-rooted, student-centered, and justice-oriented education.

The exclusion of HBCUs from mainstream music education narratives is a form of systemic exclusion. Now, however, we have an opportunity to reverse that. By listening to the stories of those who teach, learn, and create on HBCU campuses, we gain a deeper understanding of what music education can become: liberatory, inclusive, and transformative.

In the face of historical, social, educational, and sometimes musical silencing, HBCUs have always found ways to sing, compose, conduct, and teach. They remind us that music education teaches students who we are, where we come from, and how we carry our communities forward. As institutions that center self-discovery, cultural value, and transformative empowerment, HBCUs are models for the future. The field of music education cannot fully thrive until HBCUs are seen as essential. Their survival and their flourishing must become our collective concern. Only then can we say that through music we are truly educating for justice, for equity, and for liberation.

References

Allen, W. R. (1992). The color of success: African-American college student outcomes at predominantly White and historically Black public colleges and universities. *Harvard Educational Review, 62*(1), 26–45. https://doi.org/10.17763/haer.62.1.wv5627665007v701

Ashcroft, B., Griffiths, G., & Tiffin, H. (2013). *Postcolonial studies: The key concepts* (3rd ed.). Routledge.

Bonner, F. A., Marbley, A. F., Flowers, A. M., Burrell-Craft, K., Jennings, M. E., Louis, D. A., Goings, R. B., Smith, S. L., Tilley, S. D., Garcia-Powell, B., Bolton, T. J., & Tarlton, E. L. (2024). Reconciling our strivings: Historically Black colleges and universities (HBCU) in contemporary contexts. *Gifted Child Today Magazine, 47*(1), 45–64. https://doi.org/10.1177/10762175231205917

Bradley, D., Golner, R., & Hanson, S. (2007). Unlearning Whiteness, rethinking race issues in graduate music education. *Music Education Research, 9*(2), 293–304.

Buzzetto-Hollywood, N. (2023). Decolonization and culturally responsive teaching practices and the role of historically Black colleges and universities. *Journal of Education and Human Development, 12*(1), 1–15.

Cipollone, K., Zygmunt, E., Robert Scaife, P., & Scaife, M. W. (2022). "Let's create the table": Reengaging democracy in teacher preparation through radical reciprocity. *Teachers College Record* (1970), *124*(3), 61–88. https://doi.org/10.1177/01614681221086775

Closson, R. B., & Henry, W. J. (2008). The social adjustment of undergraduate White students in the minority on an historically Black college campus. *Journal of College Student Development, 49*(6), 517–534.

Coeyman, B. (1996). Applications of feminist pedagogy to the college music major curriculum: An introduction to the issues. *College Music Symposium, 36*, 73–90.

Cotton, D. R., Nash, T., & Kneale, P. (2017). Supporting the retention of non-traditional students in higher education using a resilience framework. *European Educational Research Journal, 16*(1), 62–79. https://doi.org/10.1177/1474904116652629

Dawson-Smith, K. (2006). *White faculty at historically Black colleges and universities.* Publication No. 305318255 Doctoral dissertation. University of New Orleans. ProQuest Dissertation & Theses.

Du Bois, W. E. B. (1903). *The souls of Black folk.* A. C. McClurg & Company. (Reprinted by Dover 1994).

Favors, J. M. (2019). *Shelter in a time of storm: How Black colleges fostered generations of leadership and activism.* UNC Press Books.

Gasman, M. (2025). *Why historically Black colleges and universities matter: 25 years of historical research for justice.* Teachers College Press.

Goldman, S. (2023). *Historically Black colleges are critical for equality and need more funding.* GoldmanSachs.com.

Goodwine II, V. B. (2019). *African American students' persistence in undergraduate music courses at historically Black colleges and universities.* (Publication No. 2197613536) [Doctoral dissertation, Capella University]. ProQuest Dissertation & Theses.

Guiffrida, D. A. (2004). Friends from home: Asset and liability to African American students attending a predominantly White institution. *Journal of Student Affairs Research and Practice, 41*(4), 693–708. https://doi.org/10.2202/1949-6605.1394

Hawkins, S. (2021). Reverse integration: Centering HBCUs in the fight for educational equality. *University of Pennsylvania of Law and Social Change, 24*(3), 351–410.

Hess, J. (2015). Decolonizing music education: Moving beyond tokenism. *International Journal of Music Education, 33*(3), 336–347.

Hess, J. (2019). *Music education for social change: Constructing an activist music education.* Routledge.

Jackson, C. L., & Nunn, E. F. (2003). *Historically Black colleges and universities: A reference handbook.* Bloomsbury.

Jung, H. J. (2021). *A philosophical exploration of music education and democratization: How might music education contribute to the development of a diversified democratic society?* Master thesis. University of Victoria. http://hdl.handle.net/1828/13086

Kates, J. (2005). *Essential history: Jacques Derrida and the development of deconstruction.* Northwestern University Press.

Kelly, S. N. (2019). *Teaching music in American society: A social and cultural understanding of teaching music.* Routledge.

Knowles-Carter, B. (2020). *Black is king*. Walt Disney Pictures.

Koch, J. V., & Swinton, O. H. (2022). *Vital and valuable: The relevance of HBCUs to American life and education*. Columbia University Press.

Lomax, M. L. (2006). Historically Black colleges and universities: Bringing a tradition of engagement into the twenty-first century. *Journal of Higher Education Outreach and Engagement, 11*(3), 5–14.

Love, B. (2019). *We want to do more than survive: Abolitionist teaching and the pursuit of educational freedom*. (Publication No. 2197613536) [Doctoral dissertation, Capella University]. ProQuest Dissertation & Beacon Press.

McCall, J. M. (2015). *Degree perseverance among African Americans transitioning from historically Black colleges and universities (HBCUs) to predominantly white institution (PWIs)*. Publication No. 1682266271 Doctoral dissertation. Arizona State University. ProQuest Dissertation & Theses.

McCall, J. M. (2017). Speak no evil: Talking race as an African American in music education. In B. C. Talbot (Ed.), *Marginalized voices in music education* (pp. 13–27). Routledge.

Nelson, M. K. (2013). Fictive kin, families we choose, and voluntary kin: What does the discourse tell us?. *Journal of Family Theory & Review, 5*(4), 259–281. https://doi.org/10.1111/jftr.12019

Plummer, J. A., Lares Nakaoka, S., Ortiz, L., & Ault, S. (2024). Deepening our understanding of race and community practice. *Journal of Community Practice, 32*(4), 383–395.

Ponder, H. (2023). What makes African American students successful at historically Black Colleges and universities. In F. W. Hale (Ed.), *How Black colleges empower Black students: Lessons for higher education* (pp. 119–128). Routledge.

Regelski, T. A. (2014). Resisting elephants lurking in the music education classroom. *Music Educators Journal, 100*(4), 77–86.

Ricard, R. B., & Brown, M. C. (2008). *Ebony towers in higher education: The evolution, mission, and presidency of historically Black colleges and universities*. Stylus Publishing.

Roebuck, J. B., & Murty, K. S. (1993). *Historically Black colleges and universities: Their place in American higher education*. Praeger Publishers.

Rosabal-Coto, G. (2019). The day after music education. *Action, Criticism and Theory for Music Education, 18*(3), 1–24. https://doi.org/10.22176/act18.3.1

Schmidt, P. (2012). What we hear is meaning too: Deconstruction, dialogue, and music. *Philosophy of Music Education Review, 20*(1), 3–24. https://doi.org/10.2979/philmusieducrevi.20.1.3

Schmidt, P. (2020). Doing away with music. *Journal of Curriculum Theorizing, 35*(3), 44–53.

Singleton, G. E. (2021). *Courageous conversations about race: A field guide for achieving equity in schools* (3rd ed.). Corwin.

Stein, S. (2022). *Unsettling the university: Confronting the colonial foundations of US higher education*. Johns Hopkins University Press.

Stewart, G., Wright, D., Perry, T., & Rankin, C. (2008). Historically Black colleges and universities: Caretakers of precious treasure. *Journal of College Admission, 201*, 24–29.

Talbot, B. C., & Williams, H. M. A. (2019). Critically assessing forms of resistance in music education. In D. J. Elliott, M. Silverman, & G. E. McPherson (Eds.), *The Oxford handbook of philosophical and qualitative assessment in music education* (pp. 82–100). Oxford University. https://doi.org/10.1093/oxfordhb/9780190265182.013.17

Tatini-Smith, L., Lewis, N. D., Maynie, J., McCou, K., Swanson, R., & Williams, R. (2013). I'm Black and I'm Proud: The centrality of race and racial regard at an HBCU: A pilot study. *Researcher: An Interdisciplinary Journal, 26*(2), 77–86.

Thomas-Durrell, L. (2022). Unlearning academic music education: How music education erases already-present musical identities. In D. Bradley & J. Hess (Eds.), *Trauma and resilience in music education* (1st ed., Vol. 1, pp. 110–124). Routledge. https://doi.org/10.4324/9781003124207-7

United Negro College Fund. (2023). *Annual report.*

Walker, R. (2007). *Music education: Cultural values, social change and innovation.* Charles C. Thomas Publishing.

Yosso, T. J. (2005). Whose culture has capital? A critical race theory discussion of community cultural wealth. *Race, Ethnicity and Education, 8*(1), 69–91. https://doi.org/10.1080/1361332052000341006

Additional Reading

Derrida, J. (1967). *Writing and difference.* The Threshold Press. (Reprinted by Routledge 2001)

Lorde, A. (1994). *Our dead behind us: Poems.* W. W. Norton & Co.

POSTLUDE: HOMECOMING

ABSTRACT

Growing up in a neighborhood anchored by the University of Arkansas at Pine Bluff and surrounded by a family of proud HBCU graduates, I experienced homecoming long before I fully understood what it meant. It was the sound of marching bands echoing down Main Street. It was Black style at its finest, a fashion show that could rival any runway. It was impromptu step shows erupting spontaneously with cheers. It was the best tailgate cooking, filling the air thick with the scent of barbecue ribs and fried fish that could outshine any five-star restaurant. There were the voter registration booths set up beside these tailgates with political candidates shaking hands and making their rounds. Music blasted from every direction, with each quarter-mile revealing a new decade of sound. It was the sight of alumni returning with pride and the way my family and neighbors carried themselves, with dignity rooted in a shared history of resilience and excellence.

Even when I did not yet have the language for my first experiences of homecoming, there was the feeling of a deep, ancestral pull toward something greater than myself. That is why attending an HBCU was never a backup plan for me. It was a declaration of intent. An act of self-love. A commitment to my community and my family. After I graduated from Spelman and returned years later to my first Spelman-Morehouse Homecoming, I finally understood the meaning of what I felt growing up in Pine Bluff, Arkansas. At an HBCU, "home" is not just a place, it is a spiritual grounding, a cultural inheritance. It is more than a return. It is a *coming into* the fullness of who you are and who you are called to be. For those of us whose ancestry was erased, who were severed from names, lands, and lineages, an HBCU homecoming is an act of reclamation. It is a declaration that we still belong—to a people, a purpose, and a powerful tradition.

My research visits to the eight HBCUs featured in this book were, each in their own way, homecomings. As I walked the sacred grounds of institutions shaped by generations of changemakers and artistic geniuses, I was humbled to experience what only a few are fortunate enough to do. I met no strangers, only family I had not met yet. At Tennessee State and Jackson State, I was warmly greeted as "Auntie." At Fisk and Tuskegee, I was welcomed into conversations that felt like family reunions. At Howard and FAMU, I was invited to dinner tables where HBCU memories were shared, and at Spelman and Morehouse, I was there dear Spelman Sister. Each encounter reminded me that the bonds forged through HBCUs run deep, wide, and everlasting.

At HBCUs, teaching and learning music does not happen in a vacuum. The music is the heartbeat of the lived experiences for faculty, staff, students, alumni, and the surrounding community. Music at HBCUs affirms us, preserves our history, and tells our truth, all in an environment that prepares us to serve, resist, and lead. *Beyond the Notes* honors this spirit. May this work echo the rhythm of our rich history, the harmony of our communal hope, and the promise of our collective song.

APPENDIX A: LIST OF HISTORICALLY BLACK COLLEGES AND UNIVERSITIES

As of December 2024, US Department of Education Integrated Postsecondary Education Data System lists 100 Title IV HBCUs in 19 states, the District of Columbia, and the Virgin Islands.

Alabama
    Alabama A&M University
    Alabama State University
    Bishop State Community College
    Gadsden State Community College
    H. Councill Trenholm State Community College
    J. F. Drake State Community and Technical College
    Lawson State Community College
    Miles College
    Oakwood University
    Selma University
    Shelton State Community College
    Stillman College
    Talladega College
    Tuskegee University

Arkansas
    Arkansas Baptist College
    Philander Smith College
    Shorter College
    University of Arkansas at Pine Bluff

Delaware
   Delaware State University

District of Columbia
   Howard University
   University of the District of Columbia

Florida
   Bethune-Cookman University
   Edward Waters College
   Florida A&M University
   Florida Memorial University

Georgia
   Albany State University
   Clark Atlanta University
   Fort Valley State University
   Interdenominational Theological Center
   Morehouse College
   Morehouse School of Medicine
   Paine College
   Savannah State University
   Spelman College

Kentucky
   Kentucky State University
   Simmons College of Kentucky

Louisiana
   Dillard University
   Grambling State University
   Southern University and A&M College
   Southern University at New Orleans
   Southern University at Shreveport
   Southern University Law Center
   Xavier University of Louisiana

Maryland
   Bowie State University
   Coppin State University
   Morgan State University
   University of Maryland, Eastern Shore

Mississippi
    Alcorn State University
    Coahoma Community College
    Jackson State University
    Mississippi Valley State University
    Rust College
    Tougaloo College

Missouri
    Harris-Stowe State University
    Lincoln University

North Carolina
    Bennett College
    Elizabeth City State University
    Fayetteville State University
    Johnson C. Smith University
    Livingstone College
    North Carolina A&T State University
    North Carolina Central University
    Shaw University
    Winston-Salem State University

Ohio
    Central State University
    Wilberforce University

Oklahoma
    Langston University

Pennsylvania
    Cheyney University of Pennsylvania
    Lincoln University

South Carolina
    Allen University
    Benedict College
    Claflin University
    Clinton College
    Denmark Technical College
    Morris College
    South Carolina State University
    Voorhees College

Tennessee
- American Baptist College
- Fisk University
- Lane College
- LeMoyne-Owen College
- Meharry Medical College
- Tennessee State University

Texas
- Huston-Tillotson University
- Jarvis Christian College
- Paul Quinn College
- Prairie View A&M University
- Saint Philip's College
- Southwestern Christian College
- Texas College
- Texas Southern University
- Wiley College

Virginia
- Hampton University
- Norfolk State University
- Virginia State University
- Virginia Union University
- Virginia University of Lynchburg

West Virginia
- Bluefield State College
- West Virginia State University

Virgin Islands
- University of the Virgin Islands

APPENDIX B: PROFILES OF EIGHT HISTORICALLY BLACK COLLEGES AND UNIVERSITY EXEMPLARS

Institution	Year Founded	Location	Institution Type	Music Degrees Offered	NASM Accreditation
Fisk University	1866	Nashville, TN	Private, Liberal Arts	Bachelor of Arts in Music; Bachelor of Science in Music Education; Bachelor of Music in Performance	Yes
Florida Agricultural and Mechanical University	1887	Tallahassee, FL	Public, Land-Grant	Bachelor of Arts in Music; Bachelor of Science in Music; Bachelor of Science in Music Industry; Bachelor of Science in Music Teacher Education	No

(Continued)

(*Continued*)

Institution	Year Founded	Location	Institution Type	Music Degrees Offered	NASM Accreditation
Howard University	1867	Washington, D.C.	Private, Research University	Bachelor of Music in Composition; Bachelor of Music in Jazz Studies; Bachelor of Music in Music Education; Bachelor of Music in Music History; Bachelor of Music in Music Therapy; Bachelor of Music in Performance; Bachelor of Music with Elective Studies in Business; Master of Music in Jazz Studies; Master of Music in Music Education; Master of Music in Performance.	Yes
Jackson State University	1877	Jackson, MS	Public, Research University	Bachelor of Music Education; Bachelor of Music in Music Technology; Bachelor of Music in Performance; Bachelor of Music in Jazz Studies; Master of Music Education	Yes
Morehouse College	1867	Atlanta, GA	Private, Liberal Arts	Bachelor of Arts in Music	Yes
Spelman College	1881	Atlanta, GA	Private, Liberal Arts	Bachelor of Arts in Music	Yes
Tennessee State University	1912	Nashville, TN	Public, Land-Grant	Bachelor of Science in Music; Bachelor of Science in Music Education; Master of Science in Education (Music Education)	Yes
Tuskegee University	1881	Tuskegee, AL	Private, Land-Grant	Bachelor of Arts in Music	No

APPENDIX C: HISTORICALLY BLACK COLLEGES AND UNIVERSITIES ACCREDITED BY THE NASM

Institution	Year of Initial Accreditation
Alabama State University	1972
Alcorn State University	1981
Bethune-Cookman University	2016
Central State University	1964
Claflin University	2004
Elizabeth City State University	2007
Fayetteville State University	2011
Fisk University	1952
Grambling State University	1979
Hampton University	1972
Howard University	1944
Jackson State University	1977
Kentucky State University	1971
Mississippi Valley State University	1992
Morehouse College	2006
Morgan State University	1979
Norfolk State University	1975
North Carolina Agricultural and Technical State University	1991

Institution	Year of Initial Accreditation
North Carolina Central University	2021
Prairie View A&M University	2011
South Carolina State University	1993
Southern University and A&M College	1955
Spelman College	1973
Tennessee State University	1962
University of Arkansas at Pine Bluff	1982
Virginia State University	1954
Winston-Salem State University	1974
Xavier University of Louisiana	1972

www.ingramcontent.com/pod-product-compliance
Lightning Source LLC
Chambersburg PA
CBHW050534300426
44113CB00012B/2096